Montessori:

On Religious Education

May the Apostolic Benediction which we confer upon our beloved daughter, Maria Montessori, be a pledge of those graces of heavenly favours which we wish her in order to render fruitful of good the method of scientific pedagogy applied to infant education in the case "Case dei Bambini"(Montessori Schools). Given at the Vatican, Nov. 21st, 1918.
Benedictus P.P. XV

Montessori: On Religious Education

Maria Montessori

Hillside Education

Copyright © The Montessori-Pierson Publishing Company CV 1949
Reprinted by permission, 2020.

Part 1: The Child in the Church translated by E.M. Standing.
Reprinted by permission of Seattle University

Nihil Obstat	Imprmatur
H. Canonicus Forbes, S.T.D.	J. Prapositus Ritchie
Die 23 Februarii, 1929	Vic. Gen. Glasguae

Part 2: The Life of Christ in the Liturgical Year translated by Claudio Salvucci

Nihil obstat quonimus imprimatur
Rev. J. Anghileri
† Vic. Gen. D. Bernareggi
Milan, November 29, 1949

Part 3: The Holy Mass translated by Jim McMurtrie

Nihil Obstat	Imprimatur
Paris, December 12, 1955	Paris, December 13, 1955
Pierre Faure, S.J	Michel Potevin, v.g.

All rights reserved. No part of this publication may be reproduced in whole or in part, stored in a retrieval system or transmitted in any form or by any means, electronic, mechanical, photocopying, recording, or otherwise, without prior written permission of the publisher.

Cover images: *Structure of the Mass* courtesy of John XXIII Montessori Children's Center, VA; all others courtesy of St. Dominic's Academy, PA; *Madonna della seggiola* (Madonna of the Chair), by Raphael, courtesy of Wikimedia

Feast of Corpus Christi Missal clipart courtesy of Corpus Christi Watershed, St. Edmund Campion Missal

ISBN: 978-1-7331383-6-9

Hillside Education, 2020
475 Bidwell Hill Road
Lake Ariel, PA 18436
www.hillsideeducation.com

Contents

Part One:
The Child in the Church

Preface	xi
Introduction	xvii
The Life of the Child Within the Church	1
The Atrium or Children's Chapel	25
The Spiritual Training of a Teacher	51
Some General Principles	69
The New Mistress	75
Advice to Directresses	79
Sensitive Periods	89
Child Character	95
The Montessori Method	109
A Comparison	143

Part Two:
The Life of Christ in the Liturgical Year

Calendar	161
The Two Cycles	175
Christmas	179
Epiphany	183
Easter	185
Pentecost	197
The Liturgical Calendar	207

Part Three:
The Holy Mass

The Holy Mass	229
The Open Book	231
The Missal	275

Editor's Note

"The preparation of the child for his full participation in the life of the Catholic Church is a much wider thing than the learning by heart of certain intellectual truths. It is a life in itself."
The Child in the Church, 1929

Many years ago, when I was tracking down the copyright for *The Child in the Church*, a friend sent me the French version of this book. She knew that I liked to reprint meaningful old books and that as a Catechist and Montessori guide, it would interest me. Truthfully at the time, I flipped through it and then set it on the shelf of "someday" projects. Life was busy and more than a little overwhelming as I was at the time working on the founding of a Catholic Montessori school. When I attended the Level III Catechesis of the Good Shepherd formation class, I was reminded of the book, and when I got home, I looked at it and was astounded to see the entire work of the Structure of the Mass in Montessori's book which was published years before Sofia Cavalletti and Gianna Gobbi met. This was an important artifact!

We are so blessed today to have such a well-developed program for the implementation of Montessori's ideas on religious education in the Catechesis of the Good Shepherd.

In fact, we rely on the work of Sofia Cavalletti and Gianna Gobbi and those that came after them so much that we sometimes forget the foundation of the entire work lies not only in the Montessori "method" but in Montessori herself. I felt inspired to be a kind of Montessori missionary by bringing her to you through this book.

And so began the long work to bring the book to print in English. We are grateful to Montessori-Pierson in The Netherlands for granting us reprint permission and for helping with some background information. I am also grateful to the ladies of the Cultural and Catechetical Montessori Association in Virginia for their support and encouragement, and especially among them Regina Sweeney for careful preparation of the 1929 text of *The Child and the Church*; Bernadette Goyette for sending me the Italian text for Part 2 *The Life of Christ in the Liturgical Year*; and Jennifer Miller for sending me the French compilation book so very many years ago, for careful reading of and edits to Part 3 *The Holy Mass*, and for indulging me in conversation and questions. Preparing this text has been part of my amazing Montessori journey and my life in the Catechesis with the children.

When I was working on the translations, I sought to hear Montessori's voice and imagined her saying these words to me and was filled with love. I am so anxious to share this with fellow catechists—I would love to talk to all of you about it.

Please note that Montessori wrote this at the time when all the Roman Catholic world still used the Latin form of the Mass which is now called the Extraordinary Form. So some of what she says will be foreign to you unless you attend the Latin Mass. We did not update the work to reflect the Ordinary Form Mass of today so that a true picture of

Montessori's thoughts could be presented. Her reflections are profound, however, and can inform your view of the Mass no matter what form you use. And, this work will certainly help those who are trying to adapt CGS for use in Extraordinary Form parishes.

Since this book began in collaboration, I would like it to continue as an 'open book.' If you find errors, or if you have access to the original texts and you think I have edited the translations incorrectly or misunderstood a concept, please contact me. Together we can make a more perfect representation of Montessori's ideas.

The closing words to this book bring me to tears as I see the truth in Montessori's view of the religious life. Let's pray for her soul in charity and with great thankfulness to her for opening our eyes to the child.

—M. Davidson, June 11, 2020
Feast of Corpus Christi

Part One

The Child in the Church

Preface

"Any introduction to a good book," says a critic of our time, "must necessarily be somewhat of an impertinence." How then if the book is very good indeed as this certainly is in the estimation of the present writer? May he be condoned then by the author and by all who have at heart, as indeed he has himself at heart, the business of this book. Let his apology be the fact that the editor is obdurate and holds him to an incautious promise given under the glow occasioned by a glance through the proof-sheets.

Certainly the book has no need of recommendation; its title and the name of Dr. Montessori dispense with that. These should of themselves secure a welcome from all Catholic teachers and governesses, and all mothers, and fathers too, who care about the souls of their children, and even by all priests, both for their own edification and pleasure, and because it is their privilege to counsel others in the conduct even of children's early years. Indeed it should be read by everyone of whatever creed who believes in the personal and interior religion of the young, and who would encourage and deepen these brightest, unclouded, sweetest of our human relations with Almighty God till they can be trusted, from first to last continuously, to be the support and joy of life.

How best to secure this happy result is still the burning question of Catholic School education and this little book will add much fuel to the flame. It contains a first-hand account of what has actually been done by Dr. Montessori herself for the development of the child's religious instincts in one large school. This description is followed by the record of an interview in which many questions which agitate the minds of teachers were pushed home, and very satisfactory answers secured. The whole book is very enlivening and enlightening and will no doubt freshen the smouldering fires of controversy.

This timely volume will prove an antidote to despondency, a stimulus to cheerful hope, such as was experienced a few years back when Father Drinkwater, the zealous editor and founder of The Sower, started his splendid and courageous pioneer work, still happily full of eager life and promise. The observant reader cannot fail to notice how Dr. Montessori's spirit and practice, and Father Drinkwater's suggestions meet and confirm one another on several important points of detail; while on the main principles that underlie their methods their agreement would seem complete.

In The Sower, it will be remembered, the able editor from the first devoted his reconstructions exclusively to the subject of teaching religion in our schools. His aim was to revivify and, so to say, naturalize the one lesson in the school course which alone lingered behind the rest in the rut of the old routine, untouched as yet by "the new birth of teaching power." Dr. Montessori, on the contrary, started with the general mental culture of the child. Only later, and recently, after many years of successful experimental work in that larger field, and after a deep personal insight into the inarticulate religious cravings of the unspoilt, normal child did she turn her ripe experience and acknowledged talent to the problem of the child's **spiritual needs**.

We have here in this little volume a record of a rich sample of her new work. The reading of it will re-assure and deepen that daily increasing confidence in her methods amongst those especially who have discovered "that not to every one is given the peculiar, perhaps rare, endowment of intense sympathy with the young," and who candidly acknowledge that only to such rare distinctive sympathy does the mysterious and still uncharted region of the child's mind lie open.

That distinctive sympathy, a sense of oneness with the child's interior life, is the Golden Key that admits the owner into the heart's sanctuary, where he is privileged to share the dream-visions, the mystic and poetic intimations, the musings, the fears, the expectations, the quickening wonder with which the child starts life's pilgrimage from self to God. A mystery to itself, moving in a world of mystery, the frail creature can be observed, as it were, groping silently — as a plant feels for light—in search of objects on which it may pour out some part of its immense charity, reverence, trustfulness and hope, and thereby in turn feed its own hungry and surging life.

Dr. Montessori, and those who fundamentally agree with her, possess each his own private copy of this Golden Key. But what is even better, she has discovered (and others may discover it from this sketch) that the Catholic Church is itself the ideal Master Key, in imperishable Gold, fitting all human locks exactly, however few or many may be the wards, and however simple or intricate and tortuous, large or small the chambers. She shows us here experimentally how perfectly this Lock and Key fit each other even from earliest years: how they work together smoothly, evenly, and so naturally that they were evidently meant for one another; meant to meet by the Maker of both Key and Lock, Who is withal the humble "Nurse of infant loves."

Here are her own words:

"*The Liturgy, magnificent expression of the content of the Faith, may well be called 'the pedagogical method' of the Catholic Church which, not satisfied with teaching by means of the word preached to the faithful, makes the various acts of religion real, makes them, as it were, live, and allows the people to take part in them each day. And to find life-giving food for his soul the child has but to open these portals resplendent with divine light, portals resplendent with all the solemnity given to them through the ages, by the lives of the saints, who found in the Liturgy a means of fructifying the virgin soil of their souls, open to the sweet influence of divine grace.*"

No doubt the work recorded here was carried out at Barcelona under ideal conditions. We cannot hope to find such favourable conditions everywhere, and certainly not with the short-timed lessons of our elementary schools. It is, however, very well worth while to watch things worked out, even for once, on an ideal scale under almost perfect conditions. It provides object lessons that, like a great work of art, put us on our trial, test our judgments, our aims, our sense of values. It almost forces us to approve or condemn; to say either, that is the wrong way, or that is the right way to teach realities whereby the child's free soul will freely and naturally be bound more closely to Religion and Morality. It gives us a standard, an ideal to accept as far as circumstances will allow, or to reject in favour of — well, what alternative?

Someone worth hearing has said: "It takes fifty years to get a reform taken up in a working school." Be that so, then the time is ripe. It is well over fifty years since that ideal catechist and teacher of Catholic youth, Mgr. Dupanloup, inaugurated certain new methods in his effective work in Parisian schools; and later in his educational writings enunciated and expounded these methods together with aims and ruling principles, new to the world of that day, but now accepted generally almost as obvious truisms. "Among these (says the Catholic Encyclopedia) are his conceptions of education as a process of developing mental activity instead of injecting knowledge into the mind, and his insistence on the duty of the teacher to respect the freedom of the pupil." "Je respecterai la liberté humaine dans le moindre enfant" was to him a maxim.

Reading this little book you will seem to be gathering not the spring blossom but the ripe fruit of seed sown and ground prepared some sixty years ago.

W. ROCHE, S. J.

INTRODUCTION

This book, small as it is, has not been written in one piece, but has grown, bit by bit, during the past five or six years. And it has grown rather irregularly and unexpectedly like a house that has been added to from time to time, as occasion demands. This sufficiently explains why it contains a certain amount of repetition, and is somewhat lacking in general symmetry of design.

The original part of the building, as one might say, was Chapter I. This is a translation of the pamphlet, "Bambini Viventi Nella Chiesa," which was published in Italy over five years ago. In 1924 I was about to publish this translation together with Chapter X (the Comparison between the Method of the Catholic Church and the Montessori Method), when I was told of the excellent work which was being done —along the lines of Dr. Montessori's experiment in Barcelona —by the Notre Dame Sisters at the Dowanhill, Glasgow. So I decided to wait until I had had the opportunity of seeing their work for myself. The valuable photos (Figs. I-IX) and the description of the Lesson with the Model Altar (p.173) are some of the results of this visit.

Before the MS. thus augmented had gone to the publisher, I met Dr. Montessori again in London, in April, 1927. The series of conversations which I then had with her resulted in another wing being added to the original building— viz., Chapter II on "The Atrium." The Chapter on the Spiritual Training of the Teacher was also worked out by Dr. Montessori about this time.

It then occurred to me that amongst the readers of the book there would almost certainly be some who—while interested in the religious training of children—had no ideas as to the Montessori Method in general, or—just as likely—had mistaken ideas. So it was then decided to insert a chapter dealing with the general principles of the Method. It would be impossible for any one fully to appreciate the value of Dr. Montessori's work in the sphere of religious teaching without a general comprehension of the psychological principles along which she works. So that is how Chapter IX came into being.

Finally, since it was obvious that no teacher could successfully apply her methods for the Teaching of Religion without understanding the general technique of dealing with children according to her principles, it was thought advisable to include chapters dealing with the training of the character of the child, and with the practical difficulties which beset the Directress who adopts the Montessori Method.

In such a manner then has this book come into being; and though one is conscious that it is not without defects due to the rather haphazard way in which it has grown, it bears nevertheless the stamp of Dr. Montessori's genius, and cannot fail to open up new horizons to every reader.

In conclusion I would like to express my thanks to the various persons who have been kind enough to help in the translation of the different chapters. Especially would I like to record my gratitude to the Sisters of Notre Dame, at Dowanhill, Glasgow, and to Major Dease for their generous assistance.

E.M. Standing
March, 1929.

Altar in the Children's Chapel at the Model Montessori School, Barcelona

CHAPTER 1

THE LIFE OF THE CHILD WITHIN THE CHURCH

". . . I implore the dear and all-powerful little ones, to stretch out to me their helping hands from the altar." -

BENEDICT XV.

When, at Barcelona, we began religious education in the "Model Montessori School," not only had our plan of action been long and well considered, but a significant incident was connected with the actual undertaking.

Father Casulleras, missionary priest of St. Vincent de Paul, remarkable, both as a preacher, and as an Apostle of Charity, came back from Guatemala, Central America, in 1909. He was filled with the conviction that the child should be brought into the Church, to live and grow up there, since the Church is the true place of education for the child. In the different towns of the Balearic Isles, where, as Superior, he directed the Fathers of the Mission and the Sisters of Charity, he spoke of the necessity of having "Houses for the Children" within the protecting shadow of the Church. He had not yet heard of my "Children's Houses" in Rome, and it was only in 1910 that, by chance, he came across my book, where I describe them. To Padre Casulleras the coincidence of names seemed providential, and, having read the account of my method, he judged it suited to his "Children's Houses." Straightway he went to speak of the matter to the Chaplain of the Maternity Home at Barcelona—Father Clascar, a learned man, who had translated the Bible and the Psalms into the Catalan vernacular, and who was one of the founders of the Institute of Catalan Studies. They immediately agreed to apply my method to the children of the Home; they did so, not only there, but in all the Orphanages of the Balearic Isles conducted by the Sisters of Charity of St. Vincent de Paul.

Although these Fathers neither knew me, nor knew that I was a Catholic, and, although in my book, I made no direct profession of religious faith, it seemed to them that in its very substance my method was Catholic.

The humility and the patience of the mistress; the superior value of deeds over words; the sensorial environment as the beginning of the life of the soul; the silence and recollection obtained from the children; the liberty left to the child soul in striving after perfection; the minute care in preventing and correcting all that is evil, even simple error, or slight imperfection; the control of error by means within the very material for development; the respect shown for the interior life of the child—all were pedagogical principles which seemed to them to emanate from, and to be directly inspired by Catholicism.[3]

It was not till later, when we first came into personal touch that we spoke of the importance of attempting to apply the principles of my method directly to religious education.

The Abbot Primate of the Benedictines of the celebrated Sanctuary of Our Lady of Montserrat, so kindly welcomed

---

[3] See Chap. X

this idea that he invited my colleague, Anna Maccheroni, to take part in a Liturgical Congress which was held in the Basilica of Montserrat. The pedagogical problem set before us had, in reality, already been indicated and fundamentally solved by the Holy Father, Pius X. In his Decree on the Communion of Children, he expressed the wish that they should be admitted to an earlier participation in the Holy Mysteries than was usual among Christian peoples. Another fundamental point, too, which bears, it might be said on "technical pedagogy" was indicated by the Holy Pontiff, in the words "let us educate the people to take a more active participation in the Liturgy," and with the people, therefore, little children were to be admitted to the most intimate and sublime act of religious life—communion with Jesus Christ.

The Liturgy, magnificent expression of the content of the Faith, may well be called "the pedagogical method" of the Catholic Church which, not satisfied with teaching by means of the word preached to the faithful, makes the various acts of religion real, makes them, as it were, live, and allows the people to take part in them each day. And to find life-giving food for his soul the child has but to open these portals resplendent with divine light, portals resplendent with all the solemnity given to them through the ages, by the lives of the saints, who found in the Liturgy a means of fructifying the virgin soil of their souls, open to the sweet influence of divine grace.

Formerly, when teaching was limited to telling the child the facts of Sacred History and making him memorize in Catechism answers the truths of Christian Doctrine, we were, if I may be allowed so to express myself, drawing the child away from the Church.

But if the adult needs not only to know but to "live" his religion, the need is all the greater for the child, who is more adapted to live it than to know it. Are not the limits of the problem concerning the religious education of the child identical with those of the various methods of learning and memorizing? In fact, knowledge, in our case, is nothing else but the first indispensable step in opening out for the soul the paths of life.

Here, then, is a necessary complement of the religious instruction of the child; make the Liturgy accessible to children. The grand ceremonies of the Church, the sacred symbolism, the deep significance underlying everything, the exact use and end of all the objects, the systematic distribution of the various offices—all give a fundamental importance to the place where the faithful meet, and, at the same time, afford sensible means, such as lights, colours, sounds, which help the soul, just as benches and kneelers assist the body to remain long in Church without becoming fatigued. And so the teaching of the Liturgy soon became widespread for young people but not for little children.

Now this was exactly the argument handled by Anna Maccheroni in the Church of Montserrat. She affirmed before the whole Congress, which comprised all the clergy of Catalonia, that the teaching of the Liturgy set forth by Mons. Ridolfi, Bishop of Vicenza, as the illustration of Christian Doctrine, approved by Pius X, and distributed in various books for children of different ages could be modified in the following way. The material dealt with in Vols. 4, 5, 6 could be placed in Vol. 1, and so explained to little children. She added that she was ready to try the experiment in the Montessori School of the Barcelona Deputation which received children from three to six years of age. Signorina Maccheroni's discourse, so full of the spirit of living faith, was approved, and remains as an historical document in our educational work. (*The Liturgy and the Pedagogical Teaching of the Liturgy.* Anna Maccheroni in *Report of the Liturgical Congress of Montserrat.*)

A young priest, Mossèn Iginio Angelès, was chosen on account of his simple, pure and ardent faith as the apostle of our youngest children.

The result of this proposition was the opening of "The Children's House in the Church," founded by Father Casulleras, and there began for them a new life—that of "the little ones living in the Church," while, at the same time, the Montessori Method was furnished with a long desired opportunity of penetrating deeper into the life of the child's soul, and of thus fulfilling its true educational mission.

The first step was "to prepare the place" for the little ones, that is the Chapel, which had to be the most beautiful room in the house. The Provincial Deputation of Barcelona, fired with the enthusiasm breathed into the work by a man of genius, Enrico Prat de la Riba (dead, alas! before he had completed the noble work initiated by him in Catalonia), engaged distinguished artists to adorn the "Children's Chapel" in white and gold, the walls being furnished with hangings of yellow damask. Little seats, holy water fonts within easy reach, pictures, and little statues placed at the height of one metre from the ground indicated that the new lilliputian race aspired to be received as "active members" of the Church and no longer in virtue only of the rights accorded to them by the grace of Baptism. A rich and beautiful crib was prepared in readiness for Christmas.

Mossèn Angelès, deeply moved, began to officiate and to preach in this unusual Church, and what was witnessed is, indeed, worthy of mention. One could see how little children, because of their innocence, can feel in a purer and more intense manner, even if less definitely than the adult, the need of God's presence. Their soul seems to be more open to divine intuitions than that of the adult, despite his more perfectly developed intelligence and skill in reasoning.

Meanwhile, the application of the method followed in my "Children's Houses" produced this excellent fruit—the Church almost seemed to be the end of the education which the method proposed to give. The "silence" observed in class, to accustom the child to be recollected, here found its application: it became the interior recollection observed in the House of God, amid the gentle flickering of the candlelight in an atmosphere dim, yet resplendent with gleaming white and gold. Again, the following actions were practically repetitions of what the child had learnt to do in the classroom: walking silently avoiding all noise, placing chairs quietly, standing up and sitting down composedly, passing between benches and by-standers without knocking against them, carrying objects, even fragile ones, with care, so as to let no harm come to them, for example: carrying lighted candles without covering hands and clothes with wax, or baskets of flowers, or vases of water to be filled with flowers and then placed at the foot of the altar.

Such things, therefore, must appear to their tender minds as the end of effort patiently sustained, whence issues for them a pleasing sense of joy and of new dignity. Before such an apprenticeship, these tiny members of the Church feel that they are servants executing material tasks without understanding what they do; after it, and after what they have learnt has been applied in Church, they begin to comprehend and to distinguish between the different circumstances. In order to grasp this idea one ought to know the Montessori Method in the "Children's Houses," which prepares the children, in the daily life of the classroom, by exercises which are, in themselves, quite independent of the religious education, but which seem to be a preparation for it.

In fact they aid in perfecting the child, in making him calm, obedient, attentive to his own movements, capable of silence and recollection.

When this preparation has been made the child finds in the Church the means for its application which are attractive, varied and deeply significative, and he receives, as a result, a sense of dignity and satisfaction. Moreover, the very fact of performing, for different purposes, acts, which, though similar, are capable of diverse application and signification constitutes already in itself another source of intellectual development. The child of four is not ignorant of the difference between the holy water stoup into which he puts his tiny hand, before blessing himself, and the basins in the next room where he washes his hands. Now just this appreciation of the difference between like things is real, intellectual labour which the little creature initiates when he begins to realize that he is a child of God, lovingly received in the house of the great Heavenly Father, though hitherto he has been considered almost incapable of rising to any idea or concept.

I had yet to meet many persons incredulous of the reality of such impressions. "Do you know why my little nephew wants to go to school in time for Mass?" "Because you let him put out the candles. That is all. Would it not be better to apply this pleasing exercise to Arithmetic?—for example, to hold ten lighted candles and then to put them out counting one, two, three, etc."

The critic who spoke thus to me had but a poor spiritual understanding and little knowledge of children. The arithmetical exercise with the candles would have lasted at most a week, the time necessary, more or less, to learn to count from one to ten. But those children as they grew older, and continued their instruction, either in general or religious

Notre Dame Montessori School, Dowanhill, Glasgow. Model illustrating the First Joyous Mystery of the Rosary—The Annunciation. With the aid of the movable script letters the child is making a little composition describing the scene depicted in the model. (Photo by D. L. Sewart.)

knowledge, would observe, in Church, the putting out of the candles that consume themselves, burning in the presence of Jesus descended amongst them, and they would understand that the act was not a mere childish pastime but a religious function to be reverently fulfilled, because done in a sacred place, and bearing upon the worship paid to God.

When Mossèn Angelès began to explain the Sacraments he wished to address himself to the older children only, but the youngest would not go away, and followed his words with the greatest attention. This truly extraordinary priest seemed born for his mission, and even the little children of three followed him spell-bound. He prepared the Baptismal Font, and the things necessary for the rite; chose the god-father and god-mother from among the children themselves; asked someone to bring a little baby over whom he performed, one by one, the sacred rites used in the administration of this great Sacrament. On other occasions, a bigger child acted as a catechumen and asked for Baptism. The children showed keen interest in learning that Baptism in the early days of the Church was conferred on adults, and that, to them, it is still given when they are converted to Catholicism. Thus, they gathered, little by little, their first notions of the Liturgy. They understood, for example, how the Mass is the representation, par excellence, of the Passion and Death of Christ; the older amongst them served Mass, and the younger came at the Offertory bringing their gifts to the Altar, and when the Divine Sacrifice was over they extinguished the candles.

By such means, when the time for First Communion comes, the children find that they have already "lived in the Church," for three or four years. They have a knowledge of religious things really quite unusual, considering their tender age. They are already accustomed to examine their conscience in order to purify it, and keep it free from faults. Oh! if only psychologists knew these exercises and this innate tendency of the child soul! Religiously inclined, and free in their intellectual operations and in the work which the Montessori Method offers them, the little ones prove themselves to be exceptionally "strong and robust" souls, just as the bodies of well-nourished, well-cared-for children are robust. Growing up in this way, they display neither shyness nor fear, nor credulity. They show a pleasing ease and grace of manner, courage, accurate knowledge of things, faith above all in life and in God, the author and conserver of life.

One happy result of the instruction of the First Communicants in Barcelona recalls an analogous incident in "The Children's Houses" of San Lorenzo in Rome. In those early days when my method began to be applied amongst the children of the poor and unlettered classes in one of the most destitute quarters of Rome, the fact that little children of four and a half could write made a great impression. The illiterate parents, filled with admiration and astonishment, were overcome with shame at their own ignorance. Many came to the school asking that they, too, might be taught to write. In the school at Barcelona, Mossèn Angelés had the consolation of seeing the parents of the First Communicants present themselves before him, humbly begging for instruction so that they might make their First Communion with their own little ones. "He is so small," they would say, "and explains the things of God to us with so much faith that we are ashamed; we wish to rejoice with him, and not to be separated from his soul."

But how inscrutable are the ways of Providence! Our work, although humble, might have merited a final triumph. During these years of trial, however, all who supported it died; first Enrico Prat de la Riba who had founded the school and whose work was not understood by his successors. Bishop Casulleras and Dr. Clascar also died.

And . . . the evolution of *"modern Catalan culture"* prides itself on its advanced views when it puts religion in its proper place, that is, not in the first place which belongs to it, of right, but, not too much *en evidence*, in order to leave liberty for the development of ideas which have already had their day in other countries.

Thus there creeps in a so-called "broadness" of ideas which makes religion hazy and prepares the way for future storms. This is, only too truly, the new movement of the so-called social reformers. Why did God allow us to be driven away from the first "Children's House within the Church"? Perhaps so that we may be compelled to go further afield in our Apostolate: "Go and teach all nations"—such are the strong and consoling words of Jesus Christ.

The Offertory At Mass And Communion

The following notes will serve to indicate briefly some particulars of the religious education in the school of Barcelona after the attempt was made to annex to it a Pedagogical Laboratory. A learned priest, Dr. Antonio Battle, my first assistant in the Laboratory, collaborated with Mossèn Angelès and me, generously contributing valuable work with the object of applying my method to religious education. Although Dr. Battle himself is about to write a complete account of it, I have thought it well to give here a simple indication, almost an enumeration, of the proceedings we followed.

The Child in the Church

I. THE OFFERTORY IN THE MASS

In order to make the children understand and remember that the Mass represents an offering, a sacrifice (to make sacred a thing which is separated from others in order to pay homage to the majesty of God) and consequently differs from such devotions as the Way of the Cross, Benediction, etc., the children themselves prepare and offer the species: they cultivate the grain and the vine; they make the hosts, and then they offer the bread and wine at the Altar when Mass is being celebrated.

Part of a large meadow, in which the children used to play after dinner, was destined for the cultivation of the wheat and the vine. Two rectangles were chosen by the children themselves, one to the right, the other to the left of the meadow. A grain that ripens quickly was selected. Into the parallel furrows now ready, each child cast a few seeds, so that all sowed some. The movements for sowing, care that the seeds should not fall outside the furrow, the gravity and solemnity with which the outdoor ceremony was conducted—everything made them immediately understand how the act was suited to the end proposed.

Shortly after, the vines were planted: they were like dry roots, and gave little promise of the wonder the children were henceforth to expect—namely the appearance one day of real clusters of grapes. The young shoots were placed in a trench in parallel lines, the plants being equidistant. The two little fields had to be enclosed. It seemed best to plant flowers all round as a perpetual homage of fragrance and beauty to the vines that would ripen and give the fruit, one day to become the matter for the Eucharistic Consecration. The children continued to play in the other part of the meadow; they made brick buildings, they dug trenches; they constructed little paved roads; they ran, played ball, and in their merriment they themselves were flowers around the two fields.

With the joy of playing was mingled the deeper sentiment of assisting daily at the marvel of growth. In the wheat field, parallel lines of green really began to appear, and the grain grew and rose up awakening the keenest interest in the children. At last even the dry shoots began to put forth tiny, pale leaves. The children gathered round, observing; some were chosen to disinfect the vine-plants in order to protect them from peronospora. When the wonderful clusters appeared, they enveloped them in white netting to guard them against insects.

It was decided that for the opening and closing of the school year, two out-of-door feasts should be established: one corresponding to the harvest, the other to the vintage. These feasts, we thought, might be brightened by rustic music on primitive instruments and by folk-songs, some of which were so harmonious that in ancient times the music was used for sacred hymns of the Church. A doubt then arose: could the reaping be done by the children themselves? The yellow ears, richly laden, were all in a line; the children were a-thrill with interest, so we decided to trust to their prudence. Just as at table, relying on their movement and will-training, we had placed a knife in their little hands, so now we entrusted to them the scythe—tiny scythes, made on purpose, with gleaming white handles. Everything went well. With care, with evident pleasure, with emotion perhaps deeper still, they cut all the wheat. Next came the hilarious joy of making the sheaves, binding them with coloured ribbon, placing them in rows, then bidding them farewell, to await their return as flour.

The machines for making the hosts and for cutting the large and small circles provided manual occupation.

The idea seemed so good that, at the Bishop's Palace, there was question of taking for the solemn procession of Corpus Christi, in Barcelona and its suburbs, hosts cut by the children's hands, and made of the flour from that seed which had grown amid the joy, and the vigilant care of innocent creatures. The field-work and the open-air feasts organized in God's honour, and carried out as a proof of divine love have their epilogue in the solemn offering of the Mass.

The children unite in choosing the bearer of the offering who is becomingly dressed; the little girls wear white veils. Two amphoræ are used for carrying the water and the wine. In the Ciborium is placed the necessary number of little hosts, or, those who wish to communicate at Mass can offer their host at the Altar rails where they are afterwards to receive Holy Communion. The children march in line carrying the offerings in small baskets, or on rush plates covered with little cloths ornamented with lace.

II. COMMUNION

Help given to the Communicants

The children, who, during the school year will be seven, are put forward for First Communion which always takes place in May. The final group of chosen ones is determined after consultation between the family and the school. The children, who, at all ages assist at and take part in the religious exercises, wish to be admitted to First Communion at six, or even at five.

The choice of the candidates for First Communion is a great event for the whole school; they are the object of the love and protection of everybody; their names are printed on cards with a petition for prayers that they may prepare well to receive Our Lord. Each class-room, the Chapel, even the entrance to the school, has affixed to the wall one of these cards, so that the parents, and all who enter the school are informed of what is about to take place, in order that they may all unite in prayer. Every day their companions are reminded of the need of divine help for those chosen for the Espousals of Eucharistic Communion. The preparation lasts five weeks. Each of these weeks begins at 10 a.m. on Saturday—a day on which there is only light work in school, in fact almost rest. Every Saturday, therefore, a collective ceremony is held at which assist all the children, big and small, the teaching and the serving staffs. All gather round the future communicants to help them, to support them by their presence, and their prayers, and to rejoice with them. A priest stands between the Altar and the Communion-rails, the communicants to right and left. On the table of offering are lighted candles and various objects connected with the lesson of the day: such as a facsimile of the Table of Moses, etc. After a few words of explanation, the priest solemnly bestows upon each of the communicants, a page artistically printed and adorned by a picture.

On this text, presented with so much solemnity, will turn the religious instruction of the whole week: and, at the end, the five sheets bound together will make a book—a souvenir of First Communion.

During the week the children learn by heart that portion of the matter which contains the nucleus of the teaching, the Creed, the Commandments, etc.

The following Saturday, one by one, clearly and distinctly they recite what they have studied, before the Altar and in the presence of all. This is not done on the last week, because the ceremony of that week, the 6th, is the First Communion.

All their companions and the mistresses present pray for

The Child in the Church

Notre Dame Montessori School, Dowanhill, Glasgow. Learning the names of the sacred vessels by means of miniature models made in brass. The child places a card with a name on it next to the corresponding model. (Photo by D. L. Stewart)

them and sing a hymn. The pages given to them on the five consecutive Saturdays contain the following points:

(1) Faith, the dogmas—*The Creed.*
(2) Love, charity—*The Commandments.*
(3) Prayer—*Pater, Ave, Gloria.*
(4) The Sacraments—*Confession.*
(5) Mass—*The Eucharist.*

In the last week the children go into retreat for the five days before their First Communion, from Monday to Friday inclusive. They live apart from their companions and a portion of the garden is cut off and reserved for them. In the class-rooms, too, they are separated.

They dine in school alone and recollected. This segregation is, however, neither sad nor wearisome, for numberless attentions and proofs of love reach the little solitaries. Meanwhile the older boys in the school, give all their attention to the preparation for the Solemn Mass, sung in Gregorian Chant, and the music being practiced in their honour, sweetly reaches the ears of the future communicants. The little ones in Retreat, laugh and work. They are taught by means of lantern slides, and a special and tender care surrounds them. They pass the greater part of the time in the garden, occupied in looking after the plants and the animals.

Other manual work consists in making their own silver rosaries which they will use on their First Communion Day, and they themselves bind in book form the five pages within a little cover.

Physical exercises suited to the occasion consist in practice in standing up and sitting down, in walking quietly without knocking against people or things, in genuflecting, in kneeling down and rising up, in observing silence, in keeping a becoming attitude, in not turning the head at a noise. The occupation of the heart consists in raising the thoughts to God at every action during the day, in loving and praising Him.

The suitability of a retreat of five days for little children was well considered and discussed before the experiment was tried. I had faith in the dispositions developed by education which had made them patient and tranquil workers—already given to a kind of spontaneous meditation by the "cycle of work,"[4]—observers of external things and therefore capable of finding satisfaction for themselves; lovers of silence, and the stillness which produces it, attentive to the little movements of their own muscles and capable of controlling themselves. Such children are ready to go a step further and apply the directions to their own interior movements. Not only do the principles of human justice interest them, but a simple love of Jesus is born in their hearts and with it a great desire of purification. The soul of the child is capable of high aspirations which are reflected in his behaviour and in his acts. We have had many proofs of this, in diverse conditions and places.

The retreat of our little ones really represents a temporary separation of their group (entirely dedicated to the sacred preparation) from the rest of their school companions, who are engaged in various tasks, and are therefore capable of involuntarily disturbing them in their interior occupation. But it is not a life of complete sacrifice and absolute interior recollection that is expected from them; they are left free for their own little amusements. They are to be seen for the greater part of the time in the garden, amidst the blossoming flowers of May, picking little bouquets or scented grasses which they carry to Jesus. The doves come quite near to them, and pick up the seeds thrown down by their little hands. During the class instructions they are quietly entertained by interesting lantern slides of sacred persons, places and events.

---

[4] We give the name "cycle of work" to the series of actions performed by the child when, according to my method, he spontaneously chooses his work from the apparatus put within his reach.

Illustrated books and copious collections of picture cards are at their disposal. Much time is spent in preparing the table for dinner, in clearing away, in washing up the dishes, and in putting everything in its proper place. The making of the Rosary, which begins with the choice of the necessary objects and the picking out of the silver beads, provides restful and interesting occupation. Then at times, prayer breaks forth as a necessity—little processions are organized in the garden; the singing of a hymn is readily undertaken. Zeal in bearing in mind all that is necessary; examining the conscience to discover the faults to be warded off in order to make fair and white the house where Jesus is to dwell; the joy of forgiving and loving even those who have hurt them—such are the flowers that rise almost spontaneously from hearts imbued with the spirit of the retreat. It is possible for the child to feel spiritual exaltation. The birth of the Baby Jesus in the humble stable with the shepherd visitors, the triumphant ascension of Jesus into Heaven, after the crucifixion, make a greater impression on the child than any other episodes of the divine life.

On the morning of the great Saturday the Church is adorned with flowers brought, the evening before, by the school-children, many of whom work hard arranging candles and flowers. Only the parents, who, in Spain, are accustomed to take part in the ceremony, almost with the pomp of a betrothal (in fact they give the children in sign of their espousals with Jesus, a ring, which, after Communion they continue to wear on the ring-finger of the left hand) are admitted to the Chapel, while the communicants dressed in white, with a monastic simplicity and severity, carrying their silver rosary, wait in a room far away from the chapel. Their companions, from whom they have been separated for about a week, and who had assisted them throughout the preparation, go in solemn procession to greet them, and conduct them to the Altar. The priest, in his sacred vestments, holding aloft the crucifix, leads the way. He is followed by two acolytes in surplices, with big candles, and behind them, come all the children of the school, carrying lighted candles. The procession sets forth from the Altar, passing between the rows of parents and proceeds, singing, to the room where the waiting communicants hear the strains draw near, and see the long line of lights approach. Then the procession returns: this time immediately behind the Cross come the First Communicants, and following them their companions, still carrying the lighted candles and singing until the former reach the Altar where Jesus awaits them.

The emotion aroused by this act of homage and love, has touched the hearts of priests, and the custom of going for the Communicants and accompanying them processionally to the Altar with hymns of joy has already been adopted in various religious institutions in Barcelona.

The afternoon is occupied with a religious feast, beginning with the Litany of Our Lady which the children intone on the Terrace, while the parents and their numerous friends and acquaintances answer from the garden. Then follows, with various stopping places a procession, in which all the children, dressed in white, take part, the bigger children carrying lighted tapers, the smaller, little white lilies, some bearing on their shoulders a little statue of the Infant Jesus resting on a bed of fresh flowers, others holding a banner of Our Lady.

III. SOME MINOR DETAILS ABOUT RELIGIOUS EDUCATION

Reading Exercises

According to my method, for the very young children

who begin to read words (about the age of five) we use small black cards on which are written words in white: these cards are placed beside the object represented by the name (little toys). In order to group together the names of a series of homogeneous objects, boxes are used, into which are put the things chosen for this purpose, and the cards with the corresponding names. These are, in general, the first reading exercises. We thought of using a similar proceeding, not only to teach words relating to the Liturgy, but also better to fix the idea, and to attract attention to such objects which can then be more easily recognized in Church—for example, Mass, Chapel, Baptism. In each box should be placed the objects (and the cards with the names) connected with the subject. Thus they learn the essential requisites and persons for each Sacrament, the different parts of the priest's vestments, the principal personages of the ecclesiastical hierarchy, the necessary objects for the Altar for the celebration of Mass, etc. These toys must be expressly made. The exercise consists in taking out of the box and in placing in line the various objects, then looking in the group of cards for the corresponding name, and putting it beside the object.

By frequently repeating the exercise, not only is a knowledge acquired, but the attention is prepared to follow the religious function.

Even children of over five years of age, and those who are preparing for their First Communion may employ some time (during the retreat) in similar exercises.

Everything is prepared with great exactness by a priest (Dr. Battle) and the objects are limited to what is exactly necessary, i.e., to the essentials for the validity of a sacrament, etc.

It is easy to imagine how these playthings are able to attract the interest of the children; whole scenes can be constructed—Matrimony, Extreme Unction, Baptism, with little dressed dolls, candles, missal, baptismal font and so on.

Such games are much more varied than the customary play of to-day with little tin soldiers, and they have in themselves the direct aim of teaching careful observation, reading and spelling. In the Chapel, the priest explains all the Sacraments, making the children take active part in ceremonies, whose object is instruction, as bride and bridegroom, as witnesses, as dying persons, as recipients of Baptism or Confirmation.

The toys so used, afterwards serve for individual exercise in thinking about, repeating and learning what has been taught. The child is free to choose the exercise and to entertain himself with the various objects.

IV. STUDY OF CREATION

One of our aims was to help the child, by making him observe created things, to raise his thoughts to their Creator. It is well known that very suitable work for children is the cultivation and intelligent observation of flowers. The growth of living things, the phenomena they present, their metamorphoses are generally considered useful aids in developing an admiration for nature.

Our intention, however, was to find amongst natural phenomena those most apparent and most striking, and to limit their number, as we do in all the didactic material which we offer to the child.

The principles adopted for the education of the senses are as follows: Isolate the sense; choose a few stimuli to be presented separately, and let these be attractive and different, so that the attention may be held, and the power of observation be consequently developed.

The same principles were applied in the choice and selection of plants and insects.

Our research work, for various causes, was not complete, but a few examples will give an idea of the principle. The primula conica (with little red flowers) must be watered every day, and if a child forgets for even one day the plant withers and fades.

The agobe can live on rock without ever drying up: it is sufficient to water it once a week.

The red lily of Ceylon changes its flower.

The cittorium folguera changes the colour of its leaves which become white, etc.

A very ingenious thing devised by Dr. Battle was an astronomical observatory for the children. They can daily observe the sun through a tube which assumes the dignity of a telescope; attached to the observation tube are a thermometer for measuring the heat of the sun's rays, a prism for decomposing the light, and finally a dial which marks the movement of the sun.

As well as the above-mentioned material, the object of which was to arouse admiration for the Omnipotence and

Nature Study. A group of children watching some caterpillars in a cage. L.C.C. School, Mellitus Street, W. 12

Open-air Montessori Class, L.C.C. School, Mellitus Street, W.12

Providence of God, the Reverend Dr. Battle conceived the idea of choosing from Sacred Scripture, especially from the Psalms, phrases in praise of nature, and of collecting them in little books, e.g., on the sun, on the heavens, on plants. Hence the lofty inspiration given by nature to religious souls was brought within reach of the child in the majestic poetry in which it is expressed. Short anecdotes of the Saints and of their love of nature are in process of being collected; without mentioning St. Francis of Assisi, there is, for example, the story of St. Paul of the Cross (which makes a great impression on children) who is said to have turned pale with emotion, while his heart beat faster at the sight of flowers.

These notes on our experiments in religious education represent only an attempt—but they already show the practical possibility of introducing religion into the life of the child, like a rich fountain of joy and grandeur.

CHAPTER 2

THE ATRIUM OR CHILDREN'S CHAPEL

Dr. Montessori is well aware that her work in Barcelona, described in the last chapter, is only a beginning. She herself modestly speaks of it as "un tentativo." She hopes some day to complete the work thus begun, and has already mapped out the lines along which she would have it develop.

Should time, opportunity, and means concur at some future date, and she is able to carry out the work, she will doubtless write a full account of it herself. In the meantime there are many teachers who are anxious to apply her principles without delay to the religious education of the children under their care. For these Dr. Montessori has authorized the Editor to publish the substance of a series of conversations which he had with her, in May, 1927, on this subject. We have written down the matter in an informal manner, without vouching for verbal accuracy, very much as it developed itself in conversation.

Question: "In your method you have prepared the environment of the child in such a way as to stimulate the development of the natural faculties: what sort of an environment would you prepare to correspond with, and draw out the development of the *super*-natural faculties?"

Dr. Montessori: "Such an environment already exists. It is the Church. What is the Church if it is not a specially prepared environment for drawing out and sustaining the super-natural life of man?"

Question: "But speaking practically, as a teacher, how would you set about giving what is called 'religious instruction'?"

Dr. Montessori: "People are constantly asking me about this question of religious instruction—whether it should be long or short, determined by the teacher, or left to the choice of the children, and so on. They nearly always speak of it as if it were a special school 'subject.' My answer to all this is that I should not regard it as a 'subject' at all. The preparation of the child for his full participation in the life of the Catholic Church is a much wider thing than the learning by heart of certain intellectual truths. *It is a life in itself.*

"Perhaps I can make myself more clear by comparing it with the condition of things in Protestantism. Led by Luther, Protestants took the Bible as the last word in religious matters—as the final authority. And therefore since Luther's time, and largely as a result of his influence, the reading of the Bible has come to be looked upon as the important thing for the Protestant to be able to do. Hence in religious training learning to read became the important thing. This has made it possible for Protestants very largely to combine religious and secular education. Indeed it often happens, nowadays, that a child is given no *special* religious education at all. He has been taught to read, and, thus qualified, his 'liberal' parents allow him to choose his own religion for himself. But in order to become a good Catholic it is not nearly so essential to know how to read. In fact there have been, and still are, countless good Catholics who have never learnt to read at all. But to become a good Catholic there are on the

The Atrium or Children's Chapel

other hand a number of things that one must learn how to DO.

"The child, for instance, must learn how to make the Sign of the Cross, how and when to genuflect, how to carry decorously objects such as candles and flowers without making a noise. He must be taught how to prepare for the Sacraments of Penance and of Holy Communion, and how to participate in these Sacraments. He must be taught how to follow the actions of the Mass, how to take part in processions, and, in general, how to participate in the liturgical ceremonies of the Church, as far as it is possible for the layman to do so. All these are things to be *done* rather than things to be *read*.

"In all such matters it is important that the small child should be most carefully instructed, so that he shall feel 'at home' in God's House. No one would dream of going to a ceremony like a ball without having learnt what to do, and how to comport oneself at it. Similarly it is necessary that little children should be prepared for the life within the Church. And all this requires as a preparation not so much the learning to read as a *preparation of self*.

"Now if you consider a little, you will see that many of the child's activities in the ordinary Montessori school form in themselves a valuable preparation for this *active* participation in the life of the Church. The training in muscular control, the careful deportment, the carrying of objects without shaking them, the discipline of the 'silence game,' the care and respect for material objects, the respect on the part of the directress for the interior life of the children, and, in general, the superior value of deeds to words—these are all activities which only need to be, as it were, lifted to a higher plane to acquire a new and deeper meaning."

LEARNING BY HEART

Question: "But how about the Catechism? Would you not have any learning by heart?"

Dr. Montessori: "Yes, of course I would have certain things learnt by heart; but I would have the memorizing come *at the end, as a summing up after the experience.*"

Question: "What do you mean by 'after the experience, at the end'?"

Dr. Montessori: "I mean something similar to the manner in which our children become acquainted with the definitions of geometric forms. You know how the children occupy themselves with the geometric insets in our schools. They take them out on their sockets and run their fingertips round the edges, thus getting a tactile as well as a visible impression of the various forms. They also take different kinds of geometric forms out of their drawers at the same time and mix them together. Then by comparison and contrast they sort these out again, putting each back in its right socket. All this is genuine experimental work, often involving trial and error; and by this means the children become more and more familiar with the various geometric shapes. So that when they come to learn the exact definitions, one can truly say that the learning by heart comes '*at the end, after they have experienced them.*'"

Question: "What parts of the catechism would you have the children learn by heart?"

Dr. Montessori: "That I could not, naturally, decide myself. They would have to be selected by some one in authority who would also be responsible for the wording. The important thing would be to have these statements *very exact.*"

"It would not be necessary, in my opinion, to learn *all* the catechism by heart; only certain necessary and accurate

The Atrium or Children's Chapel

definitions, such as it is essential for every Catholic to know. Nowadays there are so many people who talk such a deal of sentimental rubbish about religion that it is imperative that every child should have something clear and logical to fall back on. One cannot, unfortunately, enjoin silence on all these 'loose thinkers'—more's the pity!—so one must learn to distinguish between their vague ideas and exact definitions.

"In Italy some of the Cardinals have made up catechisms for the use of children—different ones for different ages. I am quite confident that, by teaching children religious truths according to the method I have indicated, we should be able to show that our little ones had grasped the truths as well as, if not better than, older children taught on the usual methods."

Question: "To go back for a moment to what you said about the children learning things by heart—after they had experienced them. I can see how this can be managed in a subject like geometry, but I do not quite see how you are to make it work in the sphere of religious knowledge?"

Dr. Montessori: "For this it would be necessary to have a special material, appealing to the senses, working on the same lines as our 'didactic material.' The children would learn by means of objects and actions."

Question: "Would you have this 'religious apparatus' mixed up with the ordinary didactic apparatus of the Montessori school, or would you keep it separate?"

Dr. Montessori: "I would keep it separate. I would have a separate room specially dedicated to the 'supernatural life.' Everything in this room would have a bearing on the spiritual life, and the general effect would be that here the soul of the child and all his activities would be centred in the Life and Personality of Our Lord. The work in this room would of course include: Bible History, the study of Doctrine,

Church History and the Lives of the Saints, and of course the Holy Mass."

Question: "Do you not think it might create an artificial sense of separation in the child's mind to have all the religious material kept separate from the rest—as though the supernatural life could not go on just as well in an ordinary schoolroom?"

Dr. Montessori: "No, I do not think it would have this effect at all. In our adult life the Church or Chapel is a place specially devoted to the supernatural, which with its prepared environment helps on our spiritual life; but this does not *prevent us* from having supernatural inspirations at other times, and in places which are not so specially set apart."

"It would be better to have a room specially devoted to the religious life, because such broad distinctions are a help to the immature intellect, and form the basis of more detailed subdivisions (cf. pp. 123-4). It would, of course, be possible to have the natural and the 'super-natural' apparatus all in the same room, just as it is possible to eat, sleep, work and play all in one room, though it is better to have separate rooms."

Question: "Then would you consider a school like Miss -'s, though it is equipped with all the usual Montessori didactic material, and in the hands of an expert directress, really incomplete as a means of helping a child to its full development?"

Dr. Montessori: "It is complete enough from Miss -'s point of view. She is not a Catholic and has no clear conception of the Super-natural Order. She is busy with the development of the *natural* faculties of the child, and therefore she does not feel the need of another room for the 'super-natural.' People who spent their whole time sleeping would only need a room fitted with beds!"

Question: "Would not this idea of having a separate

The Atrium or Children's Chapel

Notre Dame Montessori School, Dowanhill, Glasgow. Learning the names of the vestments worn by the Priest at Mass, and also of other objects connected with the Holy Sacrifice. The children have to place a card with a name on it next to the corresponding object. The Directress checks the work afterwards and rectifies mistakes if any. (Photo by D. L. Stewart.)

room for the teaching of religion be looked upon as rather unnecessary and newfangled?"

Dr. Montessori: "People might think it was a new idea, but, as a matter of fact, it is a very old idea—almost as old as the Church itself. In the Early Church there was, indeed, a special room called the Atrium, generally adjoining the Church, which was used for the training and instruction of Catechumens. It was—as you might say—a sort of ante-room to the Catholic Church, both in a literal and a metaphorical sense. Here, as in so many cases, we can, with great profit, take 'leaf out of the book' of the Early Church.

"This room then—which one might call the *Atrium*—would be set apart for the preparation of little children for their full participation in the life of the Church. It would not simply be a question of teaching them their catechism, but something much broader and deeper. This room would be a place where the religious sentiment would be born, and nurtured—where the children would be quite free in the expression of their religious instincts.

"Just as my first schools in Rome were called 'Children's Houses' (Case dei Bambini) so one might call these 'Children's Churches.' Not of course in the sense that they should form a substitute for the real Church—which would be absurd—but because everything in them would be directed towards initiating the children into the true life of the Church."

Question: "Supposing that money were no object, how would you build your Atrium or Children's Church? How would it be furnished? and how would the children occupy themselves in it?"

Dr. Montessori: "That is rather a big question. Well, first, I would try and find some architects and artists who understood the child spirit; and I would get them to give of their best. I have no patience with the idea that because children are very young they can be put off with the second best. I would have the room built in an ecclesiastical style, with pointed windows, which would be adorned with sacred pictures. The windows, of course, would be very low, down to the children's level—like everything else in the room. There would be statues, here and there, of Our Lord, Our Lady and the Saints; and the children would bring flowers to put in front of these images, and also light candles before them. On the walls would be sacred pictures illustrating Old and New Testament stories. The whole room would be fitted up as a sensorial environment calling out to the souls of the little children. As in an ordinary Montessori school, round the walls would be cupboards and shelves with various exercises and occupations for the children to work at."

Question: "What sort of occupations would there be in this Atrium?"

Dr. Montessori: "My principle would be that in this room *everything that the children learn and do in the ordinary Montessori school would be repeated on a higher plane, super-naturalized, as you might say.*"

Question: "Could you give some examples of what you mean by this 'super-naturalizing' of the activities of the ordinary school?"

Dr. Montessori: "Well, you know what we mean in our schools by the 'exercises in practical life'—how the children are taught to take great care of their environment—how they dust the apparatus and so on. Now they would do the same here. With an even more loving care, they would busy themselves dusting the sacred statues and pictures, the little altar and its furniture, and all the other objects in the Atrium.

"Then again, as we have already mentioned, the little ones would feel that the skill they had acquired in carrying a glass of water without spilling it would have gained a new value and significance when they carried vases of flowers to place in front of the Holy Images, or carried a stoup full of holy water. As you know, too, when they walk round the line they have to carry a little bell, and carry it so carefully that it does not ring; so now in preparing their little altar as for Holy Mass or Benediction they will feel a new significance in their power to do this, as they carry the little 'Sanctus' bell and place it without a sound in its position at the foot of the altar.

"I would arrange, too, that the children should often have little religious processions, carrying flowers to place at Our Lady's feet, or at the foot of the Altar; and here again the marching while carrying things, which is a regular part of the ordinary Montessori school routine, would acquire a new meaning.

"In a similar way the 'Silence Game'—in itself so full of mystery and awe—would now become the prelude to the still more wonderful silence of prayer and meditation.

"Even the decimal system, with which the little ones have just become acquainted, can be made use of here, in the counting and arranging of beads to make rosaries. There is a stage (when the little ones are just acquiring the notion of number) when they are interested in anything that has number and can be counted. At this stage they will begin quite spontaneously to count all sorts of things, such as the number of persons in the room, or the number of books on a shelf. It would be a simple matter to devise different exercises, of varying degrees of difficulty, in which they would be able to make use of their newly-won knowledge of number. They could begin with simple numbers as the five loaves and two fishes, the twelve apostles, the seven churches, the number of years in Our Lord's Life and in His Ministry, the number of candles used at Low and at High Mass and at Benediction. Coming to more difficult numbers, they could express numerically, with the aid of the number apparatus, such facts as the number of Sundays in the year, the different subdivisions of the Liturgical Year, e.g., the number of Sundays in Lent, or after Pentecost, etc.

"They could use the 'thousand chain' as a chain of years, and, by counting off the thirty-three years of Our Lord's Life at one end, they would be able—by marking in the centuries with number cards—to gain a clear idea as to the length of the Church's history (comparing it too with the ephemeral life of heretical sects). These are only suggestions, but one could find many facts in connection with the Church and its history which have a numerical significance, which would be specially interesting to the children at this stage.

"In the Montessori School the children are busied at a certain stage with the colour tablets. These exercises give them an intense interest in colours; and everything that they see in their environment which has colour attracts their attention. One little child, for instance, at this stage went up to a visitor and solemnly informed him, 'Your coat is brown.' Another said to a lady as she came into the room, 'Your dress is exactly the same shade as a flower in the next room.' It would be a great joy to the children, at this particular 'sensitive period,' to be given the little models of the liturgical vestments, in order to recognize their different colours and learn the significance of each.

"Music, of course, would play an important part in the life of the Atrium. I would have the children taught how to sing the old Gregorian chants, and also the old hymns which have been handed down as folk-songs.

"You know that our children have a special musical apparatus, made of bells, for learning the notes of the scale and their names. In the Atrium, too, I would have a set of bells, but here I would have them arranged as a little belfry, like a miniature church tower. The children who had already learned to play little tunes on the other bells would be allowed to use these at certain times. They would be used for calling the others to prayers—as at the Angelus, and on other occasions. These bells would be useful, too, in other ways. I would ask a priest to come and explain to the little ones the ceremony of "Blessing the Bells." He need not necessarily actually bless the bells, but it would be easier for the children to understand the ceremony with these objects before them. They could also copy out some of the passages from the prayers used at the Blessing of Bells, which are very beautiful (e.g., "May the sound of the bells drive away dangers, prevent storms and tempests from harming us; may their voice increase the devotion of the faithful and rouse them to eagerness in hastening to their church, there to share in divine worship").

Reading And Composition

"Many of the children in the Atrium will be at an age when they are just learning to read. For these I would devise the same kind of exercises as I have done in the ordinary school. As at Barcelona, I would have little cards made out with names written on them. These would correspond to various small objects which would be kept in sets in boxes, each set being accompanied by a small packet of cards with the names describing them. The child would take the objects out of a box, place them out on the table, and then read the little cards, placing each under the object it denotes. One set—for the smaller children—might contain such objects as: a cross, a lamb, a rosary, or little figures representing Our Lord, His Mother, St. Peter and so on.

"Another set would comprise the various objects used on

the altar, e.g., a Chalice, a Monstrance, a Corporal, an altar cloth, a candlestick, a crucifix, a burse, and so forth. The different vestments worn by the priest at Holy Mass would form another series; whilst still another could be made of the various things found in a church, such as a baptismal font, confession box, lectern, altar, pulpit, etc. Pictures mounted on cards could be used where it was not possible to obtain suitable models."

READING SLIPS

"It would be a good thing also to make use of 'Reading Slips' such as the children have in our schools. These reading slips, as I expect you remember, are in the form of little commands which the child on reading has to execute himself. The little one struggles eagerly and voluntarily with the difficulties of reading because it knows that—when it has wrested the meaning from the sentence—it will be amply rewarded. The reward lies in the joy of carrying out the action suggested by the card. To these little children, just beginning to read, it seems a great mystery that those small cards can, as it were, come to life and give commands like a living person."

Question: "What kind of actions would these reading slips command the children to do?"

Dr. Montessori: "In such an environment as there would be in the Atrium, it would not be hard to find many things for them to do."

Here are a few examples:
1. Go to the statue of the Madonna and Child and throw a kiss to the Baby Jesus.
2. Put a flower in the vase in front of the statue of a Saint.
3. Go to the Holy Water stoup, and very devoutly make the sign of the cross.

4. Go to the crucifix, kneel down in front of it, and tell Jesus how sorry you are that your sins have made Him suffer, and that you will always try to be good.
5. Go to a statue of an angel, think of it as your guardian angel, and thank him for looking after you. Ask him to pray for you.
6. Go and kiss the hem of Our Lady's robe, and say a "Hail Mary."
7. Take off your shoes before a crucifix, as Moses did before the burning bush, "because it was holy ground."
8. Go to a prie-dieu and say an "Our Father" for the Pope's intentions.
9. Take the big wooden cross and carry it round the room on your shoulders. As you do so think of Our Blessed Lord carrying His cross to Calvary. Make an act of contrition, kiss the cross, and put it back again in its place.
10. Make a little drawing of a boat with St. Peter in it. What does the boat stand for and why do you put St. Peter in it?

Those are only suggestions (by the Editor) of the sort of thing one could do; probably each directress would make up her own.

"As the children get older I would encourage them to write little compositions on Biblical subjects. Not indeed that they will need much encouragement; for it has often been proved that little children *prefer* writing on these subjects as their little hearts are so full of love and faith.

"Everything to be super-naturalized! that would be my aim. To take another example. It is part of the recognized equipment of a Montessori school that there should be a little washstand with soap and water and towels. The children are given the most minute instruction how the ceremony of washing and drying one's hands is best carried out.

The Atrium or Children's Chapel

Ursuline Convent, Waterford, Ireland. Instructing children in the objects of the Liturgy by means of models.

Convent of Mercy, Waterford. A "Crib" made out of a chocolate box and also painted by the child herself. She is writing a description of it in Irish.

Now in the Atrium I would have this same action (of washing of hands) done over again, but with an entirely new significance. I would ask the Priest to come and very carefully go through the action of the Lavabo, as it is done in the Mass, explaining to the little ones the significance of the ritual, and teaching them to say the prayers. After that I would have the Bambini go through the action themselves, repeating at the same time, the words that accompany it."

Manual Work

"Manual work would form an important feature of the Atrium. There would be a little carpenter's bench for the older children, where they would make little wooden models. At different times of the year they could make models appropriate to the particular liturgical season. Thus at Easter they could make a little cross, at Christmas a crib. It would be a good thing if a number of them joined together in making a more complicated model—as the Temple at Jerusalem, or the Stable at Bethlehem. There would also be plenty of scope for weaving, clay-modelling and embroidery. All these things would help to make the children understand the kind of life Our Lord Himself lived as a child; for I would have the little ones realize that the religious life is not a thing apart from ordinary every-day life; but is *one complete life which includes and takes up into itself the common things of life.* This is one of the reasons why I should like the children—as far as circumstances and climate permit—to do as we did at Barcelona, where they grew their own wheat and grapes, to obtain the bread and wine to be offered up in the Mass of their First Communion (see p. 12). It is a good thing anyhow for children to take care of plants and watch for themselves the mystery of growth; but this activity takes on a still higher purpose when the materials they have helped to produce are to be offered up in the highest act of worship—to be changed into the very Body and Blood of Christ Our Lord.

"I would also have the children become acquainted with the other elements which are used in the sacramental life of the Church—e.g., salt, oil, water, olives, incense, etc. As we did at Barcelona I would have the Priest go through the ceremony of Blessing the Water, and the children could afterwards copy out parts of the prayers, e.g., "Fill this element of water, O God, with Thy power and blessing that it may be endowed with divine grace to drive away devils."

"Water indeed is such an important element in the life of the Church—being used in Baptism, at the Lavabo, in Holy Water and in the holy rite of the Mass itself, as well as at other times—that I would have it much in evidence. I would have a little fountain in the garden with a pond containing fishes. The children themselves would look after the fishes, and I would have a little tablet near the pond—a replica of one of the ancient inscriptions from the Catacombs—showing the fish as the symbol of Christianity."

Question: "Where would you have your pond?"

Dr. Montessori: "In the cloister garden. You told me that expense was to be no object! So, adjoining the Atrium, I would have a special garden for the children. The ideal thing would be to have the school arranged like a monastery round a little cloister. The Church could be on one side, the Atrium on another, and on the other two the ordinary schoolrooms. I would have statues at the end of the cloister-walks where the children could place flowers. The children could play in the cloister garden, and I would like a tree in it with a little house up in the branches into which the children could climb, as they had in one school I visited in California.

"In this garden I would like the children to keep as many

as possible of the 'Evangelical Animals and Plants'."

Question: "What do you mean by the 'evangelical animals and plants'?"

Dr. Montessori: "I mean the various animals and plants that play a conspicuous part in Bible history and symbolism. For instance I would like the children to have a pet lamb to remind them of the 'Lamb slain from the foundations of the world.' They could have a dovecote and keep doves, because of the two turtle doves Our Lady offered up at the Temple, and the dove that was sent out of the Ark, and also because the dove is the symbol of the Holy Spirit. They could keep bees, too, and have some candles made with the wax their own bees had made. These could be blessed and placed on their school altar.

"*Nature study* would form an essential element in the work of the Atrium. In my description of our work at Barcelona I have indicated the reason for this, viz., that from the observation of created things the child's mind should be raised to their Creator. As the Psalmist says: 'The Heavens declare the glory of God and the firmament showeth His handiwork.'"

THE WALLS OF THE ATRIUM

On the walls of an ordinary Montessori school you see numbers of cards hanging up, some containing little poems, some lists of spelling examples, others the "Parts of Speech," and so on. The children are constantly reading these and spontaneously copy them down. Similarly in the Atrium, besides the sacred pictures which I have mentioned, I would hang up a variety of cards. These would be tastefully prepared, written in beautiful script, and embellished with ornamental designs after the manner of the old monastic manuscripts.

The Atrium or Children's Chapel

They would include such writings as:
    a. Sacred mottoes, such as one sees written on the walls of churches or on the altar, e.g.:
        "Sanctus, Sanctus, Sanctus."
        "Tota pulchra es Maria," etc.
    b. Definitions of the Sacraments.
    c. The Works of Charity.
    d. Acts of Faith, Hope, Charity, etc.
    e. The Fruits of the Holy Spirit.
    f. The Confiteor.
    g. The Lord's Prayer.
    h. The Hail Mary.
    i. The Gloria.
    j. The Apostles' Creed.

"To some of these sacred inscriptions I would assign a more conspicuous place than on the wall. The *'Ten Commandments,'* for instance, I would have actually engraved on a slab of stone, which I would place on a little stand or lectern, specially made, so as to be just the right height for the children. Next to this lectern I would have a statue of Moses—preferably a small replica of the one by Michael Angelo—and behind and above it a candlestick with the Seven Candles.

"On a similar stand, beside a statue of St. Peter, I would place the *'Commandments of the Church'*; and, on a third, beside a statue of Our Lord, the *'Commandments of Our Lord.'*

"The children would have these writings on the wall and on the lecterns constantly before them, and at a certain stage—when they are learning to write—they would spontaneously and with great enjoyment copy them out. They would keep their copies in a special folio, as they do the multiplication tables which they have themselves worked out, and would use them, like the latter, for learning by heart."

INSTRUCTION ON THE HOLY MASS IN THE ATRIUM

As Dr. Montessori is at present engaged in the preparation of a children's Missal, her ideas as to how best little children should be taught to understand and participate in the Holy Mystery of the Mass, will be only cursorily touched on here.[3]

Suffice it to say that the Dottoressa regards this matter of such importance that she would arrange all the work of the Atrium to be, as far as possible, Misso-centric. "For," she says, "just as all the child has to learn in the various multiplication tables is found in, and summed up by the 'Table of Pythagoras,' so all that is essential in Christian instruction is, in some way or other, connected with or summed up in the great central rite of the Mass."

This may seem a strange statement to Protestant readers, but that is because they do not realize the significance of the Holy Eucharist to Catholics. For the Mass is, as it were, the meeting place and summing up of many different lines of thought and action. It may indeed be compared to a diamond with innumerable different facets, so that from whatever point of view it is subjected to the light of thought, it reflects back a fresh significance. Thus, historically, it may be regarded as the consummation of the Old Law, and the beginning of the New Testament. It is the Sacrifice of the New Law, daily offered up for the sins of the world. Looked at in another way, it is a marvellous epitome of the Birth, Life, Death and Resurrection of Our Lord. In the prayers and readings of the book of the Mass (i.e., the Missal) the Church has preserved for us the most beautiful hymns and prayers of the Saints, and the very quintessence of the Scriptures. In the ceremonies and setting of the Mass, all the arts—music,

---

[3] *The Mass Explained to Children*, by Maria Montessori (Sheed & Ward).

poetry, painting, sculpture, architecture, even the drama—have given of their best to pay homage to the Supreme Artist. The common elements of life—bread and wine and water are taken up in It as essentials; and the most precious products of the earth—the spices of the East, gold and silver and precious stones—are added thereto in the vain hope of making a setting worthy of the Eucharistic miracle. The Mass forms the common focus of our collective worship, but is at the same time to us, as individuals, our Daily Bread. But It is not only the meeting place of all Catholic worshippers on earth; for, in the Holy Sacrifice, the Church Militant is united to both the Church Triumphant and the Church Suffering—the Angels and Saints in Heaven fall down before the Sacred Host on the Altar, and the merits of Him Who is offered there are applied to the Souls in Purgatory.

These are only some of the aspects from which the Holy Mass can be considered. They can all be summed up in the saying that in the Mass we have Emmanuel—God with us. Here, in sacramental form, we have the continuation of the sublime mystery of the Incarnation. And this is why the Mass is, and has always been, the central dynamo from which there streams, as from an inextinguishable source, the undying energy and vitality of the Catholic Church. It will be readily seen then why, believing all this, Dr. Montessori regards this subject of such importance, and would make it so prominent a feature of the life in the Atrium.

Use of Models in the Atrium

Question: "Would you approve of the use of little model altars for the children to learn about the Mass?"

Dr. Montessori: "Yes, we had them at Barcelona. I think these models may be very helpful so long as they are used in a proper way."

Question: "What do you mean by a proper way?"

Dr. Montessori: "Well to begin with, the model altar must never be confused in the child's mind with the real thing. The models should only be used for *learning the names of things and their uses.* They must never forget, for instance, that a real altar contains an altar-stone with some relics of the Saints, and that a priest could not say Mass without such a stone.

"Care should also be taken that the child's preoccupation with the model altar does not degenerate into a mere game.

"In this connection, too, I would recommend the use of the cardboard models, published by the Liturgical Apostolate (Abbaye de St. André, Belgium). These have been made to illustrate the different action of the Mass, showing the positions of priest and acolytes at the important moments of the Mass.

"In the Notre Dame Montessori School at Dowanhill, Glasgow, the Sisters have a series of beautiful models, representing the various 'mysteries,' such as the Annunciation, the Nativity, the Crucifixion and so on. The children take these models from the cupboards where they are kept, and place them on the floor. Then with the Montessori movable script alphabet they make up in their own words on a rug on the floor a little description of the incident portrayed. Such models would form desirable parts of the 'environment' in the Atrium.

"It would also be a good thing to have models of the ancient Tabernacle, the temple of Solomon, a Church, or a Monastery, with a little description written out for the children, and cards with the names on them, which the children could place, from memory, on the various parts of the models.

"I think it is very important that children should be made interested in the history of the Church. I would have

The Atrium or Children's Chapel

Dr. Montessori with some of the pupils of the Convent of Mercy in Waterford on the occasion of her visit to Ireland in 1927. She is holding an address of welcome in her hands. The large letters "B" and "S" are the first two series making the words "Benvenuta Signorina."

little stories and pictures specially composed revealing the characteristics of the Early Church—its simplicity, its fervour and its heroism. I have a great admiration for the work of one of the Benedictine Fathers in Rome. This Priest takes the boys, under his charge, to the Catacombs, explains to them how they were used by the Early Christians. He goes further than this for he actually celebrates Mass there, as was done in the Early Church, and his boys assist at it. We should do everything we can to revive the spirit of those early times.

"As in those times, I would have the children follow as far as possible the actual words and ceremonies of the Mass, and not content themselves with reading special books of devotions. The latter may be very good in themselves but they can never take the place of the actual words of the Mass."

A Special Dress for the Atrium

"In an ordinary Montessori school the children—when they come into the school—very often put on little smocks or pinafores to work in. I would have the same in the Atrium, but specially designed. I would make the children wear little coloured smocks like the one the child Jesus were. Some would be red, to commemorate the martyrs; others white for purity; and others green, which is the commonest liturgical colour. The little girls would wear a small veil like a Spanish mantilla; and the little boys would have a cowl attached to the top of their smocks at the back. On the shoulders of each of these garments would be worked a cross to symbolize that the Christian must carry his cross—big or little as the case may be—in his daily life. For even the children have their crosses to bear, sometimes much heavier than we are inclined to imagine."

THE LIFE OF THE ATRIUM

"Thus it will be seen that the work of the Atrium would be a much broader thing than merely 'teaching the child his catechism'—often with the avowed aim of making a good impression on the Diocesan Inspector, or the Bishop! It will rather be a life complete in itself, something which will affect the children at all points. It will be like a surrounding and pervading atmosphere in which they will live and move and have their being."

The light which illumines that atmosphere and gives it warmth is Our Lord Himself, Who said, "Let the little ones come to Me." Here, as in a little religious community, these virginal souls "yet streaming from the waters of baptism" will be free to expand in all their simplicity and purity, giving full expression to the ardent faith and intense devotion of childhood.

The whole trend of modern psychological research is to emphasize the permanent effect, for good or ill, of impressions in early childhood. How could these little ones, therefore, better prepare themselves for the struggle against the paganism of to-day and to-morrow than by being—in these formative years—"Bambini viventi nella Chiesa"—Little children living in the Church?

CHAPTER 3

THE SPIRITUAL TRAINING OF A TEACHER

"BUT ABOVE ALL THESE THINGS HAVE CHARITY."

A teacher must not imagine that he can prepare himself for his vocation simply by acquiring knowledge and culture. Above all else he must cultivate within himself a proper attitude towards the moral order. Of vital importance in this preparation is the way in which we regard a child. But our subject must not be approached from its external aspect only—as if we were concerned merely with a theoretical knowledge about the nature of a child and methods of instructing and correcting him.

Here we must insist on the fact that an instructor must be prepared inwardly, and must consider his own character methodically with a view to discovering any defects within himself which might prove obstacles in his treatment of the child. To discover defects that are already rooted in the conscience, some help will be required, some instruction. Thus for instance, if we want to know what is at the back of our eye, we must get somebody else to look and to tell us. In this sense the mistress must be initiated into her inward preparation. She is too much occupied with "the wicked tendencies of the child," and "how to correct its naughtiness," and "actions dangerous to the soul, caused by the remnants of original sin which are in the child," etc.

Instead of this she should begin by looking for her own bad tendencies and defects,—"first take out the beam that is in your own eye, and then look for the mote in the eye of the child." This inward preparation is not concerned with "seeking one's own perfection" after the manner of those who enter the religious state. It is not necessary to become perfect and free from every weakness in order to be a teacher. A person who is continually preoccupied in trying to improve his "inward life" is probably unconscious of those defects which make him incapable of understanding a child. And that is why it is so necessary to be properly directed and prepared to be a teacher of little children.

We have within our souls numerous bad tendencies which develop like weeds in a meadow—the result of original sin. These tendencies are manifold: let us say they can be summed up in seven groups—the seven deadly sins. A child is more or less free from sin: not only is a child, compared with ourselves, purer, but it has certain pure, occult and mysterious qualities, generally invisible to grown-up people, in which however we must faithfully believe because Our Lord spoke of them with such clearness and insistence that all the evangelists wrote, "Except ye be converted and become as little children, ye shall not enter into the Kingdom of Heaven."

The teacher must be able "to see the child as Jesus saw him." A teacher is one who can rid himself of all the obstacles which make him unable to understand a child: he is not merely a man who is always trying to improve himself. Our instruction to teachers consists in pointing out to them which states of mind need correction, just as a doctor would diagnose a definite and particular illness from which a human organism is suffering or in danger. Here, then, is positive help:

"The moral defect (peccato mortale) which arises in us and prevents our understanding a child is anger."

And, since no moral defect acts alone, but is always accompanied by, or combined with, other defects—just as Eve was joined by Adam as soon as sin made its first inroad—so anger is mixed up with another moral disorder, which appears less ignoble and is therefore the more diabolical—pride.

Our bad tendencies may be corrected in two ways: One, which is within us, consists in the struggle of the individual who, clearly and intelligently recognizing his own defects, voluntarily tries to overcome them with all his strength and purge himself of them, seeking the help of God's grace.

The other is a social corrective, which is to be found in external environment. We might point out how the resistance of external things, opposed as they are to any outward manifestation of our bad tendencies, must arrest their development. External opposition has considerable influence. It is, one may say, the chief reminder of the existence within us of any moral defect, and an external reminder which leads us in some cases to think about our inward state and then actively to set about our inward purification, if we really wish for it.

Let us consider these deadly sins: our pride is modified by others' opinion of us; our avarice by the material circumstances of life; anger by the attitude of those stronger than ourselves; sloth by the necessity of working for our living; luxurious habits by social customs; gluttony by the limited possibilities of procuring superfluous things;

jealousy by the wish to appear dignified. There is, no doubt, behind the above conditions, the desire of the individual to overcome his faults. But those external circumstances are a definite and continuous reminder which is quite salutary. In short social control affords a great support to the moral equilibrium of our personality.

We, however, whilst conforming to these social codes do not feel ourselves pure in the sight of God. But whilst our souls conform willingly to the necessity of correcting the faults which we ourselves have recognized, they adapt themselves with difficulty to the rest of the process—the humiliating one of being controlled by others—so that we feel even more humiliated by the fact of having to give in than by actually having done wrong. When we are made to restrain ourselves, and there is no way out, our instinct of worldly dignity induces us to make it appear that we have ourselves chosen what was really inevitable. The small deception of saying, "I do not like it," about something which we cannot have is one of the commonest moral traits. We resist resistance with a small deception, and so enter a battle-field rather than the road to perfection. And, as in every struggle, we shall soon feel the need of organized fighting. Individual deeds are strengthened by becoming collective. People who have the same defect, before giving in to the external causes which would go against them, are led instinctively to triumph over these by the strength of union.

Nobody would dare to say, for instance, that the equal division of wealth would be displeasing to the rich because they are avaricious or slothful; but they would say that such a distribution of wealth would benefit everybody, and is necessary for social progress; and although one may hear many rich people say that they would be resigned to it for the common good, there is a tendency to disguise our vices

The Spiritual Training of a Teacher

Notre Dame Montessori School, Dowanhill, Glasgow. Objects used for various Church ceremonies (all quarter size)

under the pretext of noble and necessary duties, just as during the war they concealed the places where there were trenches and mortal dangers with a camouflage of flowery fields. The weaker the external things which are opposed to our defects, the more time and leisure we have for constructing our camouflage and fortifications. If we penetrate a little further into these ideas we shall come to the conclusion that our vices are more fixed than we had thought, and that the devil can easily insinuate himself into our subconsciousness by suggesting that we should hide our real selves from our outward selves. This defence, not of our lives but of our evil tendencies, is the mask which we readily put on, calling it "necessity," "duty," "general advantage," etc., so it becomes daily more difficult to free ourselves from this sort of thing. Confusion arises from the fact that we are now convinced that what our conscience once suggested to us was really false, is now true.

And now the mistress, or whoever wishes to educate children, must be purged of those errors which would place her in a false position with regard to children. She must realize clearly what is her prevailing defect; and by this we refer to more than one single defect—to a combination of disorders which are allied to one another: pride and anger.

Anger is one of those failings held in check by the determined reaction of others. It is one of the things that proves how difficult it is for one man to be subjugated by another. Therefore he is a prisoner when he meets a really strong person. A man is ashamed of showing anger before others because he at once sees himself in a humiliating position; that of having to retire by force.

It is therefore a real relief to be able to mix with people who are incapable of defending themselves or understanding;

The Spiritual Training of a Teacher

people who believe everything as children do. Children not only forget our offences immediately but feel themselves guilty of everything of which we accuse them. Thus it was with that holy disciple of St. Francis of Assisi, who wept believing himself a hypocrite, simply because a priest had told him so. The teacher is here invited to reflect carefully on the serious effects of such a state of things on the life of a child. A child's understanding would not see through the deception; but its spirit feels it, and is oppressed and often warped by it. Then the childish reactions appear which really represent an unconscious self-defence. Timidity, deceit, caprice, the frequent weeping, which they seem to justify, nightly frights, any form of exaggerated fear—and similar obscure things—represent the unconscious state of defence of a little child who has not yet sufficient reasoning power to understand the real conditions of its intercourse with grown-up people. On the other hand anger does not necessarily imply physical violence. From the crude and primitive impulse which is generally understood by this word complex manifestations may be developed. A psychically developed person conceals and complicates his inner states of evil. Indeed, anger in its simplest form only shows itself as a reaction to some open resistance on the part of the child. But in the presence of the obscure expressions of the child's mind, anger and pride are interpenetrated in a complex mass, assuming the precise, tranquil and respectable form which is called tyranny.

An oppression which is not disputed places the tyrannous person in an impregnable stronghold of authority and recognized rights. The fact of being adult makes him right to the child, just because he is grown-up. To discuss this question would be to make an attempt on a state of sovereignty which is recognized and sacrosanct. In the society of grown-up people a tyrant used to be recognized as the elect of

God. But to the child a grown-up person represents God Himself. It is outside discussion; in fact the only person who could discuss it is the child, and he remains silent. He accommodates himself to everything, believes everything, pardons everything. When he is punished he does not try to justify himself, and willingly asks the pardon of any angry person, forgetting to inquire how he has given offence.

Sometimes, too, the child will do something to defend itself, but this defence is hardly ever a direct reply to the act of an adult, but a vital defence of its own "psychic" integrity, or, indeed, the reaction of a repressed spirit.

It is only when the child is growing up that he begins to direct his defences with discernment against tyranny, but then the adult finds reasons to justify himself, and helps himself, by entrenching himself more and more behind his camouflage, even succeeding sometimes in convincing the child himself that it is for his good that the teacher becomes a tyrant.

"Respect" is paid only by one side: the weak respects the strong. An offence on the part of the teacher is legitimate; he can judge the child unfavourably, speak ill of it, which he does openly, even going so far as to strike it. The needs of the child are directed and suppressed by the teacher at will, and any protest on the part of the child is an insubordination which it would be dangerous to tolerate.

Just as some peoples have succeeded in believing that everything will be secured to them through the benevolence of their sovereign, so children believe that they owe everything to the benignity of the teacher. Or, rather, it is the teacher who believes it, who, in his pride, has convinced himself that he has created everything that is in the child: he makes him intelligent, learned, good, religious; that is to say, it is he who has prepared the way necessary to put him in communication with his surroundings, with man and with God. This is a fatiguing mission. The renunciation of the tyrant completes the tyrant. There never yet was a tyrant who confessed to having sacrificed his subjects.

What our method asks of a mistress as her preparation is that she should examine herself, and purge herself of the defect of tyranny, eradicating the ancient mixture of pride and anger with which her heart is unconsciously encrusted. She must cast off pride and anger and first of all become humble before she can put on Charity. That is the state of mind which she must attain. This is the central point of equilibrium without which it is impossible to advance. This is the inward "preparation," the point of departure and arrival.

This does not imply that we should approve of everything the child does, or abstain from criticizing it, or do nothing to help the development of its intelligence and feelings. On the contrary, we must never forget that the whole point of the argument is to educate, to become the real masters (*"maestri"*) of the child.

What is called for is an act of humility; we must pluck from our hearts a rooted prejudice, just as the priest, before ascending to the altar, must recite his "Confiteor."

Only thus it can be done, not otherwise. It is not the helpful education of the child that we must abolish, but the inner state of our souls which prevents us from understanding him.

The teacher who is preparing himself inwardly by putting on charity differs from a person who is just trying in a general way to acquire that sublime quality. Charity, as described by St. Paul, includes all the highest perfections of Christianity. But the teacher must study that part of charity which is indispensible for his particular mission. Here, too, he needs a guide to direct him towards these special points.

A searchlight which concentrates its light and turns it on to a distant object—that is how one might describe the kind of charity necessary to a teacher.

It is obvious that a religious soul who is constantly seeking for perfection, and consequently for charity, will more easily direct his searchlight so as to illuminate the child mind. Yet it is true that the most vigilant and enlightened soul, with his light spread over everything, might yet pass near a child without having the special outlook of a teacher.

The charity which helps people to become teachers of little children is that which shows itself in the child, the goodness which the child itself succeeds in showing. Teachers and all those engaged in education are, however, more inclined to see evil so that they may check it at once in the most effective and thorough way. It seems rather as if in that alone consisted all the essentials of a moral education. In this way the roots of good which are beginning to sprout in the child's soul may remain unrecognized and denied.

An unobservant person might often believe that it was he who had sowed the seed of good in the child's soul, and be blind to many delicate and childlike expressions of goodness, just as one who suffers from daltonism is blind to certain colours.

Instead of this the teacher should prepare himself to recognize goodness; for it is towards goodness that all the help of education must be directed.

AN ILLUSTRATIVE ANECDOTE

The Dead Dog

A dead dog had been lying for several days in a sunlit street of one of the cities of Palestine. A group of people had collected round the disgusting object. Some said: "It is horrible"; others,

"It is monstrous," and kicked it away. A youth passed that way and stood a moment to look, then said, "What beautiful little teeth!"

And, in fact, the dog's teeth still remained white and shining. Somebody asked, "Who is that young man who can see beauty in this dead body?" And the reply came—so runs the legend—"He is called Jesus, and He is the son of a Nazarene carpenter."

This short story illustrates a sensibility capable of seeing good wherever it may be found, even if it is something quite small and hidden away. Such a sensibility is allied to the perfect love of which our Master, Jesus, was the Exemplar. And that love, which lights up everything, we call "charity."

We must not confuse this kind of charity with vague forms of optimism. It does not make us regard all existing things as good, but only what is really good, and on that account, to be clearly distinguished from evil. Our Lord did not see the dead dog as a beautiful object, but He saw the one beautiful thing that remained amid corruption. In the same way the eye of a great artist recognizes at once a really precious object, even if it is small and mixed with many ugly and vulgar things; whilst, on the contrary, an uneducated person, insensitive to beauty, might regard the ugly things as pleasing, and be blind to the beauties of a real work of art.

The kind of goodness to which everything seems good, and evil non-existent is, therefore, something totally different from the charity which is necessary to become good teachers of the young.

The Cornfield—An Illustration

In a field of ripe corn the ears seem at first sight all alike, but on looking carefully one notices several kinds of corn and, especially, that some ears are more beautiful than others -they are full, and bent with their weight. The grain of these, when ground, not only gives more flour, but a very white flour, especially rich in nutritive value. Not only that, but these ears of superior quality are almost immune from the disease which are liable to attack the weak and inferior corn.

Cultivators have only recently become aware of these important facts, and have busied themselves in selecting the better kinds of grain and discarding the inferior, with a view to cultivating only the best kind in their fields.

The result, however, cannot be attained as easily as appears at first sight, for the better grain requires more care to make it grow; and that is the reason why so little of this variety grew in ordinary fields. To make the kind of corn with heavy ears flourish, the earth must be intensively cultivated with special manures; and only by preparing a new and perfect medium can intensive culture succeed in getting a field uniformly covered with this valuable and wonderful corn. If the intensive care of the field is in the least neglected, the beautiful ears begin to dwindle and get lighter in weight and finally become diseased. "This is degeneration," thought the agriculturalists who had sown the field entirely with selected seed. But the biologists, led by de Vries (The Theory of Mutations) have given an "experimental" explanation of the above phenomenon. It was not a case of "degeneration." Grains of the poorer quality had remained hidden in the earth of the field, and had not sprouted because the ground was intensively manured in such a way as to vitalize the large seeds which, so nourished, prevent the growth of the inferior seeds; and these, smothered by the stronger kind, remain concealed and latent, with no room to germinate. But it is well known how corn can survive; even if it does not sprout

The Spiritual Training of a Teacher

Montessori Schools in Italy

The girl in the foreground is studying "Fractions," the boy behind her is doing a Grammar Exercise.

Note the child on the left at the table counting along a bead chain; the girl opposite is using a number frame.

properly it still remains alive and capable of germinating. Thus, when the cultivation of the ground was neglected, it happened that the large grains, which required a great deal of manurial nourishment, could not grow, whilst the old seed, which did not need so much, grew quite easily. And the more the grower neglected the land, the more the inferior seed, poor and sickly, found its chance of living and springing up. The grower who had sown his seed entirely with the strong-growing grains could not explain the appearance of so many kinds of inferior corn. But the bad seed which was sown had persisted, awaiting its opportunity. Superior grain cannot live poorly, it needs a great deal to make it grow. Thus we see that it is not sufficient to have good seed without the necessary care of the environment. Good seed and bad seed are always there: the cultivation of the good is more difficult, but when it finds the conditions favourable it overcomes the bad and gives prodigious results. Want of care does not leave the field barren, for, in the place left empty by a heavy ear, light ears spring up. Good conquers evil or evil conquers good. The field is always full either with good growth or bad.

The fact is, therefore, that if good things are not nourished we suffer not only from the lack of them but also from the presence of worse things.

In a neglected field, or in one short of water, there is not only the absence of good tender grass, but also the presence of rank nettles, intruding all the more where the vital conditions for good grass are wanting.

And it happens also with the soul somewhat as it happens with the cornfield and the meadow. Progress in agriculture began with discovering and studying the best ears, and then solved its problem by procuring the necessary things for their cultivation. There will not be a good harvest merely by exterminating the inferior plants. The surest way of keeping down the bad seed is to encourage the growth of the good.

The sudden extermination of evil is not a thing to be recommended; this is clearly taught by our Divine Master: it is better to let tares also grow, than to destroy the good grain along with them. The key to the problem is, therefore, not to destroy evil but to cultivate good.

The Two Fans (An Allegory)

We may now illustrate the same principle in the case of two folding fans with long handles, which, when closed, completely conceal the central part or web, but which, when open, spread it out into a circle.

The two fans, one black, the other transparent, light blue and silver, are half-open; the blue semicircle—light and glittering—is at the top, whilst below is the black one, solid and heavy. The handles, by which the fans may be manipulated without touching the folding part, are placed one upon the other in the same horizontal line. We will represent Good by the transparent, luminous fan which is spread above, and Evil by the black fan which is spread below—heavy, opaque, very visible and tangible.

If the bright fan be opened further it not only becomes larger, but at the same time limits and shuts off part of the black fan. And vice versa: If it is the black one that is opened the result is not merely an augmentation of the dark part, but also a diminution of the bright part. If the whole of the luminous fan could be opened it would totally eclipse the black one. However, between the two blue handles turned towards the earth, the whole of the black fan would be still there, packed together and compressed.

If, on the contrary, the black fan should be completely opened, the beautiful slender fan would not completely disappear, but, folded together with the handles closed, it would seem to point out Heaven to the dark, triumphant fan.

Both remaining present, and both touching in the same space, this manipulation of the fans represents the changes in the struggle between Good and Evil. Even in the soul nearest perfection through the complete triumph of good, there is still suppressed evil; whilst there is no soul, even one apparently steeped in wickedness, which does not enclose a fan of light, compressed, but turned towards heaven like a lightning-conductor which calls out to God for Grace. The two webs are thus separated to form two different things, and the handles seem like a double dividing-wall. Fusion is not possible—only the prevalence of one over the other.

The acquisition of one good quality is at the same time the conquest of a bad one, and every evil quality which triumphs has overcome a good one.

There is a double gain and a double loss which yet do not call for a double act. There is no doubt that the easiest and most natural way of overcoming evil is to let it fold up and close, by developing good, and not tear to tatters the resistant and solid part of it.

No one ought to be more careful to cherish the luminous fan of good than the teacher. Even if he should forget the black part, he would yet have the wisdom to suppress it, and would possess the simplest and most practical secret of success. Nothing could better illustrate the existence of these two irreconcilable elements than the conception of "Justice" relatively held in the earthly, and in the celestial world. Justice, in the earthly sense, is something which causes fear; it concerns itself with evil, and signifies punishment for a gross offence. Whoever breaks human laws feels the "terror of justice"—Justice is a cruel tribunal, a prison, a hard chastisement, a long torment. He who has not committed sin feels no fear. Such a one would say, "I have nothing to do with justice"—that is to say—for him justice does not exist, he has nothing to do with it, and it does not concern him. And he is proud and satisfied to live without ever having anything to do with justice. . . . Such expressions are in contrast to another conception of justice. The word "justice" signifies something high, something noble, something for which every soul hopes. Everyone repeats with a sigh of longing "Justice will be done to me. . . . My hope is in justice."

What is this justice? This kind concentrates on goodness. It has no material tribunals; it is a light of faith which assures to each one of us a reward for every good action we have done. Nothing escapes God's justice, which takes account of every good deed we do, and compensates us for every ill done us by others. If one really thinks that the only justice which exists is the gloomy justice of this world, and if all hope of heavenly justice were lost, then the soul would feel like something heavy which sinks into hell.

Hell is the loss of God.

How have we been able to remain under the mistaken impression that a child should be judged according to the evil which he does, and that his education should be directed according to the gloomy standards of "human" justice? When Jesus was teaching us about love, he pointed to the child as an example for us, and as a guide to the Kingdom of Heaven.

CHAPTER 4

Some General Principles with Regard to the Instruction of Children in the Mass

One of the greatest steps forward in the religious education of children was that of introducing them to liturgical practices in such a way that they might participate in them with full knowledge.

From that moment the question of a missal for the children, and their preparation so as to be able to follow the Mass, assumed an importance parallel to that of their instruction in the Catechism—which, previous to the great reform of Pius X, was almost the only thing left to them.

But in the practical carrying out of this new step forward the ordinary methods of education of our time have been used; that is to say, the adult has still looked upon the personality of the child from the same point of view as he regards his own. The continuous and direct intervention of the adult with the child has been regarded as necessary in order to deter him from disorderly actions, supposing the child only capable of good through the exhortation and example of the great. Even so did people think at the time of

Christ; when the children approached the divine Master, the adult drew them back. So much so that Jesus was obliged to admonish them, saying, "Let the little ones come unto Me." Moreover Our Lord was moved by this action to one of His moments of severity, and made of it the occasion for one of His divine revelations, "Verily I say unto you, that unless ye be converted and become as one of these little ones, ye shall not be able to enter the Kingdom of Heaven."

Jesus perceived in the children something which the adult of 2,000 years ago—like the adult of today—does not perceive, while in the Gospels it is clearly affirmed that there are many mysteries which will be revealed to babes and sucklings.

The teachings of Jesus with regard to children touched on a point which is central for their education; viz., that the child has a personality different from ours, and in him are to be found spiritual tendencies which, in the adult, have now been hidden under a hardened crust.

This idea must constantly be present with us, in order that we may be disposed to offer to the child the highest things; and not only so, but that we may offer them in an elevated manner.

We should assist the child by giving him the religious knowledge he needs; at the same time, however, not forgetting that the child can help us by pointing out to us the way of the Kingdom of Heaven. A great respect for the personality of the child should form an essential part of our most profound Christian sentiments, while the practical application of this sentiment should be a characteristic refinement of every religious teacher.

We may hope much for the spirituality of children; let us not forget that His Holiness, Pope Benedict XV, during the European conflagration, placed at the beginning of an encyclical letter—to be read to the faithful in every church throughout the world—these words: "I pray that the all-powerful children may stretch out their hands to the altars."

What is therefore of great importance to us adults, in this question of the liturgical education of the children, is not only the manner of our teaching them the necessary things, but also the preparation, in our own souls, of a greater sensibility.

We are, it must be confessed, still far enough away from the attitude of mind which should be ours. It is too common a thing to hear in church harsh, and therefore injurious words addressed to the child: "Keep still! don't be such a nuisance!" "You're not attending, you naughty boy." Many lay teachers lead into church files of children, dragooning them about like a sergeant-major with a set of new recruits under him. "Down, on your knees! not that way, all together!"; or you may see a teacher seizing the children by the shoulder, and shoving them, one by one, into the pew, as though he were putting fruit into a basket.

Another evident mistake is that of teaching during the divine office. It frequently happens nowadays that one meets in churches meritorious persons who have laid on themselves the mission of assisting and instructing—during the divine office—these groups of children, or even of older boys (who may be already doing Algebra at school or making commentaries on Dante). During the Elevation—a time of silence and inward recollection—behold there resounds the voice of the zealous teacher, voice without harmony or expression, explaining loudly, in the tone of one who performs an arid duty, what the Elevation signifies, and what sentiments it should arouse in the hearts of the faithful. The lesson finished, a loud "sit down" recalls to their seats the youthful platoon, in whom—though with the best of intentions—all spontaneous uprisings of the soul have been suffocated.

Illustration from "Little Children's Thoughts and Prayers on the Rosary," by Sisters of Notre Dame, Glasgow (Sands & Co., 1s. 6d.)

Some General Principles

Certain errors of a similar kind are to be found in many of the little books on the Mass composed specially for children. These books are overburdened with instructions, whether in the words or the illustrations, which things attract the attention of the child, absorbing all his energy. Anyone reading one of these books is bound to have his attention caught by the appeal of the illustrations, which point out the position of the officiating priest—now situated on the right, now on the left, now turned with his face to the altar, now turned instead to the congregation—and is obliged to put the words of the text in correspondence with these attitudes.

In addition to all this there are also found, in some of these little books, illustrations representing the symbolical significance of the various actions which form part of the rite: that represents the Birth of Jesus, this His Ministry, that other His Death and Burial. Now we have all experienced how difficult it may be genuinely to follow the Mass even when we are accustomed to so doing and almost know the words by heart. How then is it possible to follow it and be instructed in it at the same time?

May we not say that the purpose of the Mass is that we should participate in the mysteries, abandoning the soul to God in that state of inward recollection which is only made possible by shedding for a moment from our minds all external wrappings? It was for this reason that in early Christian times the catechumens were sent away at commencement of the mystical parts of the Mass. For it was considered that it was not meet that they should receive instruction in an exterior act at a time when they should be united with Jesus Christ in the most intimate offering of the soul. Instruction and participation in the mysteries are two very different things and should remain separate.

The first subdivision of the Mass into parts is precisely this:

The Mass of the catechumens and the Mass of the Faithful. And this is of very great significance.

It is not necessary that the child should be a sage in order to follow the Mass, but it *is* necessary that he should be spiritually free. That is to say, instruction in, should not be confounded with the practice of the cult.

The missal should be, then, for the child as well as for us a simple reproduction of the liturgical text; and the part containing the instruction should be reserved for the "Atrium," at another time than that of assisting in the rite itself.

That the children's missal should be a reproduction of the liturgical text is already agreed upon by the vast majority of those who are researching, at the present day, to elevate the religious preparation of the children.

But to do this effectually the disposition of the sacred liturgical text should be arranged in a manner accessible to children: it is just here that the main problem of a children's missal remains to be solved. That text, though immutable, might however be adapted to the child in the manner in which it is offered to him; in the way in which it is analysed and graduated; above all in the manner in which it is made to arouse, concurrently, the corresponding activity of the child himself, for it is now admitted that it is the activity of the child that brings out the best that is in him.

CHAPTER 5

THE NEW MISTRESS[1]

Inexperienced teachers generally attribute immense importance *to lessons*, imagining that their own preparation ends when they have presented the material in the right way. The truth is far otherwise: the mission of the mistress is much more important than this. She has to direct the development of the child's soul. The limited rôle of a simple observer of children is quite different. Such a one does not aim at *knowing* the children, but simply *helping* them.

It is, then, useful to know certain fundamental principles capable of aiding this work of direction. The chief thing here is to be able to recognize those states of polarization of the attention which we have called *Concentration*. When the child is wrapped up in attention to his "great work," the mistress must respect this attention; she must not interfere either by correction or encouragement. It is *then* that she must absolutely observe the principle of non-intervention. Certain teachers have absorbed this principle off-hand, *en passant* as it were; they have told themselves that all they have to do is to distribute the material, then withdraw and be silent whatever happens.

---

[3] Extract from an article by Dr. Montessori in the *Call of Education*, July, 1927.

Result, frightful disorder in the school! But non-intervention—the sign, that is, of respect for the child's activity—*is only appropriate when some interesting phenomenon is* taking place in the child's life; it is quite out of place when disorder reigns and the attention of the child is all astray.

I have seen, in a school, disorderly children who took all sorts of material and used it in an absolutely wrong way. Amongst them glided, sphinx-like, the mistress, without words. I suggested: "Wouldn't it be better for the children if you went for a stroll in the garden?" Whereat she started, going from child to child, speaking softly in the ear of each. "What are you doing?" I asked her; and she replied, "I don't want to disturb them; so I whisper."

Her mistake lay in fearing to disturb disorder! If she had feared upsetting order she would have been in the right.

A mistress once said to me, "You would have us respect the child's concentration as a very superior thing, comparable to the inspiration of an artist or of a man of science? Why then, do you tell us we can interfere when the children play with the Didactic Material?" "It is quite true," I replied, "that I respect the normal inner activity of the child as much as I do the inspiration of an artist, but *it is the inspiration and not the artist which calls forth my respect.* If I dropped in on the artist and found him sitting at home smoking and playing cards, I should not be afraid of trespassing, nor should I scruple to call to him, saying, 'My dear friend, why sit woolgathering here? Come out for a stroll in the sunshine!' "

Our method does not insist upon respect for the futile or the erroneous!

As a fundamental thing, therefore, in her knowledge of the method, the mistress must learn to distinguish between good and evil. By Good, we mean—in this connection—the psychological states favourable to the child's development, to his health of mind. By Evil, we mean the psychological states void of formative influence or actually unfavourable to his development, since they lead merely to a useless scattering of his forces.

Not only to school mistresses do we recommend this fundamental knowledge, but above all to mothers.

Without any doubt the mistress might well admonish the child somewhat briskly in order to get him out of this state of disorder. But a capable teacher possesses other and more efficacious means than force, although these means require sustained attention and persevering effort. One of the principles to be observed will be the minute supervision of the environment in which the child moves, which will become a veritable work of foresight and love.

As a wife supervises the arrangement of her husband's house so as to make it pleasant and attractive to him, so must the mistress busy herself about the child's surroundings. Constant attention is needed, and even this is not enough; she must know all the child's needs. More still, she will work with her own hands to embellish the cradle of the new-born soul.

In addition to the perfect presentation of the material, in addition to this fundamental psychological knowledge of the child, she must take the most minute care of the smallest details in the environment, keeping a continual watch over the objects it contains.

By the habit of observation the mistress will arrive at understanding, little by little, but clearly, what her mission is.

On this observation of minute details depends the order or the disorder, of the children; on it depend the results she will obtain in her school. It is, therefore, essential that she should train herself if she wishes to arrive at the right observation of these details.

It would be easy to give an example of the serious consequences derived from errors apparently trifling. Let us suppose a house belonging to working-men in which baths have recently been added. If the tenants use these baths to store coals in, they can obviously not wash in them any longer. Not only will this be bad for the house, but the error, trifling if you will in itself, will result in a state of inferiority; they will not be able to take advantage of the gifts of civilization placed within their reach. Thus going back to the teacher, she will obtain very small results instead of the great ones that were expected, disorder instead of order. The ability of the mistress in our method depends on the enlightened application of principles which inspire her to strive against little obstacles and thereby achieve great results.

Analagous to the way of spiritual perfection is the path the mistress has to follow. It is not that the trifling venial sin overcome leads straight to perfection. It is rather that the soul, freed from these trifles, is capable of rising. The overcoming of the trifles has brought into play all the energies of life; by the overcoming of the little difficulty an obstacle is removed from the path to perfect order. It is not the child himself that we take into consideration, it is the error that we have to track down. Our work is the dealing, not with the sinner, but with the sin.

CHAPTER 6

ADVICE TO DIRECTRESSES[1]

I would like, in the present number, to anticipate certain questions which are sure to be set by readers of *The Call* by a few suggestions which have been borne in upon me, in proportion as I have visited various schools and observed their mistakes. These errors, apparently trifling, are in their nature psychological rather than technical, and are concerned with small matters. These may appear to be very small, and are indeed so; yet nevertheless they are such that they succeed in preventing that full and harmonious development which every directress wishes to see reigning in her class. It is precisely because they appear to be so insignificant that they are so hard to detect and difficult to eliminate.[4]

As they fall under four headings, I will divide what I have to say into four sections.

THE ENVIRONMENT

The directress must not simply content herself with having prepared a suitable and agreeable environment for her class; but this environment must remain the object of her

---

[4] From *The Call of Education*, Vol. II, No. IV.

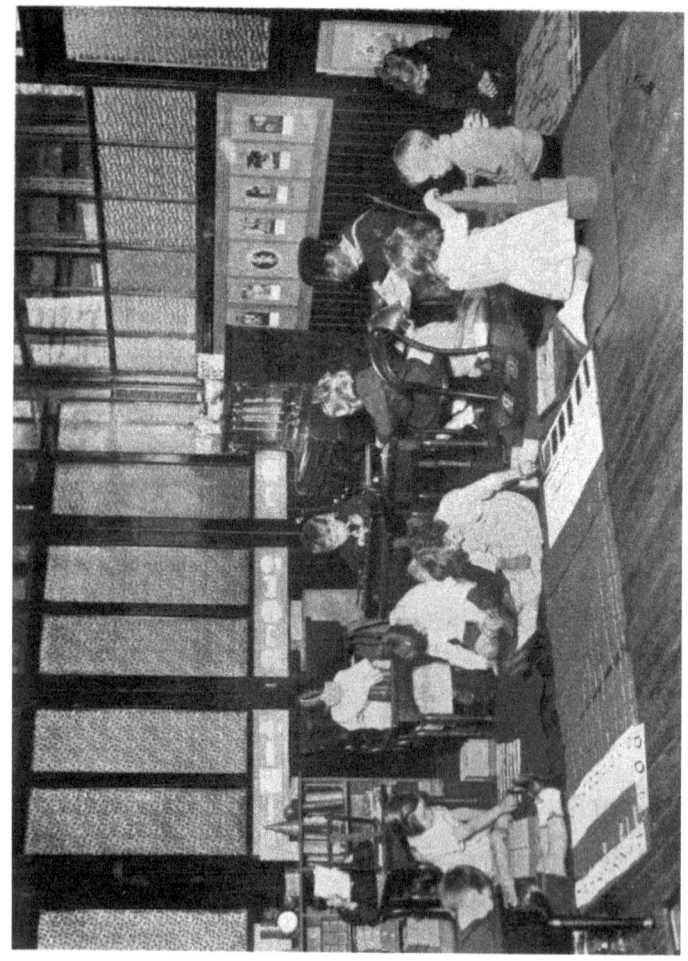

Notre Dame Montessori School, Dowanhill, Glasgow. Children working with sensory apparatus, e.g., Pink Tower, Colour Tablets, also Number Rods, numbers from 1-1,000, notation on Frame, etc. (Photo by D. L. Stewart)

unceasing care, because a great amount of her success will depend on this. The directress must therefore:

(a) Keep the material for the development in perfect order. If she neglects to do this the material will not interest the children, and will therefore lose its value; for the whole essence of the Montessori Method lies in the spontaneous activity of the child, which can only result from the interest which it shows in the material.

(b) She must take care that every object used by the children has a fixed place, and one which can be easily reached by them. Thus, for example, the pencils, coloured crayons, the pens and the ink, etc., should be kept in such a manner that the children can find them easily without the assistance of the directress.

(c) It is the order in which the objects in the environment are kept which teaches the child the idea of order. The directress should therefore, in this respect, occupy herself rather with the environment than with the child and permit the former to teach the latter. To give an example. If for each little broom there is something to hang it on which prevents it from touching the floor, and therefore from getting spoiled, the children will quickly learn to put it away in this manner; and if there is a special hook for every towel used, and if the towels are hung up in such a way after use that they will dry properly, the child will be interested in this order, and will learn to do the same.

Exercises in Practical Life

There should be exercises in practical life for all the children, corresponding to the age of the child, passing from the easy to the difficult, the simple to the complicated.

Every directress should study to find out which are the

exercises in practical life at once interesting and possible to carry out in her particular surroundings, and then draw out a list of them; because, while the didactic material is in a manner fixed and absolute, this is not the case with the exercises in practical life. The latter vary according to the possibilities of the particular environment; nevertheless they always remain a most important part of the work, *because they take the place of the formal gymnastic exercises of other methods.* For this reason, therefore, the exercise should be interesting and sufficiently difficult.

The Exercises in Practical Life should be done when they are necessary, at any hour, and not according to a fixed time table. For example, the children should wash their hands when they are dirty, sweep the floor when there is anything on the ground that needs sweeping up, etc. Many will object that, if this permission is given to them, the children will do nothing else but the exercises in practical life, and drawing. This is not so, and if such a situation comes about it is solely because the directress has not known how to present the material to the children in a manner which has rendered it interesting to them, or because she has given them work either too easy or too difficult.

The directress must not remedy this state of affairs by forbidding the exercises in practical life, or by permitting them only at certain times of the day. She must let the children work at these exercises if they want to, even for the whole day if they wish it; only she should make the other work so interesting that they will not wish to devote themselves exclusively to one thing. She should not, however, become alarmed even if the children give themselves up exclusively for several days to one kind of work: this is what we call an *"explosion"*; and this continuous application to one kind of work -*provided it is done with intensity, that is to say, with sincerity*—always produces the best results.

The directress should herself study to find out the best way of carrying out the exercises in practical life in order to be able, afterwards, to teach them with success to her children. She should point out every detail of the action with absolute clearness, and then leave the child the means of perfecting itself, without correcting it, even if it does it badly. *What is important is that the child should do the work itself* without a word, or any other assistance—even a glance—from the directress.

She must give her lesson; plant the seed in the soil, and then slip away; observe and wait expectantly, but not interfere.

Use of Material Corresponding to Age

The material must correspond to the intelligence and therefore to the age of the child in order to interest him.

If the material interests him, the child repeats the exercise, and this repetition of the exercise develops not only intelligence but also character; therefore the progress of the class, as well as its discipline, depends on the interest of the children in their work. The directress should always bear in mind the ages of the children, and the material adapted to the different ages, in order that she may be able to present to each that occupation which really interests him; she should know the precise order of the progression of the material, though she need not always follow it. When, for example, a child comes to the school at a relatively late age, she should give to it the material corresponding to its age, *not that which precedes it, even though the child may never have had the elementary material in its hands.* Perhaps, later, he will turn back spontaneously and do the preliminary exercises after he has, as you might say, saturated himself with the work which has interested him.

To facilitate the task of the directress I will give here an outline of the material and the exercises which correspond to the different ages. I omit the exercises in practical life, which, as I have said, should be given at all ages, in degrees of difficulty and complication suited to the ages of the children.

Three years. The three series of solid insets, the "Pink Tower," the easy buttoning frames, etc., the "rough" and "smooth" boards, the first series of colour-matching.

Three-and-a-half years. All the buttoning and lacing frames, the first geometric insets, the stereognostic exercises, the broad stair, exercises in touching different stuffs, the long stair, all the colours for matching, the more difficult geometric figures, the first gradations of colours, geometric insets with cards, the first drawings.

Four years. Continuation of all the preceding exercises, colour gradations with all the colours, the bells, all the geometric figures with the figures on the cards (with the teaching of their names also), geometric insets, with eyes bandaged, touching the sand-paper letters, counting with the number rods, counting with the spindles, odd and even numbers, touching the sand-paper numbers and learning their names, memorizing the numbers.

Four-and-a-half years. Making up words with the movable alphabet, much drawing, reading cards, first exercises in arithmetic with the number rods, learning the notes of the musical scale, reading.

Five years. Continuation of the foregoing exercises, especially exercises with the movable alphabet, writing, written sums in arithmetic, and reading.

Five-and-a-half years. Writing in ink, first exercises in musical notation, the grammar boxes, repetition of exercises with solid geometric figures, the three series of solid insets with the eyes shut.

The Intervention of the Directress

Many directresses intervene with the children's activities with prohibition, advice or praise, when they should not do so; and, on the other hand, hold themselves apart when such intervention is necessary.

The directress must not interfere with an action when the impulse that prompts it is a good one—neither with approval or assistance, nor to instruct or correct. Her intervention destroys this impulse, or at least causes the real "ego" of the child to remain hidden, which draws itself inwards like a snail into its shell.

I give herewith a few examples to illustrate these facts:

(a) A child runs up to some one and embraces him affectionately, but in a rough and awkward manner. Now if the directress chooses this moment to correct the child, and instructs it as to how it ought to salute another, the child will feel offended, or at least embarrassed and confused—to such an extent that, for a long time, it will not forget this disagreeable impression, and it will not wish to salute anyone, and may not, indeed, ever be able to salute anyone again in such a free and spontaneous manner. If on the other hand the directress recognizes that it is her fault for not having instructed the children properly, and prepares herself to give an animated and diverting lesson on the different ways of saluting another person, and gives this lesson several days later, the child will not feel itself offended, but will learn with pleasure how to salute another politely, without losing its affectionate spontaneity.

(b) A child is trying to wash a table; not knowing how to do it, he does it badly. The directress chooses this moment to teach him how it ought to be done. The child loses interest, rubs the surface of the table two or three times with half-hearted interest, then leaves it and goes away. If the directress had only waited the child would possibly have discovered for himself how to wash the table, and would thus have perfected himself. But in every case the directress should choose another moment to give the lesson, that is to say, when there is no danger of destroying a good impulse.

(c) A child has not long been in the school; he is small and very timid. Up to the present he has remained motionless at his place, looking round him without interest in anything. To-day he rises: softly, softly, as though he were trying to hide himself, he goes to find his first work. The directress sees him, and makes gaily towards him to encourage him with a few words. The child feels himself discovered, is embarrassed, is indeed as much frightened by the approval of the directress as if she had given him a scolding. He is covered with confusion, returns hastily to his table, puts down the object which he had been seeking and remains there without using it. For another month, perhaps, this child will do nothing more, but will remain seated, looking around him, more depressed and more timid than ever.

(d) A bad-tempered and ill-mannered boy does an act of kindness to another child. If the directress seeing it, nods her head to him to demonstrate her approval, encouraging him to persevere in the good path, the child will feel a sort of shame at his first display of gentleness (which perhaps seems to him a form of weakness) and will do his best to suppress and conceal it in future—thereby becoming more unsociable and impolite than before. If on the other hand the directress acts as though she had not noticed anything, the child will feel a real pleasure in doing these little secret acts of kindness, and will perfect himself by continuing to practise them.

The directress should intervene and correct the children every time the latter commit impolite and disorderly actions,

Ursuline Convent, Waterford. Exercises in Practical Life. Left. Using the washstand—note the concentration. Right. Lunch in the class room: the children lay the tables, wait on each other, and clear away afterwards.

i.e., actions which do not spring from a good impulse or lead towards perfection. For example, when they:
(a) pass in front of other persons without asking permission;
(b) drag chairs along the floor instead of carrying them;
(c) bang doors;
(d) throw paper on the floor instead of into the waste-paper basket;
(e) leave the table in disorder after working at it, etc.

The directress should not only intervene when there is disorder, but also beforehand to prevent it coming. She should therefore reprove those actions, which, without being disorderly, are useless; because these are actions which lead to disorder. For example: two children are playing together stupidly. If the directress does not intervene to direct their attention to something interesting and intelligent, after a few minutes other children will have joined them, causing a great disturbance and disorder. Or again; a child instead of washing his hands, is playing with the water. If the directress does not intervene, in a little time the child will begin throwing the water at his companions, who will imitate him at this game, putting the whole class in an uproar.

These observations which I have made, one here and one there, on various occasions and with different persons, have always led—when pointed out to the teacher—to a great improvement in the class; and this to the great astonishment of the directresses, who have often confessed to me that they would not have imagined that such a small thing would have so great a result. But it is precisely the little details which change a work of mediocrity into a masterpiece.

CHAPTER 7

SENSITIVE PERIODS[1]

I would like to draw your attention to one of the most interesting conclusions arrived at by the Dutchman, Hugo de Vries, in his classical experimental studies on the development of living things. It is this: that certain determining conditions in the environment are able to bring about different results if applied at different stages in the individual's development.

Conditions which are extremely favourable to development during a certain period may become ineffectual, or even unfavourable during a later period.

It follows that the moment through which the living thing is passing should be regarded in itself, and not in relation to the necessity of the life of the species, or—in other words—to the life of the adult individual. Actual development depends, not on a precocious orientation or adaptation of the infantile being to the completeness (*finalità*) of the species, but in the possibility of realizing the conditions of life necessary for the *present moment* of its own individual evolution.

Such conclusions do not concern themselves with a generic principle, but with a number of facts which have been established from the observation of the manner of

---
[5] From *L'Idea Montessori*, June 1927.

development of the most diverse orders of living beings. When one speaks (in experimental biology, such as de Vries has described) of conditions in the environment, favourable at certain determined periods to the development of the individual and not at others, it must be understood that this is because the individual itself is different at different times. Not only has vegetative life generic needs which are diverse, but there are also different "attitudes" and different "sensibilities" which exist only for a period which will pass, and then become weaker or even disappear.

In these periods, which de Vries has called "sensitive periods," the living being has, what one may call, creative and transforming attitudes; and these instincts conduce appreciably to the realization of fundamental necessities on which the future of the species depends—and furthermore, these periods are such that, having passed, the possibility of such realization has passed with them. For example, it is known that the feminine sex of the worker bee is incompletely developed. Only the queen bee is perfect, but this condition depends on its nourishment. The *pappa reale* is that food which will assist the larva of the queen to reach its own particular development; and, if this particular nourishment is wanting, the larva, destined to maternity, remains a worker bee. There is, in the life of the feminine larva, a sensitive period when it needs a certain food on which its whole future depends. If, however, this nourishment becomes accessible to the larva "when it has become too old," its own development is no longer possible; for its growth has now preceded too far towards the form of the worker bee; and it cannot come back. In this case the end of the "sensitive period" is clearly determined.

As an example of a sensitive period of another genus one may compare, with the above, the case of the larva *(bruco)* of the Porthesia, a very common species of butterfly. These caterpillars, when scarcely out of the egg, move towards the light; that is to say, they have a definite sensibility towards the light. They live on trees; and, being attracted to the most luminous part of the tree, they come into contact with the young leaves, which are tender enough to form their first nourishment. As soon, however, as they have absorbed a sufficiency of this tender nutriment and are able to digest tougher leaves, they lose this sensibility towards light. Thus they are now no longer obliged to remain always at the extremities of the branches, but are able to advance towards the darker parts of the tree where they find nourishment more adapted to their later development. The loss of this sensibility is therefore as necessary as its appearance.

My experiences with children have led me to describe in my books a large quantity of phenomena, which are strikingly parallel to the above. These are the periods in which children show aptitudes and possibilities in the psychical order, which afterwards disappear.

Thus, for example, they interest themselves with an extraordinary intensity in certain exercises, which one may in vain expect them to repeat at a more advanced stage. When their energy spurs them on to concentrate on a particular exercise, they will remain at it absorbed for a long time, and display in the execution of it an accuracy and a patience which the adult would not be able to imitate.

It is during this sensitive period that a function can be more perfectly established, or an ability can be acquired in a more perfect manner. For example, it is only at a certain period that the sounds of a language can be reproduced to perfection, and thereafter established as a definite and perfect acquisition. Since, during this period, the child is near his mother, the language which results is called the "mother-tongue." In this period, however, any language whatever could be "fixed" perfectly—as we see in the case of children who have emigrated sufficiently early to foreign countries. In vain does the child of a later age, or the adult, tire himself out in trying to pronounce perfectly the sounds of a strange language; in spite of all their efforts they carry in their accents the "stamp of a foreigner." On the other hand, the grammar and the rules of the new language are accessible to the child more developed in reasoning powers, because he is particularly interested in words and the construction of phrases; and this is beyond the power of the little child. The boy will learn the spelling and the grammar of the new language successfully. It will, however, be rare if an adult succeeds in learning these things as easily and as well as the boy; he will always continue to make mistakes in spelling and grammar.

If in education one takes into due consideration these sensitive periods, one may sometimes arrive at results which are surprising, and, above all, contradictory to our prejudices concerning the uniform progression of the intellect, and our ideas with regard to fatigue in learning. When the child does exercises which correspond to the needs of his "present sensibility" he advances and reaches a degree of perfection which is inimitable in other moments of life; and, even without fatigue, increases his own strength, and proves the joy which comes with the satisfying of a real need of life.

That is to say, he grows and is reinforced by his work, and is not consumed by it. Children who are able to commence writing at the proper age (*i.e.*, four-and-a-half or five years of age) reach a perfection in writing which you will not find in children who have begun to write at six or seven; but especially you will not find in this later stage that enthusiasm and the richness of production, which has made us call this singular phenomenon "the explosion into writing."

There follows from all this, not only a putting back of the various things to be learnt to a younger age, but also a surprising efficiency in the results, in every exercise which occurs in its "sensitive period."

As soon as the Montessori Method began to be known, these facts prevented many persons from giving it due consideration. The so-called "miracles" of the Montessori children deterred cautious students from a serious examination of the Method. It seemed to them an absurdity to allege that smaller children should be able to accomplish things which not even older children were able to do. In Holland, however, where the researches of de Vries had prepared the way for such observations, it was precisely this fact which aroused such interest -viz., the recognition and the utilization of the "sensitive periods" of the child. Especially Professors Fortuyn and Godefroy were supporters of it and made it known. I will conclude with the following quotation from Professor Godefroy.

"The term 'sensitive period' to describe the phenomenon of a temporary and extraordinary sensibility of an organism to actions of a definite kind which relate to its own development, is admitted to-day amongst biologists on every hand. When one considers education put into harmony with the nature of the child the 'sensitive period' reveals itself in a new light. We are in fact called to consider the origin of education on a natural plane, and to turn to the child in its more tender years. The instruction also of the adolescent reveals itself on new planes, because the adolescent also has 'sensitive periods.'

"We who are already acquainted with the idea of 'sensitive periods' can affirm that the Montessori Method is based on just such a principle, is new and original in psychology and differs from all other systems. This also explains, up to a certain point, the success of the Method itself, and the possibility it reveals of obtaining results markedly different from other systems.

"Those who are not favourable to the Montessori Method ask, sceptically, what will become of the Method after a number of years, meaning to imply that before long a new system will have taken its place.

"It is not difficult to make clear to such that the Montessori Method is founded on general characteristics of life, proper to all organisms, and that it will therefore last as long as life itself lasts. It is not possible to imagine that such a principle, having once been introduced into Pedagogy, could ever be abandoned."

CHAPTER 8

CHILD CHARACTER[1]

We have chosen intentionally the title: "Child Character." By character, here, we mean not merely the traits of moral character but also the child's personality, which is not composed of separate moral, intellectual and physical factors but is a whole, and can be analyzed only in theory by psychologists. [6]

We intend giving here a general survey of children's characters, of their activity which is so often not taken into consideration, and which is still more often misunderstood.

Suppose that the development of their work is represented by lines.

Suppose then that a horizontal straight line represents the state of quiescence. Suppose again that all the lines in the upper part represent orderly work, *i.e.*, "order," and those in the lower part disorderly work, or "disorder." Take a look at this scheme, and with this guide let us follow a child's actions in school.

Let us consider the different circumstances: the child enters the school; he keeps quiet for a while, and then starts working. The line moves upwards into the division of "order."

---

[6] An address given by Dr. Montessori at Brussels, and published in *La Femme Belge*.

Dr. Montessori amongst the Irish "Bambini" on the occasion of her visit to the Convent of Mercy, Waterford, 1927

He grows tired and commits disorderly actions, and the line falls instantly into the division of "disorder." The child takes up some new work. He had, for instance, first taken up the Button Frame and now the insets. Up to this time he has been assiduous, but all at once he begins to hinder his neighbours, and the line drops; he amuses himself by teasing his comrades, and thus deliberately enjoys being disorderly. He then chooses the musical bells; he makes them ring; for a moment he will keep quiet and the line rises again into "order." When he has finished this he will begin to annoy his teacher.

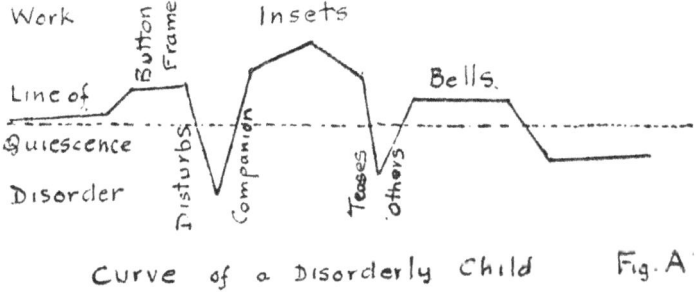

Curve of a Disorderly Child   Fig. A

This line (Fig. A) would give us an idea of the daily acts we have just spoken about, and at the same time a diagram of the individual work of a child at school.

Such a diagram can demonstrate at one glance the development of a continued phenomenon which we might be able to follow, thanks to a law, provided one existed.

But in this line we do not see any law which is capable of interesting us in it; it is a diagram of those many children who do now this, now that, without being able to fix their attention upon anything, and who handle in half a day all the material which suffice for a whole year's work. This is the type of a disorderly child.

We shall leave this child for a time, and after an interval we shall go back to the same child when we shall see that the phenomenon of concentration, namely attention, has begun to show itself.

Now I will give you the diagram of a child in the transition stage, *i.e.*, no longer disorderly, but not yet quite orderly, a state we might consider as being just between order and disorder (Fig. B).

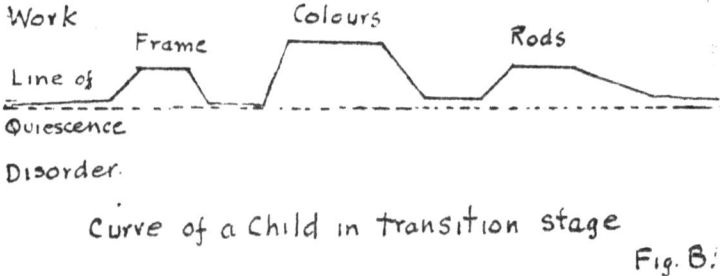

Curve of a Child in transition stage

Fig. B.

On coming into school the child chooses some simple work, very easy to himself, one or other exercise of practical life. He leaves it to take up from the material a familiar object, and repeats certain exercises. Then we see him get tired, restless, and his line falls under the line of "order." This may happen not merely with one child alone but also with a whole class. What would the inexperienced teacher say in that case? She would conclude that the children were tired after having done exercises of practical life, or after having worked with the material, that the phenomenon of concentration has not shown itself, and that she is powerless to do anything.

If the teacher is kind-hearted, she may conclude that the children need a rest, that she ought to stop their exercises or change their surroundings, and she will take them with her into the garden. You will see them playing in a "disorderly manner," filling the garden with their shouts, and when back again in the class-room, they will be much more restless than before leaving it; they will do nothing but change about from one work to another, and their seeming fatigue will be as evident as before.

How many teachers have not said to themselves: "It is *not* a fact that free choice of work brings rest and calm to little children; for I have actually seen them choose their own work and apply themselves to it for a moment, but yet their unrest grows; it is of no use whatever to make them rest, or to take them to another scene; I shall never succeed either in making them work or in giving them restfulness."

Such teachers have faithfully studied our method, but they have not had the required confidence in it to respect the child's freedom. And they cannot refrain from reasoning, from having recourse to their scientific knowledge, from interfering, from trying to direct; and by doing so they interrupt the process of the phenomenon and thus they spoil all.

If, on the contrary, a teacher respects the child's freedom, if she trusts sufficiently to it, if she has a strong enough character to forget for a moment all the science which aids her own intelligence, and if she be humble enough not to think that her interference will be of any use, she will then have the patience to wait. Then she will see this phenomenon: after the preliminary work, after the spiritual unrest of a child seeking in the depths of his consciousness where light has not yet appeared, he chooses a fresh, and to him difficult work; he gives himself wholly to it; he becomes engrossed in it for a long time, devoting his whole soul to it; he isolates himself from his surroundings: this is what we call the *"Great Work."*

When finished, the child leaves the object alone which was the instrument of his concentration. Now he shows an entirely different character from that shown when he was supposed to be tired. Then he looked tired; now his face bears a radiant expression; calm and repose reign on his features, as if he had been given a strength-giving injection.

This makes us understand that there is one whole and complete cycle of work, composed of two parts—the first one being that of preparation or training, followed by the second one, the "Great Work"

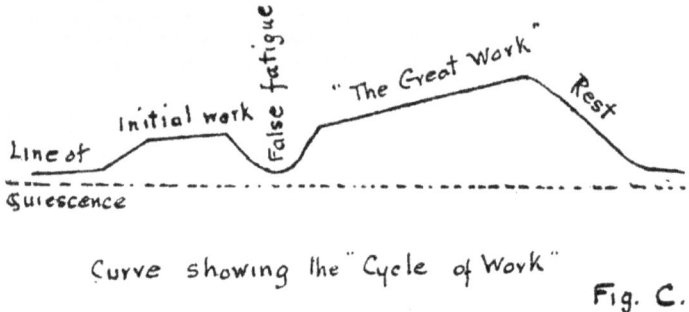

Fig. C.

Let us compare the child with a hearty eater. He is hungry. Olives are brought to him, and then soup. In the child's case, he will not let himself be served with the hors d'œuvre—his intellectual aperitif—but chooses it himself, with an instinct which teaches him that before eating the substantial dish he must prepare himself for it.

After the soup comes the nourishing meat, and the person at table eats his fill. If a friendly neighbour were to see him eating his olives without eagerness and slowly drinking his soup, looking impatiently to the right and left, that neighbour might say: "This man has had enough; he is tired and he wants to be off. I know what I shall do. I shall suggest to him a stroll in the garden."

Then they both go out, and, in passing, the neighbour gives the order to keep the roast for the next day. How embarrassing the stroll would be! By what means could repose, cheerfulness and strength be brought back to the soul of the poor hungry man?

If, on the contrary, the neighbour has more perspicacity, he will say to himself, on noticing the man at his olives and soup, looking impatiently round him: "This man is hungry, he is eager to eat his roast", and he will take a real pleasure in seeing the other eat with a good appetite.

How many well-meaning people, anxious about the welfare of others, would say to themselves: "This man is eating too much; I, who am familiar with anatomy and physiology, know that his jaw has to expend a force of several kilograms to reduce this slice of beef to chyme, I must stop him": "Sir, leave your dinner, your jaw is getting tired."

Here is a case when we have to forget some of our science. After the "Great Work" the child is rested; one might even say that during it he was really resting! His radiant cheerfulness and his quiet repose, proclaim a new truth to us. As a matter of fact the child does not display the signs of fatigue after his "Great Work"; on the contrary the physiological characteristics indicate a superabundance of vitality.

It is the same phenomenon which shows itself after a good dinner or bath, which are really exercises or work, which, instead of diminishing our strength, serve to restore our vigour; in the same way there is a psychical work which invigorates the spirit.

To enable the child to rest it is necessary to enable him to do the "Great Work."

As a matter of fact, what *is* rest? To us it does not mean being idle; our muscles do not rest when inactive, but only when acting normally. So psychical rest consists of an exercise which renders the intellect vigorous.

That is all as mysterious as the essence of life. A teacher cannot say: this child needs this or that work just now to be vigorous; that is beyond her power, for only the child is capable of choosing the work which suits him. Herein lies the respect due to the child's work and the confidence to await it.

The child that is rested is a merry, cheerful child, who will perhaps be disposed to confide in his teacher, because his soul has awakened and he is going to see in his teacher a person superior to himself. He now observes a great many things in his surroundings which he did not remark before. Assuredly he has become richer, and hence even more openhearted.

The diner, too, who has dined well, will greet a friend affably whom before dinner he might have passed by without even a glance. This need not astonish us.

Before being able to expend our forces we must first collect them. A teacher who would try to instruct a child morally weak or ill-nourished would find that child wanting in the power to come to her to confide in her and to obey her, and even were he to do so, it would be feebly and with difficulty.

Though it may seem strange, it is this way that we should teach children the manifestation of this inner wealth, without imparting it to them beforehand, as if these manifestations of inner wealth were something that could be learned.

Let us rather look for the way by which those inner forces develop, and as a result we shall see the same forces unfolding themselves abundantly.

According as these phenomena recur, and calm and rest develop, another complex phenomenon will appear which might be called *the discipline of the children*. Those teachers whose experience has taught them this point, comprehend the language of our schools. Thus one teacher will ask another: "How is your class getting on? Is it orderly yet?" and the answer may be: "No, not yet." Or one might hear a remark of this kind: "You remember that child who was always so disorderly? He is quite orderly now." When teachers speak

Notre Dame Montessori School, Dowanhill, Glasgow. Children preparing miniature altar and vestments as for Benediction. (Photo by. D. L. Stewart)

in this way they have learned what they had to learn. All that follows is but a natural consequence. The phenomenon begins to grow as soon as it has manifested itself.

The children in whom it has shown itself are on the way towards psychical development; gradually they will become "Great Workers," and finally it will be impossible for them ever to be idle. If, for instance, they have to wait for some one, they will not be long without finding something to do; they will begin some work or other in order to be able to wait patiently. Work becomes then an *attitude* of the child.

As this development continues we see that the period of the *pseudo-fatigue* gradually decreases, while the line of rest becomes longer.

This rest *sui generis* is an active rest. Without doubt it is also an inner activity which has no connection with any object.

Let us go back to our comparison with the diner. There is a period for digestion which also belongs to the process of nutrition, but which takes place internally and is in nowise connected with the different dishes. The child's mental digestion also has particular traits of activity which are those of a meditating person; this activity is very like that of persons in contemplation. The child also contemplates his environment, notices the smallest trifle and appears to be making discoveries.

Concentration is thus divisible into three phases; the preparatory phase; that of the "Great Work" which is connected with an exterior object; and the third phase which is entirely an inward one, full of joy and light which, like a reflector, illuminates the environment and enlightens objects which would otherwise pass unobserved.

Only in the spiritual life do we find similar phenomena. Thus it has been written: "Eyes have they but they see not, ears have they but they hear not." It is not the senses only which must open these. These senses have thus become more and more the instruments of the mind.

In the same way there is a kind of parallel in purely intellectual matters. Ill-bred people on leaving a room collide with others or with the furniture they did not see; they make their mistake worse by profuse apologies, by which fact they prove their inferiority; a quite common excuse is: "Sorry, but I didn't see. . . ." A blind man would do the same: he would tread on his neighbour's toes and stumble over the furniture, and might say with equal truth: "Sorry, but etc. . . ." We do not think, however, that the education of the blind consists in teaching them to make apologies, and it would seem to us almost the same if this were to suffice for the normal child.

Let us consider another phenomenon: the child becomes obedient; we are much astonished at this, for we have not taught him obedience; moreover no one could ever imagine such marvellous patience as we now notice in the children.

Imagine a person who could not keep his balance, who could not stand upright, not daring to use his arms for fear of falling, but only stumbling forward. But once having learned how to maintain his equilibrium, he will be able to leap, to walk as he likes, to bend to the right and left. It is thus in psychic life. Imagine an unbalanced mentality, to whom it is impossible to fix upon, and hold fast, a mental attitude dictated by the will. Could such a man submit to another's will infallibly? How could he obey another's will without being able to obey his own? Obedience is a kind of pliability of the mind, which is supported by the mental equilibrium. This obedience, which springs from strength of will, has in itself the greatest possibilities for what we call *"adaptability to environment."* To adapt oneself to an environment, biologists teach us, one has to be strong. The monks also know this. To be obedient one has to be strong and well-balanced. These are acknowledged facts in religious life, but nobody had thought of employing similar phenomena in the intellectual world. Just as in biology the strong creature is able to adapt itself to circumstances, so will the vigorous intellect be obedient.

This is more or less the same phenomenon. If great wealth allows us to do all we wish to do, great strength will allow us to do all we are told to do.

By these gentle and patient means of development according to natural laws, by concentration and attention, by contemplation, which one might say is the digestion of the concentration, the individual fortifies himself, and once strong, he can finally do more than we would venture to ask of him.

Do you see now what the little child has done with his fundamental activity, his concentration of attention and his contemplation which is the starting point of all else? Now he is master of his body, his muscles and his voluntary movements; he is able to follow them and direct them with attention. We have seen how far the child can master his movements, since he is able to keep motionless in the deepest silence (*cf.* the Silence Game); his self-command is often greater than that of grown-up persons. Neither must we forget the mechanism of this development, nor the control of mistakes, together with the influence exercised by environment.

If we consider all these facts together we shall find a striking resemblance to the religious life. A prepared environment, a life of peace, the required concentration for meditation and contemplation, mastery over the body, silence, the same exercises repeated from day to day. The monks have produced the greatest heroes, namely the saints, those who were ready for every strife, struggles against temptation, endurance, martyrdom. Such heroes are not formed by heated speeches, nor by sounding the trumpet of war; on the contrary they have traversed the noiseless road of formation.

If what is wanting could be supplied by exhortations, by threats or by commands, we should try this treatment to give back sight to the blind. This would be a miracle which is beyond our power. All the same, pedagogists still suffer from such delusions. What is essential are the bracing exercises. What do the monks do? They remain in that prepared environment day after day; now these same principles can be applied to the entire psychic life for the training of character.

If man be a unity, his path must be equally so. In the inner life there is also unity.

This is only a comparison of course, and no one will suppose that I should think of educating children of three with the same discipline as the monks, those saintly heroes. No, I have gained my experience in quite another way. Children in freedom have revealed to me the laws of inner life—general laws, which are not exclusively followed by monks. It is the children who led me to discover the narrow way for the development of that life which has freed itself from materialism. Children have spontaneously sought and have instinctively found the way of strength. Concentration is the centre of development. As a matter of fact every force must be conducted into channels before becoming motive power. The water of a flood is evaporated by the sun, but canalized water is heated and becomes motive power. This is the reason why we venture to say that it is useless to teach the principles of strength; our aim must be to make strong men.

CHAPTER 9

The Montessori Method

Although the primary object of this book is to set forth Dr. Montessori's ideas on the religious education of children, it will not be out of place to devote a chapter to the principles of the Montessori method taken as a whole. For it will be seen that her method of work in the religious sphere is simply an extension of the same principles to the study of the Supernatural Order.

It is not possible in a single chapter to give an adequate idea of the principles which underlie the Montessori method: we can but briefly point out some of the salient characteristics and refer those who wish to go further to Dr. Montessori's own works; and, what is equally important, urge them to go and see the method actually at work in a well-managed Montessori school.

If it were necessary to compress the description of the principles of the Montessori method into a single phrase, perhaps the most comprehensive would be that it was a method based on "Liberty in a Prepared Environment."

The Prepared Environment

Modern biological research has emphasized the importance of environment in the development, and therefore in the study, of all forms of life. This does not imply that environment is the *cause* of the growth; it is rather the means towards it. The wonderful successes in biological research achieved by such men as Darwin, De Vries, Fr. Wasman, Fabre and others have depended on the fact that these naturalists have been careful to place the developing forms they wished to study, and have studied as they grew up, in their proper environment. As Dr. Montessori says, "the function of the environment is not to *mould* the growing form of life, but to *reveal* it." Every schoolboy knows that to rear caterpillars successfully you must give them air and light and a particular kind of food; otherwise their development will be arrested and they may die.

And the important point to notice is that unless the right environment is given to an organism it cannot reach full development or reveal its true nature. To take rather a crude example. Suppose (by an effort of imagination) that you had never seen or heard of such a creature as a monkey, and that one day you were given a present of a monkey, shut up in a small box with smooth walls and a glass side so that you could observe it. Under such conditions you would never come to realize the monkey's extraordinary propensity for climbing. But now, supposing someone came along who had observed monkeys in their natural environment—and said to you: "Place that creature in a large cage with a tree inside it and you will see it display an agility that will put the cleverest acrobats to shame." You could verify the statement by preparing an environment and putting the monkey into it. The true environment would not be the *cause* of the monkey's agility; it would only *reveal* it.

In the same way, says Dr. Montessori, if you wish to understand the nature of the growing child—to discover the capabilities and talents within him—you *can never properly do so until you place him in an environment suitable to his needs, and allow him to be free in it.*

The higher and more complex the organism, the greater the number of factors in the environment which are necessary to draw out the latent faculties of the living creature. Thus for the growth of a plant you require suitable soil, fresh air, light, moisture, and suitable temperature; and for an animal you need, not only all these, but, in addition, space and liberty for it to move about freely. But man is an intellectual being, and therefore in the environment of the growing child, you will need not only those factors in the environment which support the vegetative functions, and also the opportunity to move about like an animal, but in addition something which answers to the need of his growing intellectual faculties as well. Now a Montessori school is just such a "prepared environment."

It would not be sufficient to leave a child all day to his own devices in the middle of a field, or in an ordinary living room. True, he would have fresh air and liberty to move about. But this would be no more true freedom for him than it would be for a bird shut up in a cage. For the child—by his very nature—longs to spread out the pinions of his intellect and rise to the use of reason. He would therefore soon become restless and unsatisfied without opportunity and means to develop these rational faculties.

But now place that same child in an environment which has been carefully prepared so that it will correspond not only to his vegetative and animal needs, *but also to his intellectual and moral needs*, and leave him free in it, and you will see a wonder that beggars description. You will then see—as I have often seen—in different countries—some forty to fifty children, of ages varying from three to seven years, all in the same room and all quite at liberty to move about and talk as

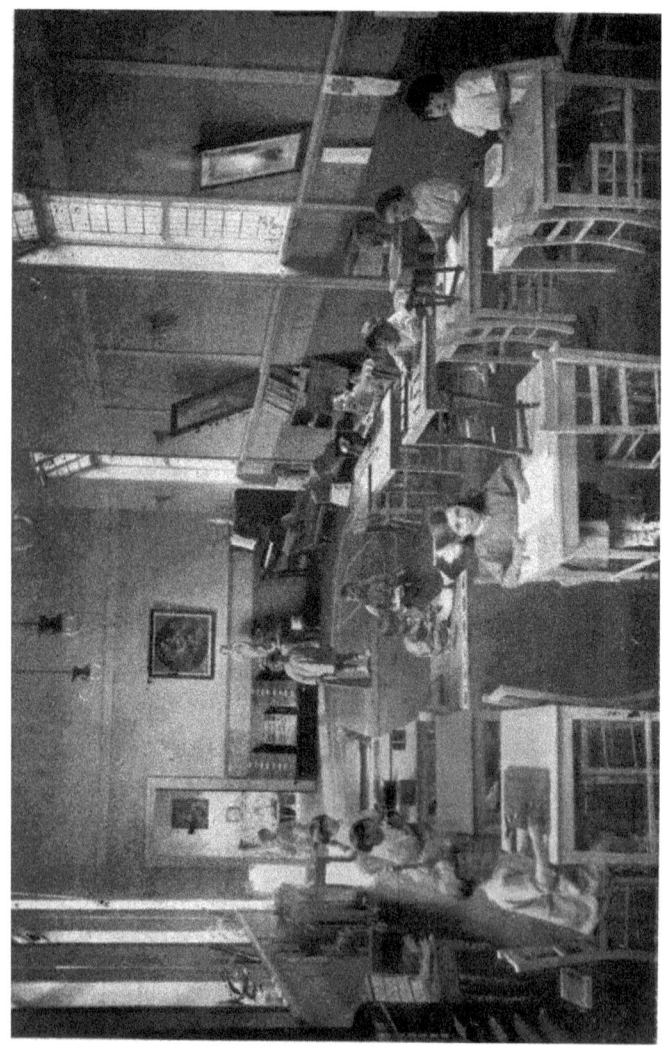

Montessori Room, Convent of Mercy, Oak Lea, Sunderland. Notice piano at far end, and lines on the floor for children to march on. The child in the foreground on left is using part of the music apparatus. (Photo by Taylor's Studio)

they wish. And yet in spite—or rather—*because* of this liberty (taken in conjunction with the prepared environment) there is no more disorder or confusion than you will find in a large bank or emporium, where everyone is quietly going about his own business. In fact the children are all so busy with their various occupations that I have often seen the teacher go out of the room without the children even appearing to notice it.

The orderly, yet spontaneous behaviour of small children, their astonishing concentration—often for prolonged periods of time, their manifest joy and serenity in their work, their mutual helpfulness and courtesy, the avidity with which they throw themselves by their own choice into such occupations as arithmetic and grammar—all this seems almost incredible to persons who have never seen it for themselves. Yet it all comes from placing the child in an environment specially prepared for his mental needs. If this is done he shows a mental agility comparable to the physical agility of the monkey taken out of the small box and placed in an arboreal environment.

A very important part of this prepared environment consists in what is (rather clumsily) called the Didactic Apparatus.[7] This is not the place to enter into a description of this Montessori material. Suffice it to say that in the earlier stages the material is used to bring about a concentration of the child's attention on sensorial objects, thereby developing and refining his sense perceptions; and later, to lead through combined operation of the senses and intellect, to a knowledge of reading, writing and arithmetic.

At the same time as he is thus employed the child, by finding himself a free member in a community of children of varying ages, has the means of learning day by day, and

---

[7] Dr. Montessori prefers the phrase "Material for Development."

week by week, those lessons in self-effacement and courtesy which make social life possible.

It must not be forgotten that another and the most important factor in the child's environment is the teacher or directress. For though the rôle played by the directress is not the same as that of an ordinary infant-school teacher, it is no less important. It is indeed even more important and requires more tact and discrimination; for without this sympathetic guidance of the directress all the rest of the environment would be almost useless.

It must be remembered too—in connection with this question of the environment—that what is left out of the child's environment is as important, in its way, as what is put in. Things which are not essential, which have no purpose in assisting the development, are to be excluded.

"Montessori Freedom" in Education

Dr. Montessori has remarked that there are two kinds of objectors to her method. First, there are those who, hearing that liberty for the child is an essential part of it, are at once frightened off. These are generally people who have never really studied the method and jump to the conclusion that it is based upon the Naturalistic Theory of Rousseau as to man's nature, in accordance with the prevalent New Pelagianism.

The other objectors are found amongst those who have made a more intimate acquaintance with her work. Curiously enough *they* complain on just the opposite score—viz., that Dr. Montessori does not allow the child *enough liberty!* How can this paradox be explained? The answer lies in a juster appreciation of the true meaning of liberty.

Let us try and make this clear by an example, of a kind which frequently occurs in a Montessori school. Amongst the "didactic apparatus" there is a set known as the Number Rods. This consists of ten rods of varying lengths, the smallest being ten centimetres long, and the longest a metre. The intermediary ones form an ascending series varying by ten centimetres. The purpose of these rods is to acquaint the small child with the idea of number—and in particular the numbers one to ten. To this end the child is taught to use the rods in a particular way. By so doing the rods assist him to gain a clear notion of number; and even start him doing simple sums in addition and subtraction. "Now," says Dr. Montessori, "if you find the child is no longer using the rods for the purpose for which they were intended, if for instance he begins building a tunnel with them, or using one of them to ride a-cock-horse on, then the apparatus must be taken from him." Dr. Montessori has no objection whatever to a child building a house or tunnel, *but not with those particular rods,* because they are of a special nature, and destined for a special purpose, and so made that, used rightly, they will bring about a certain intellectual development. The same principle applies to the use of the other pieces of apparatus. *The child must respect the end for which they are made.* This refusal to allow the children to play with the apparatus in any way they like seems to some people an unwarrantable interference with the liberty of the child.

But this is—most emphatically—not Dr. Montessori's idea of liberty. She is very strict with her teachers in insisting that *no child may be allowed to use any of the apparatus until he has been definitely taught the use of it,* and the child may only occupy itself with it as long as he respects that use.

On the other hand she insists that the child should have the liberty to choose—from those pieces of apparatus of which he understands the use—this or that particular one he wants to work at (providing no other child is using it). But he may only choose from amongst those which he has learnt how to use. No words could better express Dr. Montessori's idea of liberty in her school than those used by the Holy Father Leo XIII in his Encyclical "Libertas praestantissimum." He says:—"Considered in its nature it (liberty) is the faculty of choosing means fitted for the end proposed; for he is master of his actions who can choose one thing out of many...

"Now since everything chosen as a means is viewed as good or useful, and since Good as such is the proper object of our desire, it follows that freedom of choice is a property of the will....

"But the will cannot proceed to act until it is enlightened by the knowledge possessed by the intellect—and this is the more so because in all voluntary acts choice is subject to a judgment upon the truth of the good presented, declaring to which good preference be given....

"No sensible man can doubt that judgment is an act of reason not of will....

"The end, or object, both of the rational will and of its liberty is that good only which is in conformity with reason. Since, however, both these faculties are imperfect, it is possible, as is often seen, that the reason should propose something which is really not good, but which has the appearance of good, and that the will should choose accordingly...."

Again in another passage the same Holy Father says that since the intellect of man is weak, "it is necessary that it should have light and strength given it to direct its actions to good and restrain it from evil, and without this, freedom would be its ruin." And again, "First of all there must be *law: that is a fixed rule of teaching what is to be done, and what is to be left undone*" (the italics are ours). Again, "Nothing more foolish can be uttered or conceived than the notion that because man is free by nature he is therefore exempt from law...."

Many of Dr. Montessori's own followers have grievously misunderstood her on this point, and done much harm to the movement by confusing liberty with licence. She herself is absolutely clear on the issue. "We must always consider choice in relation to things we have already presented to the child." "A child might come into the room and 'choose' for example the numerical rods out of *curiosity*: that is not free choice. Choice is what he takes from a variety of things, but only from those he knows." "Some people think," says Dr. Montessori, "that true liberty of thought consists in thinking and believing what you like, not what is true—forgetting the word of Our Lord Who said, 'it is the Truth which shall make you free.'"

Again and again she insists that the Freedom given to the child must be *a freedom to do right*—not what is wrong. That the possibility of doing wrong is not an essential part of freedom is evident from the fact that the Angels and Saints in Heaven are perfectly free. "Never fear to destroy evil," says Dr. Montessori, "it is only the good that you must preserve." But she is careful to add that, sometimes, actions in the child which have really a good motive and serve a useful purpose are not understood by the teacher or parent, and are suppressed to the child's detriment. It is only the experienced eye that can distinguish the weed from the useful plant in their very young stages; and similarly it often needs an experienced and sympathetic observer to distinguish between those actions on a child's part which are the outcome of an orderly impulse, and those which spring from a disorderly one. Too often, for instance, in the past, good behaviour in the schoolroom has been made synonymous with the immobility of the child.

Numberless comments have been made by visitors on the decorous behaviour of the little children in Montessori schools—their graceful precision of movement as they walk in and out amongst the little tables and chairs, their careful treatment of the apparatus, their courteous behaviour to each other and to visitors. They seem to combine the purposefulness of adults with the naïve, spontaneous charm of childhood. All this is the result of a liberty which has come after knowledge. Nothing is left to chance. There is a right way and a wrong way of doing everything, even such a small matter as moving a chair, handing a pencil to another person, or folding a rug. From the very beginning—in the Exercises on Practical Life—the tiny children are given what are called lessons in grace and courtesy. Again, one of the fundamental principles of the method is that the apparatus is devised in such a way that it corrects mistakes automatically. Thus Dr. Montessori insists that the little tables and chairs should be light and portable so that they can be easily knocked out of place. This being so, the children soon learn to correct any clumsy or awkward movements in their efforts to avoid these minor accidents.

The Superior of the Vincent de Paul Society in Spain very happily summed up the whole matter of Montessori Liberty when he said: "Do not fear a Method of Liberty which counts the words in the teacher's mouth and makes the children walk along a line on the floor."

The Right Environment Reveals the "New Child"

We have said that, according to Dr. Montessori the function of the environment is not so much to mould as to reveal the growing child. It must not be forgotten that, to this end, it is not enough to have the right environment, but you must give the child liberty in it. To make this clear let us revert once more to the simile of the captured monkey. Suppose you put the monkey into a spacious home, furnished with trees to climb in, but at the same time kept it chained tightly to the foot of a tree; you would not even then realize its acrobatic possibilities. It is the same with the child. If you place him amidst a prepared environment—*i.e.*, prepared to answer to his intellectual needs—it would all be to no purpose unless you allowed him to be free to move about in it, and to use it as he likes.

But—given this freedom in the prepared environment—the most astonishing results appear; and the child reveals itself as possessing characteristics and virtues not usually credited to it.

It must be borne in mind that in singing the praises of the "New Child," so revealed, Dr. Montessori is referring to what theologians would call "natural" virtues as opposed to "supernatural." The question of the relationship of the unsuspected natural virtues of the "New Child" to the Doctrine of Original Sin we shall discuss on a later page (see Appendix, p. 158).

Meanwhile we shall consider some of the characteristics of the Child as revealed by the combination of Liberty with a prepared Environment.

Auto-Education

Dr. Montessori insists on the principle that the only real education is Auto-Education. The child's mind is not a sack to be filled with information; it is a dynamic principle. As food is useless to the body—indeed injurious—unless it be thoroughly assimilated and made one with the whole organism as a living part in a living whole, so mere knowledge is useless, unless it is thoroughly assimilated and made one with the child's mind as living part of a living unity. Thus assimilation of knowledge is best effected as the result of the spontaneous working of the intellect. That is why the facts

St. Oteran's Convent of Mercy, Waterford. A corner of the "Babies' Room" which contains over a hundred infants. St. Oteran's is a large National School and was the first to introduce the Montessori Method into Ireland. "Cead Mile Failte" is Celtic for "A Hundred Thousand Welcome." (Photo by Philip & Whitney)

we cram up for an examination generally disappear from our minds as soon as the examination is over. They are not organically related to the rest of our knowledge. "A truth discovered and conquered by one's own efforts exercises a much more compelling power than the same truth learnt from another, . . . Acquisitions so made are stable, because, each having come in its own time, does not interfere or become confused with others—each rather preserving its unity in clear contrast to the others."[8]

"You cannot educate directly," says Dr. Montessori, "any more than you can make silk directly." In the latter case all you can do is to place the silkworm in its right environment, give it the right kind of food and *leave it to its own spontaneous activity;* in time it will spin its silken cocoon. So with the child. You can give it the right environment and the right intellectual food—but the active work of education must be the spontaneous exercise of the child's own faculties. One of the most striking and charming features of a Montessori school are the Montessori "explosions" which are constantly occurring in the child's development. These are moments when the child's intellect, working spontaneously, suddenly makes a new generalization or sees some unexpected relationship. At such times the child visibly experiences the thrill of joy which always accompanies such expansions of the intellect.

IMMENSE SPONTANEOUS ACTIVITY OF THE CHILD

Most people do not realize the immense spontaneous activity of the intellect in the growing child. Many persons think children are as a rule naturally indolent and have to

---

[8] *Psychologie et Psychothérapie Educatives* par Abbé d'Agnel et Dr. Espiney—an excellent book which ought to be translated into English.

be urged on continuously to mental work. This is a profound fallacy, and usually results from the fact that grown-ups imagine the child's intellect to be torpid because it is not working in the way they expect or wish it to work. Some of the most interesting of Dr. Montessori's lectures to her students deal with the spontaneous work of the intellect in children of two years *and under*. The work of the intellect is going on incessantly even before the child can speak, striving without pause to reduce the chaos of its impressions to order and arrangement. "To the new-born baby," says Professor James, "the world is one big, booming, buzzing confusion," and the marvel of infancy is that the child is able to sort things out as quickly and as well as he does. In the growth of the "microcosm" (*i.e.*, the individual) there takes place something analogous to the operations described in Genesis in the Creation of the World. First, there were made the broad divisions—light separated from darkness, land from water, and so on. So in the child's mind one may have these rough, primary classifications. For instance, a small child may not yet have learnt to distinguish the different colours, or the different numbers, or the different notes from each other. Yet he has already made the broad classification between number, colour, and sound. He may say "one, two, three, twelve, seven"; he may confuse blue with green, but he will not say, "one, two, three, blue, *eight*." This means that his opening intellect is already creating certain broad differences, as between colour and number. And later on—as in the creation of the world—his spirit, made in the likeness of the Creator, will go on to a more detailed differentiation. Seen properly these facts have immense significance as being evidences of a great spontaneous activity of the intellect; for it is the intellect which compares, contrasts, arranges in categories, and distinguishes individuals and universals.

In the same way Dr. Montessori has pointed out, and every observant mother will agree with her, that very small children—at the ages of two, three and four—display a most extraordinary passion for having things in their right places. You will often observe, in a roomful of people, that it is the smallest person present—of two or three years of age—who is most upset if a door is left open, or the corner of a rug turned over, or a cloak or hat left lying on a chair. At this age the small child feels a passionate desire that things in the environment should maintain a certain repose, and this longing to set the objects in its little world in their right place reflects the growing sense of order which is developing in the child's mind. In the Montessori school the small child has the fullest scope for giving vent to this very useful activity. Curiously enough this passion for having everything "just so" in the environment is much more strikingly evident in a child of three than in one of six or nine years of age. This introduces us to another very important principle in the Montessori method.

Periods of Special Sensibility

"When I was a child," says the apostle, "I thought as a child, but when I became a man I thought as a man, and put away childish things." Dr. Montessori goes much further than this: she would say "When I was a child of two I thought as a child of two, but when I became a child of six I thought as a child of six and put away those things I had thought as a child of two," and so on.

In other words the life of the child is a series of different stages, each having its peculiar mental and physical characteristics.

At each stage the mind of the child tends to be peculiarly

active in a particular way; and, as a consequence, has a special urge to occupy itself with certain factors or aspects in its environment at each particular stage.

AGE OF SENSATION

Between the years of three to six the child is at a stage when the activities of the senses predominate. It is hard for us adults, who possess a vast store of abstract ideas and conceptions and the garnered memories of more years than some of us care to think of, to imagine what the life of the senses means to a little child. We have, *by the very nature of our intellectual processes,* become, most of us, much more independent of our physical environment than the child of three. At any rate we can, for long periods, detach ourselves largely from things sensible, as we follow a line of abstract reasoning. But the child has only a very slender stock of abstract ideas; and it is for this very reason that he is so interested in the objects of the physical world around him. For it is only by the work of his senses, combined with the work of his intellect (*Intellectus agens* and *Intellectus patiens*) that he is able to build up a storehouse of abstract notions and concepts, according to the Aristotelian maxim, *Nihil est in Intellectu quod prius non fuerit in sensu.*

Through the windows of the senses innumerable sense impressions are pouring into his soul, and it is the business of the intellect to cope with these multitudinous and heterogeneous impressions, and reduce them, by classification and comparison, to some sort of an orderly system. The material world around him, so varied, so bewildering, so manifold, so alluring is a South Sea of discovery for the small child. His little life is a perpetual and wondering exploration. His constant mental attitude is like that of Miranda in the

Tempest (though his admiration is concentrated possibly more on things than on people):
"O wonder!
How many goodly creatures are there here!
How beauteous mankind is! O brave new World

¹*THE SENSE OF WONDER*

"A great deal of man's happiness comes from the power of admiration. To admire something is like a stream of fresh water flowing over the soul's surface; children are so happy because for them there is so much to wonder at. The deep solemnity of their untarnished eyes is the solemnity of wonderment. Woe to the man who has nothing to wonder at! his soul has lost all freshness, and his eyes are lustreless and vacant. ***N.B. Not capitalized in the original text

"If at any time of our lives we cease to wonder, the fault must be all ours. The world in which God has placed man is an eternal wonder; admiration is the only thing which establishes a kind of equality and proportion between man and the vast world in which man lives. We do not understand the marvels of the universe. We see very little of the universe; we live, each one of us, in a very small corner of it; the universe is not ours, but it becomes ours through admiration. . . .

"It is the saddest thing in the world to have one's lot cast with people who have lost the gift of admiration. It is the cruellest and darkest captivity of heart; it is external and internal darkness. It is the hardest purgatory of the soul; it would be hell itself but for the hope that the day will come that will set us free from the companionship of unwondering souls, and place us amongst the spirits whose life is unending admiration.

"Let me be surrounded with the young and the infants, whose every sound is the expression of some wonderment, and

I shall feel that my heart swells again with a happiness it has not known since childhood."—The Personality of Christ, by Dom Ascar Vonier, Abbot of Buckfast.

That has such people in it!"

Now the Montessori apparatus is so designed as to assist the classifying work of the intellect by presenting to it colours, shapes, surfaces, and all manner of objects, in such a manner (by careful grading or striking contrast and so forth) that the child's mind is drawn on to abstract from them *clear* and *definite* ideas.

Indeed, one might almost say that the object of the Montessori sensory apparatus is a super-sensible one. Hundreds of observers have commented on the almost uncanny concentration of children of two and three years, on the sensory apparatus. Let us take for example the apparatus called "the cylinders." This consists of ten cylindrical pieces of wood, each with a little nob on top for a handle. These cylinders vary by half a centimetre in diameter, from the first, which is half a centimetre in diameter, to the last which is five centimetres; and each fits into a socket exactly corresponding to its particular size. All the child has to do is to take the cylinders out, mix them up, and replace them in their right sockets. At first the child seems to have no idea of the right size, and begins by putting the cylinders in the wrong sockets; but the apparatus automatically corrects the child's error. Children of two and three years of age will repeat this exercise twenty and thirty times consecutively, and use it sometimes for days together, gradually learning to do it more quickly and more accurately.

A casual observer might think the child's enjoyment consists in the delight of simply putting them in and out again; but the source of its joy is deeper than that. Every time the exercise is performed the child is obliged to make a series of comparisons—comparing the sizes of all the cylinders. At first it means the most ridiculous mistakes; but in the end it learns to pick them out in their right order without a mistake. The real joy of the child lies in the psychological fact (not of course consciously realized by the child itself) that in repeating the exercise it is acquiring an ever increasing sensibility. It is acquiring the power to discern at a glance the different grades of cylinders. It is this inner growth, this development of an increasing sensitiveness, of a new power, that is the really important element in this apparently simple and meaningless exercise; and it is this that makes it so fascinating to the child.

So is it with all the rest of the Montessori apparatus. It is not the preoccupation with the material in itself which is of special value, it is the inner growth which accompanies it.

This brings us to another of the important principles of the Montessori method -one which stands in close relationship to that of liberty.

The Value of Spontaneous Repetition in Infant Education

Most persons have observed the tendency in small children to repeat a saying, or an action, or game over and over again. We believe that Dr. Montessori is the first who has clearly recognized the significance of this trait. It is often assumed that when a teacher has explained a thing to the child that is the end of the business, but Dr. Montessori says: "To have learnt something is, for a child, only a point of departure." What is necessary after that is a period of digestion or maturation, a period of intense and prolonged mental activity. A child on being shown how to use a piece of Montessori apparatus—whether it be the colour tablets,

Ursuline Convent, Waterford, Montessori Class in open air. (Photograph by Poole.)

or the letters of the alphabet, or the multiplication board etc.—is not content to use it only once. It feels the need for more; and an inner impulse urges it to settle down, day after day, to a process of repetition which often seems incomprehensible to adults. *We* should get terribly bored if *we* had to repeat these exercises over and over again as the child does spontaneously and with such obvious delight. Indeed, in training her teachers, Dr. Montessori makes her students settle down at a piece of apparatus, and repeat it over and over again for a quarter or half an hour—as the child does—until the students are thoroughly sick of it. Then she says, "Now by your very boredom you will be able to gauge something of that imperious inner impulse which drives the child to this prolonged repetition. It is the very urge of life itself, the tremendous impulse of the developing intellectual faculty which drives it on and sustains it through these—to you—tedious labours."

There is a passage in G.K. Chesterton's *Orthodoxy* which I cannot forbear quoting, as it illumines this point with his characteristic vigour. "All the towering materialism which dominates the modern mind rests ultimately on one assumption—a false assumption. It is supposed that if a thing goes on repeating itself it is probably dead. People feel that if the universe was personal it would vary, if the sun were alive it would dance. The sun rises every morning: I do not rise every morning; but the variation is due not to my activity but to my inaction. The thing I mean can be seen for instance in children when they find some game or joke they specially enjoy. A child kicks its legs rhythmically through excess not absence of life. Because children have abounding vitality—therefore they want things repeated and unchanged. They always say 'Do it again' and the grown-up person does it again until he is nearly dead."

"What interests the child," says Dr. Montessori, "in these repetitions is not only the sensation of doing the exercise, whatever it may be, but also the fact *that he is acquiring a new power of perception, enabling him to see what he did not at first notice.*"

It will be seen from this how necessary is the principle of liberty, for the child must be allowed the freedom to go on repeating the exercises as long as he likes; otherwise this inner ripening of the faculties has not time to take place.

Each Stage a Preparation for the Next

The preparations of life are often indirect. This is frequently the case in the sphere of education. To make this clear let us take an illustration. The caterpillar is destined to become a butterfly which flits about from flower to flower, living on honey; but it would be no good, while it is at the caterpillar stage, expecting it to fly, or offering it honey as a means of sustenance. If you are anxious for a caterpillar to develop into a successful butterfly, you can best *help it by giving it what it needs as a caterpillar*. Froebel, the inventor of the Kindergarten, saw this truth very clearly, but he was not so successful as Dr. Montessori in providing the right kind of nourishment for the child at the different stages. He says, "The child, the boy, the man, should know no other endeavour but to be at every stage of development wholly what this stage calls for. Then will each successive stage spring like a new shoot from a healthy bud . . . for only the adequate development of man at each preceding stage can effect and bring about adequate development at each succeeding stage.[9]

The child when it first comes to a Montessori school, at the age of three or four, applies itself for the most part to

---

[9] *Education of Man*: Froebel.

the purely sensory apparatus—colour tablets, cylinders, long stair, etc. It would be no good giving such a child the advanced apparatus, for it is still at the stage when sensations predominate. The great thing is to utilize each stage as it comes. Every one must have noticed how little children are always touching objects—running their fingers, for instance, along the edges and surfaces of chairs, tables, plates, in fact, of all the objects they come across. How often one hears a grown-up say to them "Don't touch those things," "Keep your hands off," and yet the child persists in these forbidden activities in spite of threats and punishments, as if impelled to them by some uncontrollable internal impulse. Instead of repressing these tactile explorations so natural to the child at this stage Dr. Montessori encourages them, and has harnessed them to educational ends, as, for instance, in learning to write. The child learns the shape of the letters of the alphabet by means of letters, cut out in sandpaper and pasted on cardboard; and it does so by feeling over the sandpaper letters with its first and second fingers, lightly touching the surface of the sandpaper. It does this many scores of times and soon acquires a muscular memory of the letters.

DROPPED STITCHES IN THE MENTAL LIFE

But it would be useless to give the sandpaper letters to a child of eleven or twelve, because he has passed the stage when he is so feverishly interested in tactile impressions. Hence the importance of making full use of each stage as it comes, for there are certain ideas and activities which, if they are not acquired at a certain particular stage, can never be learned quite so well, or in such an easy manner. Indeed one might say of these "sensitive periods" (adapting Shakespeare somewhat) "There is a tide in the affairs of the child which, taken at the flood, leads on to fortune, omitted, all the voyage of his life will be spent," if not in "shallows and miseries," at least, in a poverty of development compared with what might have been. There are many grown-ups who will remain to the end of their lives gauche and awkward in their movements, or lacking appreciation in the finer shades of colour, or untidy in their person simply because, at the critical stage when a natural interest in these things was to the fore, there was no environment or person in it to secure that the "sensitive period" was made full use of. Thus there are, what Dr. Montessori calls "dropped stitches" in the structure of the mental life which can never be wholly picked up. It is true that even in spite of the dropped stitches a garment may be completed, and it is true that the child will in any case grow up somehow, but the final result will not be so perfect.

Training of the Imagination

The objection is sometimes raised against the Montessori method that it lays an over-emphasis on the training of the senses to the detriment of the development of the imagination. There is not enough make-believe, it is said, in the Montessori school, and the child's imagination is starved. If this were true it would be a serious charge; but it is not true.

There is no outstanding educationalist who appreciates better the value of imagination than Dr. Montessori, nor has displayed in his writings and conversation a more vivid and telling imagination than Dr. Montessori.

She would be indeed one of the last persons to wish to limit the development of imagination. She devotes over a hundred pages of one of her books to this faculty—its development, its function in art and science, its use and its misuse.

Her own reply to her objectors on this score takes

something of the following form. Far from agreeing that the child's preoccupation with sensorial objects is likely to thwart its imaginative development, she asserts that it will *materially assist it.*

Discussing the creative work of the imagination she says: "What is called creation is in reality a composition, a construction raised upon a primitive material of the mind, which must be collected from the environment by means of the senses. This is the general principle summed up in the ancient maxim: *'Nihil est intellectu quod prius non fuerit in sensu.'* 'We are unable to "imagine" things which do not actually present themselves to our senses.'"

Or again: "The sensory education which prepares for the accurate perception of all the differential details in the qualities of things is, therefore, the foundation of the observation of things and of phenomena which present themselves to our senses, and with this, it helps us to collect from the external world the material for the imagination.

"Imaginative creation has no mere vague sensory support: that is to say, it is not the unbridled divagation of the fancy among images of light, colour, sounds and impressions, but it is a creation firmly allied to reality; and the more it holds fast to the forms of the external created world the loftier will be the value of its internal creation.

"So it may be said that in order to develop the imagination it is necessary for everyone first of all to put himself in contract with *reality.*"

True and False Use of the Imagination Especially In Religion

If the imagination be not based on a solid foundation of reality it may become a danger. And here we might put in a word about fairy tales. Contrary to what is generally supposed Dr. Montessori has no objections to fairy tales in themselves, so long as the child is old enough to distinguish between what is real in them and what is not. If the child is too young to realize this distinction it may grow up in a world of unrealities which it may find it hard to outgrow. Indeed it may not even grow up, as in the case of the little girl who went to see *Peter Pan* and afterwards, in her childish simplicity, jumped from her bedroom window, expecting to fly away like Peter and Wendy, and was killed.

IMAGINATION AND RELIGION

Still worse is the case of those who have confused imagination with reality to such an extent that it becomes an obstruction to their religious development. I was present once at a Theosophical school, when a visitor gave a serious "talk" to the children on Fairies and Elementals; she actually passed round, *as genuine reproductions,* some photographs of "real" fairies flitting about in a garden in Yorkshire. Those who are acquainted with the extravagant imaginations of Theosophical writers know only too well how dangerous such seductive phantasies may be to the immaturely developed minds of children, and how hard it is for those who have been brought up in this world of false imaginations to break through them to a solid bed-rock of reality. As Dr. Montessori well says—"The way of Truth is difficult through the crust of imagination which is fixed without being first constructed upon a basis of truth."

As so often happens in education, we must educate the imagination indirectly by giving the child the opportunity of storing up a supply of true images. We must not treat the imagination as an isolated and special faculty to be developed separately by itself. Rather we must have faith in the spontaneous working of the child's mind according to its own laws. Our business is to present the external world to the child in a manner that helps him to understand it, to help him to organize an inner life corresponding to it. The flight of the imagination will come at the right time, even as the caterpillar will acquire wings and fly if you give it time and the proper nourishment. The nourishment of the caterpillar may seem heavy, coarse material for a creature destined to flight—but it is nevertheless the best preparation for it. So the preoccupation with tangible objects, their forms, colours, sizes, etc., may not seem a very imaginative occupation, but it is nevertheless a necessary preparation for true imaginative flight.

Spontaneous Ascent form Concrete to Abstract

Similar to the objection we have been considering is the criticism that the child's pre-occupation with the Montessori material is a hindrance to the development of purely abstract and intellectual activities. To learn multiplication by the multiplication board, or work out long division with the "division apparatus," is not all this keeping the child back in the concrete and particular, when it should be soaring up to the region of universals? Observation of children in Montessori schools has again and again shown this to be a vain objection. Experience shows that the children, *of their own accord,* when the time comes, discard the apparatus and work without it. I remember in one school watching a little girl doing subtraction sums with the "number frame," beside her on the table. I noticed with interest, however, that she did not use the bead frame at all but did the sums in her head.

Mellitus Street L.C.C. School, W.12.

Boy playing a tune of his own composition on the bells.

Child busy with the "Thousand Bead Chain." The cards are "hundreds" placed like stations along the line.

"Why do you not use the frame?" I asked. "Because I can do it quicker now without it," was her sensible reply.

A concrete basis (such as is supplied by the didactic material) is necessary so that the child can abstract from it clear and definite "concepts." When this has been done the child abandons the concrete and particular for the universal. "This process," says Dr. Montessori (*in a simile which is in itself a perfect example of the right use of imagination*), "this process has led us to liken the child's mind to an aeroplane which requires the ground to rest on for a short distance, but only that it may arise and fly. These ascensions, due to work accomplished with such attention and constancy, remind us of the joy felt by the souls in Dante's *Purgatory*, while they are undergoing the suffering necessary for their purification and for their ascent into Heaven; and the teacher, a silent and gentle director, but at the same time strong and sure in pointing out the path which leads to perfection, is like the angel who guards, helps and comforts. These spontaneous ascents of the mind are accompanied by the most intense joy, and give rise to what we have above referred to as the 'Montessori Explosions.'"

Concentration and Character Building

It cannot be too often pointed out as a fundamental and far-reaching principle, that the *child is constantly acquiring qualities which have no direct relation to the material means of development which are offered to him.*

One of the most astonishing features of a Montessori school is the intense and prolonged concentration which the children display when they are working with the apparatus.

This concentration is of great practical value educationally, as it results in the children learning to read and write and do elementary arithmetic more quickly and more easily than in an ordinary school.

Still more important, however, is the effect of this prolonged concentration in the sphere of the child's moral character and growth.

When a child comes to a Montessori school first he is often restless and distracted. He will try now this piece of apparatus, now that—"everything by starts and nothing long." At this stage he may go from table to table, sometimes even interfering with the other children who are working; in short, he behaves as a "naughty" boy. Then one day, sooner or later according to individual circumstances, he begins to show an intense interest in one of the exercises. It does not matter which: the important thing is not the external object but the internal action of the soul which accompanies this profound concentration. For, when once a child has shown this intense interest in any one of the exercises (it does not matter which), when it has settled down to it in such a manner that he is oblivious of everything that is going on around him—*then* something seems to happen inside his soul. He comes out from this experience a changed being.

It is the beginning of a new phase, almost a new life. A new polarization of his whole personality now takes place. It is as if the steady concentration of all his faculties had acted as a magnet acts through a piece of paper on a heap of iron filings; suddenly and mysteriously the confused mass of particles arrange themselves in a definite and orderly form. So is it with the elements of his personality: the child becomes, often with surprising suddenness, docile, good tempered, hardworking, and considerate to others. He goes on to show a like interest in other exercises, often the very ones he passed over before.

"It is after these manifestations that a true discipline is established, the most obvious results of which are closely related to what we call 'respect for the work of others and consideration for the rights of others.'"

So profound and lasting is the effect of this first prolonged concentration on the child's soul that Dr. Montessori compares it to the phenomenon of "conversion" in the supernatural world.

Of course, as in the case of a convert, this "conversion," important as it is in it-self, is only the starting point of a new development—towards more complete self-mastery. "To ensure the continuance of this attitude and of the development of personality, it is essential that *some real task should be performed each day*, for it is from the completed cycle of an activity, from methodical concentration, that the child develops equilibrium, elasticity, adaptability and the resulting power to perform the higher actions, such as those which are termed acts of obedience."

"This is comparable," says Dr. Montessori in another place, "to the method of the Catholic religion for the preservation of the forces of the spiritual life, viz., a period of 'spiritual concentration' which opens up the possibility of acquiring 'moral powers.' It is from methodical 'meditations' that the moral personality must draw its powers of solidification, without which the 'inner man,' incoherent and unbalanced, fails to possess itself and dispose of itself for noble ends."

Exercises in Practical Life

No outline of the Montessori method would be complete without a mention of what are called the Exercises in Practical Life. The Montessori school is, as we have said, a specially prepared environment which calls out the child's activities, and in so doing instructs and disciplines him. During a large part of his time he is occupied with the specially prepared apparatus—whether purely sensory, as in the first stages, or, later on, with that which leads him along the path of the "Three R's." Of no less importance, however, in the child's development (according to Dr. Montessori) are the exercises of practical life. In these, too, the child is brought into relationship with a prepared environment. The child is taught carefully how to wash his hands, to pour water from one vase to another without spilling any on the floor, to move about amongst fragile objects without breaking them, to touch things without spoiling them, to clean things and put them in order, to sweep, and dust the furniture of his little world, to arrange flowers, to set the table, to wash dishes and so on.

In this connection, too, we should mention the "Silence game," which combines a number of these activities, and in addition presents to the children the mysterious fascination of collective silence—an experience not usually attainable with such small children.

Of great value, too, in developing that poise and refinement of movement so noticeable in Montessori children are the rhythmical exercises, in which the children are taught to march and dance to music along a line on the floor.

The New Child

It will be seen from the foregoing pages that the Montessori method claims to be much more than a particular way of teaching this or that special subject, more than a general method of instruction.

More fundamental than this, its object is to influence the whole life of the child: it aims, in short, at a total development of the personality, a harmonious growth of all the potentialities of the child, physical and mental, according to the law of its being.

We have seen that to make possible this inner growth the child is placed in a special environment, so prepared as to meet its inner needs; and that *in* this environment the child is given an unusual degree of liberty. Further, that as a result, the personality of the child is developed and strengthened in a remarkable way.

The supporters of the method claim, in fact, that the children, when placed in these circumstances, reveal themselves as possessing capabilities and powers not usually credited to them. "It has been proved beyond a doubt, that under these circumstances many of the defects or limitations usually associated with children disappear as if by magic. These children display quite spontaneously a love of work, a respect for the work and property of others and for property in itself. They show themselves capable of prolonged concentration, of great delicacy and precision of movement, of mutual forbearance, of swift and willing obedience. Furthermore, it frequently happens that physical defects such as indigestion, stammering, nervousness of all sorts, are removed. In short there results such a toning up and heightening of the whole personality that again and again observers have found themselves using the expression that Dr. Montessori has revealed a *'New Child.'*"

It is of course absurd to imagine that Dr. Montessori's method—or any method could *make* a new child, since human nature always remains the same. But what she has done has been to show that, when treated in the right way, the child reveals itself as possessing higher capabilities, both intellectually and morally, than those with which it is usually credited.

CHAPTER 10

A Comparison Between the Method of the Catholic Church and the Montessori Method

It is a curious but undeniable fact that amongst the leading advocates of the Montessori method in America, England, Holland, Austria, Sweden, and Ireland, are to be found converts to Catholicism. It might be supposed that this circumstance was due to a proselytizing zeal on the part of Dr. Montessori. But this can hardly be the case because Dr. Montessori does not, as a rule, touch on the question of religion in her training courses for teachers. On these occasions she confines her lectures to the psychology and practice of her method in general—a procedure, both wise and politic, since her audiences usually consist of members of many different denominations, with no particular interest in religious education.

Yet we do not think that the existence of this group of

persons, who are at the same time converts to the Montessori method *and* to Catholicism, is entirely a matter of chance. It is true the method has received express Papal Benediction, and we would be far from denying that this might have something to do with it. But taking into consideration only purely natural causes, the important factor appears to us to lie in the fact that there is a *striking resemblance between the method of the Montessori school and the method of the Catholic Church, in the manner in which both institutions adapt themselves, in practice, to the psychological nature of man.* In this chapter we shall briefly point out some of these similarities and show how they arise from a common psychology.

(1) A Prepared Environment

No institution understands better than the Catholic Church the importance of a "prepared environment" in assisting the development of the soul. Every Catholic Church is, in fact, such a specially prepared environment, with objects in it carefully selected and so presented to the individual as to help on his inner development. Still more completely selected and so presented to the individual as to help on his inner development. Still more completely is this principle carried out in the case of Religious Orders, where it is applied to every department of life. In such cases too, as in a Montessori school, what is left out (of the environment) is almost as important as what is put in.

(2) Use of Didactic Material

A teacher of the old-fashioned type, on going into a Montessori school for the first time, is usually surprised— not to say appalled—by the *material* nature of the education

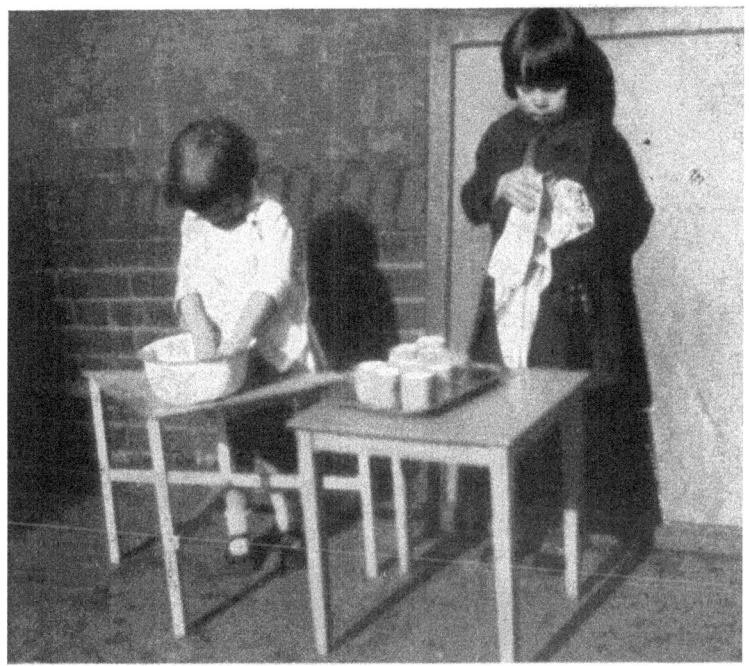

St. Anne's School, Southwark (Notre Dame). Exercises in Practical Life — washing up

in progress. All round the room he sees rows of shelves and cupboards containing a great variety of material objects. He sees the children going to and from these cupboards, selecting their occupations, returning the apparatus when they have finished, and making a fresh choice. They seem to be almost entirely preoccupied with these things; to him, they appear to be simply wasting their time—"fiddling about" incessantly with wooden blocks, wooden rods, beads, colour-tablets, cards, button frames, number frames and the like. Or if they are not doing any of these things, he may see them walking round the room in a sort of procession to music, carrying vases or flags or little bells; or perhaps going about the room dusting the furniture or sweeping the floor. It does not seem possible to such a teacher—used, as he is, to the rigidity and immobility of an ordinary class-room—that any real intellectual development can be going on amidst all this bustling about and "playing" with material.

Exactly similar, though on a different plane, is the impression received by a person of Puritanical training (like a Quaker for instance), on entering a large Catholic church for the first time. He beholds everywhere about him, with astonishment, not to say horror, a similar emphasis on the material side of things. He sees the worshippers with their attention fixed upon all kinds of material objects—rosaries, images, candles, incense, pictures; he sees them moving about from place to place *doing things*, carrying flowers, lighting candles, genuflecting, making the sign of the cross, going in processions. The very central devotion of Catholicism, the Holy Mass itself, appears to the Quaker as something material and unspiritual. Believing as he does that the spiritual life is a purely interior one, he finds it impossible to believe that this preoccupation with all manner of visible and tangible objects can assist in the development of the spiritual life. In fact he imagines that these things must tend to act as hindrances and distractions, serving to keep back the soul from soaring into the supersensible regions of true spiritual experience. In precisely the same way, the old type of teacher believes that the Montessori child's preoccupation with the didactic material must tend to keep its mind from soaring into the region of purely intellectual operations.

(3) From the Sensible to the Supersensible

The trouble in both cases—with the Quaker in a Catholic church and the teacher in the Montessori school—lies in this, that neither realizes that the end of all this preoccupation with external objects is not in the objects themselves, but in the reactions which they evoke. I remember once hearing an experienced and successful Montessori directress trying to explain to a group of student-teachers the significance of the child's constant repetition of its exercises with the material. "It is not the exercise that matters in itself," she said, "but the development that goes on inside the child's mind—a development of which the outer action is but a sign. It is, in fact," she continued, "very much like what Catholics say of a sacrament, viz., that it is an outward sign of an inward grace." The lady herself was not a Catholic, but the analogy had impressed her as a striking and useful one.

It is of course *only* an analogy, because the operations of Grace belong to the supernatural order. The analogy would have been more exact if she had referred to sacramentals rather than sacraments.[10]

Even, however, in the case of the sacraments the simile used

---

[10] "Sacramentals are rites, blessings, blessed objects, that is to say, outward signs and symbols productive of salutary effects in the soul. They do not remit sin nor produce grace of themselves, as do the sacraments, but they act *ex opere operantis Ecclesiae, ex sua impetratione.*"—*Catholic Liturgy*, Lefebre, p. 111.

by the Montessori directress is a just one, to this extent at any rate, that the operation of grace, resulting from a right use of the sacraments, is often something of which the individual is unconscious. The effects of the sacraments can be observed afterwards in an increased development of spiritual powers and a finer moral susceptibility. Similarly the right use of the didactic material leads to a development of the intellectual powers by a process of which the child is not conscious.

(4) Freedom to Choose One's Occupation

In a Montessori school, as we have seen, a child so long as he knows the right uses of the various pieces of material is allowed a considerable degree of freedom as to which he may use at any particular time—except of course when some collective lesson like the Silence game is in progress. Similarly in a Catholic church, except at such times when he is joining in the collective worship of the Mass, the individual is free to move about and choose the particular form of devotion which answers to the needs of his particular soul at the time, be it the rosary, or the "Stations of the Cross," or the offering of a candle, or going to confession and so on. The child in the Montessori school is given the most minute instruction as to how to use the material, down to the smallest detail, and is left free to use it when he likes.

Similarly in the Church the child is most carefully taught how to go to Confession and to Holy Communion, and is then left free to choose when he will go.

The Catholic Church is not based on the coercion of the individual, but on the assumption that Divine Grace operates in every individual, as the source of his religious life. So, in a Montessori school, the intellectual development is not a thing that needs to be forced; it is based on the assumption that there is in the child an inward urge or prompting, which shows itself in the spontaneous operations of the intellect. Neither the operations of Grace in the one case, nor the promptings of the intellect in the other are things that can be seen; but their presence can be proved by the results which they bring about. As it is the Faith of Christians, under the operations of Grace, which—humanly speaking—keeps the Church going, so it is this inner, imperious, spontaneous working of the intellect that forms the driving power of a Montessori school. It is a power akin to those mysterious forces of life which keep going the vegetative and animal functions of our bodies. If anyone doubts its efficacy, as a driving power in education, let him sit for half-an-hour with his eyes open in a well-managed Montessori school.

(5) Method of Catholic Priest and Montessori Directress

In the old type of infant school, where class teaching predominated, the teacher was the continued focus of the child's attention, the medium, *par excellence,* through which he learnt. It was the teacher's business to talk, the child's to sit still and listen. The successful teacher was the one who, by various artifices, managed most completely to rivet the children's attention to herself. It is quite otherwise in a Montessori school. Here the personality of the directress does not obtrude itself. She is called a *directress,* not a teacher, because it is her business, not so much to teach, as to direct the spontaneous energies of the child into useful and formative channels. A certain amount of instruction, of course, must be given by the directress in the meaning and use of the didactic material.

In adopting this role the directress relies, for the child's development, on the inner unconscious growth which results from its work with the material. This is a process which, once started, goes on independently of her, and is the more successful the more completely she is able to efface herself. From this point of view she may be regarded as a link between the child and the material, putting him in touch with the means of his own self-development.

If one compares the role of a Catholic priest with that—let us say—of a Free Church minister a similar contrast comes to light. The Catholic priest performs his high office, as dispenser of the Sacraments, with an impersonal self-effacement, whereas the personality of the Protestant minister, with his sermon and extempore prayers, is strikingly prominent. In fact what is called the "success" of the service very largely depends on him. It is true that it is part of a priest's duty to give instruction, and this must be accurate; but this does not occupy so prominent a place in a Catholic service as in a Protestant, where, in point of fact, the sermon has to take the place of the Elevation. It is interesting to note, too, that Dr. Montessori has been criticized for insisting that the instruction given to the children in her schools should be in a particular and prescribed form. The words the directress has to say are (so these critics affirm) too stereotyped—which is exactly the complaint of many Protestants against the words used by the priests in the Catholic Church.

As the dispenser of the Sacraments, the priest may be also regarded as the link between the materials of the Sacraments and the individual who is to make use of them. Furthermore—like the Montessori directress—the priest knows that his duties are most successfully accomplished when he has brought the individual to the use of the Sacraments, and is content to keep himself in the background, leaving the spiritual development of the soul in his charge to the unseen operation of Divine Grace which accompanies their proper use.

(6) Faith and Works

The principle of auto-education means, as we have already stated, that, intellectually, the child must work out his own salvation. The teacher, however expert and willing, cannot do it for him. Merely being told things by the teacher is not enough for the child to learn them; there must be a corresponding self-activity on the part of the child before the knowledge becomes real and vital. The teacher's part is, of course, an essential one, and the child could not progress without it. At the same time it is equally true that without the child's active co-operation, *i.e.*, his "works," his knowledge would be dead as—"Faith without works is dead."

(7) Use of Externals to Focus Attention

Everyone knows how easily the attention of little children is distracted from one thing to another. In this connection it is interesting to note the useful effect of the didactic material. It frequently happens, when a child is working at some piece of apparatus, that its attention becomes diverted by something else in the room. It may be by another child who asks a question, or by the entrance of a visitor, or by some unusual noise, or by the divagations of the child's own imagination in the realm of fancy. The noteworthy thing is that as a rule these periods of distraction do not last long. The presence and the nature of the material combined, somehow seem to act as a check on mind-wandering, almost as though there were some mysterious power of attraction in the material itself which draws the child's attention once more back to it. It reminds one exactly of the manner in which one's rosary beads assist in keeping the mind on one's devotions. Who has not, in saying his rosary, sometimes discovered—when he has come to the end of a decade—that his attention has been wandering, and found, moreover, his distracted thoughts brought to heel by the check imposed on them from without, as his fingers pass on to the next decade of the "specially prepared didactic apparatus" of the rosary. Indeed the whole environment of the worshipper in a Catholic church is so designed as to turn back the wandering attention to devotional channels, just as the whole environment of the child in a Montessori school is so devised as to direct the child's attention to things of intellectual interest.

(8) Authority

I have heard it said (by Protestants) that the Montessori method ought to be better adapted to a Protestant than to a Catholic atmosphere, because—so it is averred—the large measure of freedom permitted to the child is inconsistent with the Catholic idea of authority and dogma. We need not repeat here what we have already said as to the true nature of liberty (pp. 115-119). This point happened to come up in a conversation when Dr. Montessori was present. She remarked: "There is dogma as well as liberty in my method if you can only discern it. When you say to the child 'This is red,' or 'This is seven,' what are these but dogmatic statements?" It cannot be too often repeated that the Montessori idea of liberty is a liberty only to do what is right, and to think what is true. It is the teacher's duty not only to encourage all right and useful spontaneous activities, but vigorously to correct all that is evil and imperfect.

There are other similarities in method to which attention

A Comparison

Dominican Convent, Sion Hill, Blackrock, Dublin. Children using models of the liturgical vestments

might be drawn in this chapter, such as the use of "silence," or the voluntary undertaking of arduous occupations for some higher end (which, says Dr. Montessori, reminds one of the attitude of the souls in Purgatory), or the performance of practical duties (the "exercises of practical life") not for their own sake, but as a means of inner development, like the "obediences" of the religious life—but enough has already been said to show that in the method of a Montessori school there is a greater similarity to the method of the Catholic Church than is to be found in that of the ordinary type of school.

A Common Psychology

The root reason for this similarity of method is not far to seek. It is simply this, that they are both based on the same psychology, viz.—that man is a twofold being, made up of body and spirit. If man were a purely spiritual being there would be as little use for a Montessori method of education as for a sacramental system of religion.

It is true that the intellect of man is a supersensible faculty, by reason of which he is raised above the animals, and made capable of "immortal longings," and "thoughts that wander through eternity." Yet, though the intellect is a super-sensible faculty, and though it is by no means essential to an intellectual being to have a body (the angels are intellectual beings and have no body), in man the operations of the intellect are inextricably bound up with the activity of the bodily sense organs, to this extent at least, that the material with which the intellect works has its origin in the senses. St. Thomas Aquinas, the great Catholic theologian, accepted the Aristotelian maxim to which we have already referred, that there is nothing in the intellect which was not first in the senses. The human intellect depends, then, on the bodily senses for the raw materials from which it abstracts incorporeal ideas.

Thus a man deprived of sight from his birth can form no true concept of the idea of "redness." The only idea he can form about it must be by analogy, by using ideas derived through the other senses. He may think of redness as a quality like the sound of a trumpet; or he may imagine the proportions of a beautiful cathedral as being something like the harmony of a piece of music (did not Goethe say that Gothic Architecture was like "frozen music"?) but his ideas on such matters must always be based on the impressions supplied by other senses than sight. The process is different in the man who was once able to see and has later become blind; for his intellect (*intellectus agens*), working on his previous visible impressions, has already abstracted from these, ideas which remain long after the sense which supplied their material has ceased to function.

With the angels, however, the case is different. Having no bodies they can have no sense organs, and therefore their ideas cannot have a sensory basis. Their ideas are, in fact—so theologians tell us—directly infused. There could, therefore, in the nature of the case, be no such thing as a Montessori school for little angels! This is the reason why the operations of the intellect in the angelic mind are of a different order from those of man; for the angelic mind—to use the scholastic phrase—works "intuitively," *i.e.*, it apprehends truth with a complete and instantaneous comprehension. The intellect of man however works "discursively" [*species intellectualis abstractiva est propria ex alienis*].

The writer once heard a conversation between Dr. Montessori and a learned Dominican. The latter, who had read her books carefully, remarked that he had been struck by the agreement between them and the principles of the scholastic philosophy. It would be easy to cite many examples to illustrate this, but the following must suffice:

(*a*) In her chapter on "Intelligence" Dr. Montessori says: "The first characteristic which presents itself to us as an indication of intellectual development is related to *time*. The masses are so much alive to this primitive characteristic that the popular expression 'quick' is synonymous with intelligent." Thus we can have various degrees of intelligence. At one end there is the very dull, "slow" mind which seems often to be specially hampered by its gross material connection; then the quick mind—more agile and "spirituel" (sic) (as the French would say); and, at the other end of the scale, the instantaneous comprehension of the angelic mind. It is interesting in this connection to recall one of the stories told about St. Thomas Aquinas himself. Asked on one occasion what he regarded as the greatest gift that God had bestowed on him, he replied that, in all his life, he had never read any author without understanding his meaning at the first reading. Well, indeed, was he called the *angelic* Doctor!

(*b*) To take another example. We have seen how great an emphasis Dr. Montessori lays on "auto-education," viz., that the child should as far as possible be guided into discovering things for himself. St. Thomas says: "There are two ways of acquiring knowledge: (1) By invention or finding out, and (2) by discipline or learning. Invention is the highest mode and learning stands second. We read in *Ethics*: 'He is best who understands all things by means of himself, but he is good who obeys him who talks well.' "

(*c*) We will conclude with another passage from St. Thomas. "There are three degrees of the cognitive faculty. There is first the act of the corporeal organ, *i.e.*, the sense, which knows particulars; secondly, the power, which is neither the act of the bodily organ nor conjoined with corporeal matter, and such is the intellect of angels, the object of which is form as it exists without matter; and thirdly, there is the human intellect, which stands midway between the other two, which is the form of a body, although not the act of a bodily organ. . . . We must therefore admit that our intellect knows material things by abstraction from phantasms; and that by material things so considered it becomes in some manner able to understand immaterial things."

The Catholic Church has never for a moment countenanced the belief, so common in Eastern philosophies, that matter is somehow a mistake, a drag on the spirit, something from which the soul must disentangle itself in order to be free. The doctrine of the Incarnation, and all that it involves, is a flat denial of this point of view. Our Blessed Lord Himself, by sharing our human bodily nature, raised material substance to the highest possible degree. And, knowing its weaknesses, in this the most intimate manner possible, He instituted the Sacramental system. Here matter, far from being a thing to be despised, becomes the very means to our highest spiritual good.

And the Catholic Church—a thing visible and tangible in itself—a city set on a hill -has always followed the example set by her Founder in making use of material things for spiritual ends. In her "Sacramentals," and in general, in the infinite variety of her liturgical developments, she has always worked on this principle.

It only remains to point out that a method of education based upon so similar a view of the educative value of a prepared material environment would—*ipso facto*—lend itself most readily to religious education on Catholic lines.

Part Two

The Life of Christ in the Liturgical Year

CHAPTER 1

CALENDAR

When one has duties to perform, a calendar is indispensable, because it is a guide that orients us through the scope of a year, as a clock is a guide through the scope of a day.

The years follow each other more or less the same, as also the days and hours. And if there was no such thing as a calendar or clock, we need to divide time by the natural phenomena that always repeat themselves in a uniform manner: the snow and the burning sun, the light of the day and the darkness of the night. The regular recurrence of phenomena that mark time is tied, as we know, to the revolutions of the earth around the sun. It takes one year for each orbit. In completing them, the circle returns to itself: and every time it spins marks a day.

From these two familiar and indispensable measures—the year and the day—we can then orient ourselves to the external world, in order to observe how the earth germinates through its various seasons, and how the temperature changes and the many natural phenomena that depend on it.

When a season peaks in its fulness, we already feel that we are in the vigil of another season, which we await with anticipation. Autumn makes one dream of Winter and snow. Winter brings the desire for a green and flowery Spring, which sees us awaiting the Summer that follows, with its burning sun, its tranquil seas, and the fruits of nature. And in Summer we are caught up in nostalgia for the melancholy Autumn, with its falling leaves and refreshing rains.

Why do we not feel the need for a calendar that, instead of revolving around the phenomena of the external world, takes ourselves as the center, and, so to speak, makes time gravitate around our own souls?

The soul is the most important thing for us; and that is why it ought to be the most interesting, because the hours, the days, and the years pass away for each of us, marking the limits of our lives and of the time to do good.

Now, we must say that there is not just one particular way to look at the calendar, but that it is indeed determined with the greatest accuracy in the times and the seasons.

What would the seasons be, if the life of man was like the years that repeat their cycles?

These seasons would be two: Birth and Death. Even for the earth, there are really only two seasons: Winter and Summer, for which Spring and Autumn are the periods of passing from one to the other, and the preparation for each. So too in human life we can conceive of periods of preparation: preparation for birth and preparation for death. And like the farmer prepares the seed through Winter and prepares for the harvest in Summer, we too can prepare ourselves, counting the months and the days and the hours, seeking to understand ever more the value of our lives. Working for our betterment in every time of the year is without a doubt the most important thing for us.

But what would such a calendar refer to? Where is the sun that shows us the seasons of life or allows us to distinguish the light from the darkness? No—not the sun itself, but the Creator of the sun, would be the measurement of this calendar that deals not with the life of the earth, but the lives of men. Such time will, therefore, be measured as between man and God.

This is why we must study the division of the year in Christ: not just as an interesting general idea, but as a concrete fact that is exactly and minutely established in a calendar. This division, like the fundamental subdivision of time, is tied to the solar year; but its seasons, the fruits that it yields, the relationships that it permits us to establish with people all over the world, are different, because all refers itself to Christ.

After all, how do we count the years? Where did it all begin, from the first to the 1949 years that we count to today? It began in Christ.

All the peoples of the world, those who are a part of Christian civilization, and even those who are not a part of it, count time from that cold night in which a little Babe was born in a grotto in Bethlehem.

If so, how could we orient ourselves in time and direct our actions outside of Christ?

"Brothers," St. Paul tells us, "you know it is already time to rise from sleep because the night is advanced, and the day approaches. Let us cast away, therefore, the works of darkness and clothe ourselves with the arms of the sun. (Rom. 13:11-12)"

The Life of Christ in the Liturgical Year

The Liturgical Year

In the liturgical year, there is a period of time that serves as a unit of measurement to organize the long series of 365 days, of the year, and of the week. "God created the world in six days, and on the seventh He rested and sanctified it," Genesis says. The day of rest is taken into the highest consideration in the Liturgical Year. Even more than rest, it is a day of detachment from one's regular life, and it is necessary to enter into a kind of life that is superior. Even in that day there are essential duties and strict obligations; but in view of a higher world we must frequently enter, if only to return afterward to our regular lives.

These periodic elevations, the offering of a day to God, prepare the way for us to join ourselves to the Kingdom of Heaven.

That is why the Liturgical Year is composed of weeks: neither months nor seasons are counted. There are 52 weeks in the year, thus 52 days to sanctify ourselves in an absolute way; that is, not by recurrences or anniversaries, but by the simple division of an entire year of 365 days into groups of seven.

The 52 weeks of the Liturgical Year, which represent a subdivision corresponding to that of months in the common year, are considered together in groups, just as in the common year, where the months are grouped in threes corresponding to the four seasons.

The groups of weeks, however, are not called *stagioni* (seasons) in Italian, but *tempi* (times).[3]

These *times* are then grouped into *cycles*.

The word "cycle" immediately gives an impression of a center around which something rotates, or at least from

---
3 In English, however, we are accustomed to say "liturgical season"

which everything departs and radiates.

And that is, in fact, just it. In the liturgical conception, the times of the year stem from two centers, or two great feast days. And from there the groupings of weeks are counted: one group that precedes the feast-day (preparation); a group that prolongs the idea of the central feast-day with a series of related feasts; and finally, a group that ties one cycle to the other.

The two centers, which are the origin points of the distribution of time, correspond to the most important moments in human Redemption. First, that moment in which the Word became incarnate and was made Man, to live amongst us,

> ET VERBUM CARO FACTUM EST,
> ET HABITAVIT IN NOBIS

that is, the feast of Christmas. And then the other day in which the Messiah, having completed the expiatory sacrifice by Death on the Cross, rose again, signifying victory over death, and at the same time our Redemption:

> EGO SUM RESURRECTIO ET VITA

that is, the Pachal feast, the Sunday of Easter.

The cycle of Christmas and the cycle of Easter meet in the middle in an intermediate time.

To illustrate this concept of the meeting of seasons that are developed around the birth and the death of the Savior, we need to have recourse to a symbolic representation.

We can draw a bar that represents birth: a white bar laying horizontally, that is to say, in the same prone position of the Infant Jesus that he assumed at birth.

The Life of Christ in the Liturgical Year

Diagram 1.

Another bar, longer and violet, is then used to represent the death of Christ; and we draw it vertically, positioning it in the orientation of the crucified Jesus.

Now we can superimpose the two bars: the result is a cross, symbol of the guiding principle of the Liturgical Year, in the position of the crucified Jesus, the symbol of our religion (*Diag. 1*).

CHRISTMAS AND EASTER

The date of Christmas is fixed in the Liturgical Year: it is very close to the beginning of Winter, and is marked in the moment of midnight between the 24th and the 25th of December. And since the day of Christmas can vary, it can fall on any day of the week.

The day of Easter, on the other hand, is fixed within the week, because it always falls on Sunday (Jesus died on Friday and rose again after three days). Yet it varies on which calendar day it falls. In fact, celestial phenomena are used to determine the day. It occurs at the beginning of Spring, and it falls in the week of the full moon that follows the equinox: the Sunday of that week is the Sunday of Easter.

Marking the orbit that the earth follows around the sun in the span of one year, let us try to ascertain the subdivisions of the Liturgical Year.

Diagram 2 indicates the trajectory of the earth around the sun and the four positions of the earth that mark the boundaries between seasons: namely, the Winter Solstice (December 21) and the Summer Solstice (June 21), and the two equinoxes, the Autumn Equinox (September 21) and the Spring Equinox (March 21).

Christmas falls a little after the Winter Solstice, and in the image it is marked with a comet that goes in search of the house at Bethlehem.

Easter, the Resurrection, is the first Sunday after the full moon brightens the nights at the beginning of Spring, and in the image it is marked with a little cross, after the Spring Equinox.

The moon completes its orbit around the earth in about four weeks, with enough divergence, however, to make an extra calculation necessary to make it agree with the monthly subdivisions of the year. Every quarter of the moon lasts a week (see fig. 2 of Diagram 2). It is, therefore, necessary to carefully determine the recurrence of Easter from year to year.

The two great feast days are found at the boundaries of the Winter season: one at the beginning of Winter and the other a little after the Winter has passed, at the beginning of Spring.

Christians all over the world have their liturgical feasts on these same days, corresponding to the historical celebrations of the life of Christ, born in Winter and sacrificed at the beginning of the Passover among the Hebrews in Palestine.

However, those who live on the opposite side of the earth, have the seasons opposite to ours—their Winter is our Summer. They therefore have a Summer Christmas and an Autumn Easter.

Thus, these feasts of Christ are present in all four of the seasons of nature.

Calendar

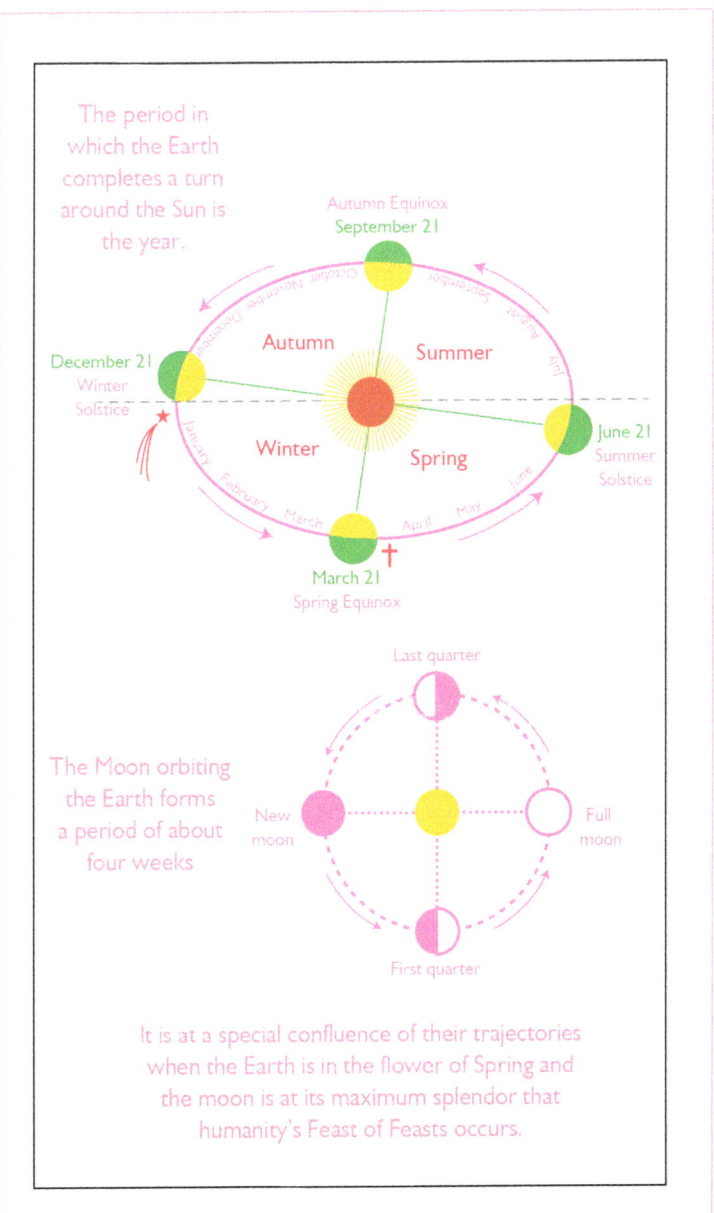

Diagram 2.

THE SEASONS COMPARED TO JESUS CHRIST

The seasons of the Liturgical Year radiate outward from these two points: Christmas, until Easter, and Easter, until Christmas.

It is the cycle of Jesus Christ that determines the seasons in the Liturgical Year, just as the Sun determines the seasons of the civil calendar.

In the calendar thus divided we can distinguish various commemorations. This is the same as the civil calendar, where one finds commemorative dates overlaid on a base of seasons and months.

In the liturgical calendar are recorded the events concerning our Savior: "*Tu solus Sanctus — Tu solus Dominus — Tu solus Altissimus, Jesu Christe* (You alone are Holy, You alone are Lord, You alone are the most high, Jesus Christ)." And there are daily commemorations of the Angels and the Saints. The hosts of Angels assist at Mass around the altar, and they accompany all of mankind as guardians and defenders; and the Saints also come around the altar, placing all their merits alongside ours. Thus, there also exists a cycle of Angels and a cycle of Saints; but the cycle of Christ is that which determines the seasons, which all the rest just serves to crown.

The Church did not establish merely one day of Christmas and one day of Easter, but a season of Christmas and a season of Easter.

The times of *preparation* for Christmas and Easter are called Advent and Lent, respectively. Advent and Christmas are therefore joined together just as Lent and Easter are joined; and they form the two great and distinct seasons of the year.

In times of *prolongation* the Church reflects on the divine

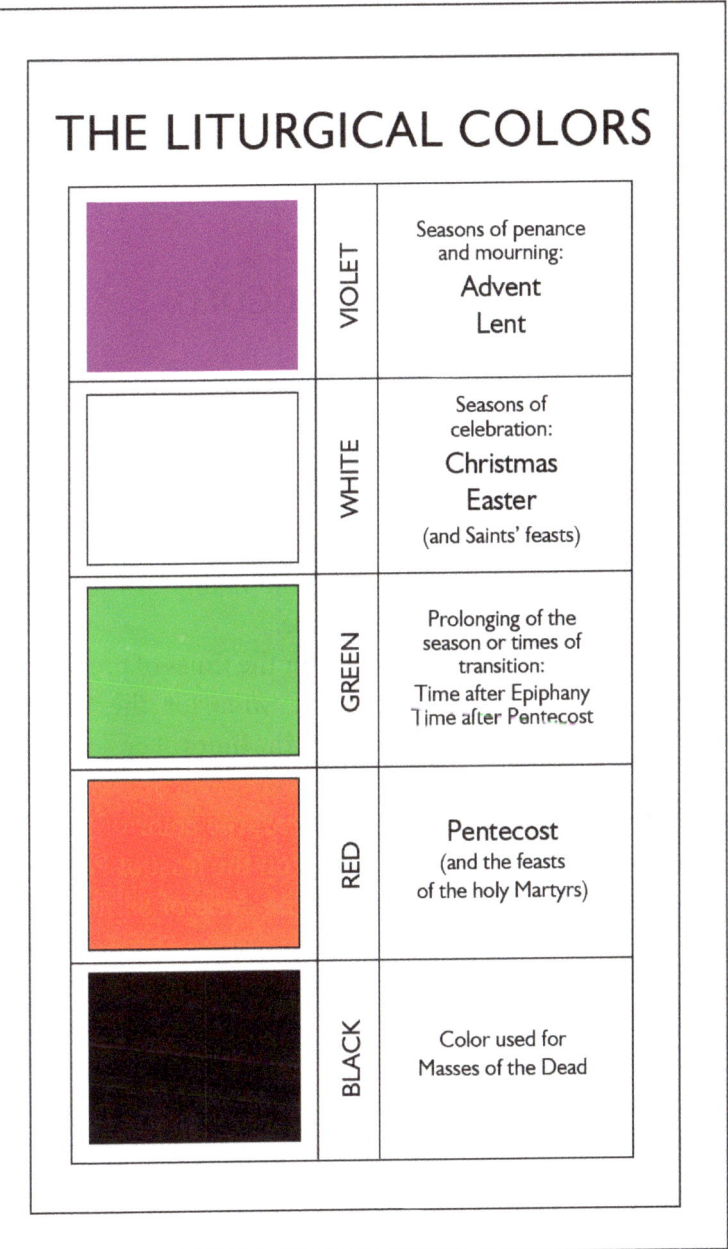

Diagram 3.

splendor of the feasts just passed, which remains until we reach the beginning of another feast.

These periods of transition to mitigated colors, like that of the earthly Autumn and Spring compared to Winter and Summer, are called *Time after Epiphany* and *Time after Pentecost*. [4]

THE LITURGICAL COLORS

In order to make these subdivisions more evident, the Church makes use of different colors to indicate the ceremonies celebrated at the altar, according to whether these pertain to periods of preparation, feast, or prolongation.

These are the meanings of the liturgical colors of the altar—that is, the chasuble, stole, and maniple of the priest, and the veil and burse of the chalice.

The colors are as follows: *violet* for the times of preparation (Advent and Lent) and penance; *white* for the feasts of Christmas and Easter; and *green* for the times of prolongation, after the Epiphany and after Pentecost (Diag. 3).

To these colors we need to add *red*, the color of the Holy Spirit, who sends down His flames on the feast of Pentecost. Some of these colors reappear in the cycle of Saints (called the Sanctoral cycle) and in particular feasts of the Savior and the Most Blessed Mother.

Feasts of Jesus, the Virgin, the Angels and Saints call for white. Certain feasts of Christ—like the Holy Cross, the Precious Blood, etc.—call for red, which is the color of blood and also of enflamed love, because it is blood shed for the love of mankind. The same color red is also used for the feasts of the Martyrs, who are heroes of love, having died for the Faith.

---

[4] In the current 1969 calendar, these are referred to as Ordinary Time

Black, the color of grief, is reserved for Good Friday, for the commemoration of the Departed, and for Masses and funeral rites for the Departed (see Diag 3).

The seasons of the Liturgical Year are not as uniformly divided as the natural seasons, which are tied to the perennial rotation of the stars that move like the gears of a clock.

Liturgical time is correlated to the life of man, consisting of preparations, sacrifices, merits won and rewards obtained; things that do not proceed from invariant mechanical movements, but that relate to the fire of the soul and to the graces tied to the will of God.

This is why we must orient ourselves to different rhythms, no longer ones established by the exterior order of created things, but ones that remain tied to the Almighty who never ceases to act.

CHAPTER 2

THE TWO CYCLES

Instead of seasons, therefore, we will speak here of the divisions in the Liturgical Year as times and cycles.

These correspond symbolically to episodes in the life of Jesus Christ: the entire story of our Redemption.

As the Mass is a brief, symbolic commemoration of the life of Our Lord, so the Sundays and liturgical feast-days also form one—stretching through the space of a year that which the Mass covers in the space of a half hour.

And just like in the Mass, there are two divisions, which recall Jesus as Divine Teacher and Jesus as mystical Sacrificial Victim and worker of our Redemption, so in the year we can distinguish one period of life and one period of death, the period of life in the birth of Christ, and the period of death in Easter that signals the Redemption of Man.

Let's follow the path of the calendar, therefore, and see how the liturgical cycles unfold.

The Liturgical Year has already begun for a few weeks, when the civil year begins with the clamor of January 1st.

The first day of Christ's year is the first Sunday of Advent, and it falls in the very last phase of Autumn, because four Sundays need to pass before we reach Christmas.

The year begins, like the Mass and like the history of the Chosen People, with the yearning to reach God. The Mass, with Psalm 42, repeats the aspiration to present oneself at the altar of God; Sacred History, with the lamentations of the Prophets, invokes the Redeemer; and the year, during the time of Advent, prepares itself for Christmas.

The expectation of a good that delays its coming is distressing. Christians know that to reach God it is necessary to pass through penance first: and, as Giovanni Battista taught, it is through the effort of purification that one must await the Lord.

The expectation coincides with the physical characteristics of the Autumn season, cloudy and without fruit, but with the seeds already hidden in the earth. Christians feel themselves in a desert, but one in which they are preparing the way for the Savior.

When priests celebrate the Mass in Advent, they vest in a color of *penance*, in a color of sadness, with the chasuble, stole, maniple, veil, and burse in violet. During the Mass is sung the beautiful chant of the *Gloria in Excelsis*.

In the primitive churches arose spontaneously the custom of a period of penance and fasts as preparation for the birth of Christ.

Christians placed themselves on the lookout, and they prepared themselves for the fight against the darkness; and it was during Lent and then during Advent when the use of the *stations* began.

Station (*statio*) was a military term used by the Romans to designate guard posts in foreign lands. Tertullian, affirming that Christians were also a militia, exhorted them to remain vigilant in their stations, just like soldiers. That military term remained as is in the Church; and the first places named "stations" were the great ancient Basilicas of Rome.

In the second and third century, the observance of the stations consisted of getting up at daybreak to travel, fasting and by foot, to a far-away place, where the divine mysteries were celebrated. Later, however, the stations were observed in a more solemn and social manner.

The faithful mostly gathered near a church, and there they awaited the bishop with the clergy. Often it was the Pontiff himself who arrived from far away with his retinue, walking with bare feet. All together they went in procession, singing psalms and reciting the Litany of the Saints, into a basilica where the bishop was celebrating the Divine Office.

Only between the 7th and the 9th century was the duration of Advent limited to approximately four weeks before Christmas. To establish when it begins, which is then the beginning of the Liturgical Year, it is necessary to count four Sundays retrospectively from Christmas, and then we name these Sundays (counting in the opposite direction), the first, second, third, and fourth Sundays of Advent.

CHAPTER 3

CHRISTMAS

The day of Christmas, on the 25th of December, is one of the two central dates as we have mentioned. But how was it determined?

Jesus is the Sun who wraps us in light and in warmth. His dates are approximately determined, like those sidereal days relative to the equinoxes and the solstices, indicating that the 21st day of the month is the limit between seasons. They are always precisely defined by men—either by observers of the stars or by the legislators of the Church.

For a long time January 6th was considered the day of Christmas, especially in the Orient.

In the opinion of some, an extraneous circumstance intervened to move the date into December. The 25th of December, in the West (and in Rome), was one of the most solemn festivals of paganism to celebrate the birth of the "Sun God." The Church, to combat the influence that the suggestive splendor of this magnificent feast-day may have had over new Christians, celebrated on the same day the birth of another Sun: the Sun of Justice, the Sun of Truth, the Sun that came to enlighten the nations.

But the opposite is more probable, that the date of Christ's birth, December 25th, was determined by calculating nine months from the Incarnation (March 25th), and that the coincidence with the pagan festival was fortuitous.

One day, however, is not enough to celebrate an arrival this great. Likewise in the world, if an extraordinary event occurs like the coronation of a great king, or a great date of particular importance is commemorated, as the flight from Egypt was for the Hebrews, one mere feast-day is not enough to contain the solemnity and the jubilation that goes with it. And although there remains only one central day of the event, it brings with it a period of preparation and a long celebration to follow.

The same happens for Christmas, for Easter, and for many festivals that recall the most salient facts pertaining to our Redemption.

There is, thus, a vigil day of immediate preparation (like the day before Christmas) and a period of successive feasts that last throughout 8 days—that is, until the "octave." At the octave the same festival repeats itself, similar to how a weekday returns after 7 days.

The Octave-day of Christmas has a particular importance, because on it we celebrate the Circumcision of the Baby Jesus, and it corresponds to the civil New Year, on January 1st.[5]

Because of that fact, the religious recurrence of the octave-day of Christmas was for a long time dissipated by the joyful and inaugural games that filled that day, as relics of paganism. For this reason the Church in the 5th century instituted a sacred Mass *Ad prohibendum ab idolis* (for the prohibition of idols).

Later people began to celebrate the Circumcision on this day: "And after eight days were accomplished, that the child should be circumcised, his name was called Jesus, which was called by the angel, before he was conceived in the womb," as Luke states in his Gospel (Luke 2:21).

The feast of the octave was historically established. The name of Jesus as given by the Angel was a secret of the Most Holy Mary, received on the day of the Annunciation. The Virgin Mary, the Gate of Heaven, was therefore united to

---

5 In the current calendar, the Solemnity of Mary, Mother of God, is also celebrated on this day.

the God-child in one feast that closed one of the doors of perdition (9th century).

When, after 40 days from the Birth, the Most Pure Mother will present the Baby at the Temple, "to be purified" after the ritual, Jesus will be recognized as "the Light come to illuminate the Nations."

The feast of the Purification, which is counted among the Messianic revelations, can be considered the ultimate natural end of the season of Christ's birth. In fact, like all of the feasts of Christmas, it has a fixed date occurring on February 2nd.

The Liturgical season of Christmas, however, is necessarily shorter (we see that it extends 20 days). It should be a period full of joy over the birth of the Savior, without shadow of penance or fasting. But comparatively, February 2nd is a far-away date, often overlapped by the beginning of the Paschal cycle, namely the preparation for Lent.

Another feast pertaining to the revelation of Jesus as the Messiah falls during the Christmas Cycle: the manifestation of Jesus to the pagan world, to the Magi and to cruel Herod. *Epiphany* literally means "manifestation."

Epiphany recurs 6 days after the Christmas Octave-day, on the fixed day of January 6th.

Epiphany also has an octave as well; and this octave closes the festal period of Christmas, which thus extends from December 25th to January 13th and lasts 20 days total.

It is evident that, if a feast-day can fall on any day of the week, its octave will have a Sunday within it, which is then called "Sunday during the Octave" (as in Sunday during the Octave of Christmas, Sunday during the Octave of Epiphany, etc.)

The liturgical calendar commemorates all these days from which the Christmas feasts are developed—days that, just like Christmas, are fixed on a specific day of the month. After

Christmas and its octave follows Epiphany and its octave, along with the intercalated Sundays within these periods.

The two seasons, a season of preparation and a season of festivity, are marked in the calendar with their own liturgical colors: violet and white.

CHAPTER 4

EPIPHANY

The day after the octave of Epiphany begins a calendar period that is distinguished by the color green.

It is made up of 6 weeks. The first week may be incomplete, because we are counting by Sundays, and the first Sunday can fall quickly after the day of Epiphany, or indeed on the same day when Epiphany falls on a Sunday. To be more precise, the season is comprised of six Sundays rather than six weeks; and these are referred to by ordinal number of their position after the Epiphany.

However, it only happens rarely that all six Sundays occur, because there is only a limited space allocated for them. And that limited space does not depend on the Christmas Cycle but on the Paschal Cycle.

In fact, the day of Easter is determined on its own. The movement of the stars sets the date, not the succession of weeks.

The Paschal Cycle does not begin when the Christmas Cycle ends, but rather when its time to begin has arrived. And Easter is a central point on which various related seasons depend, all the way back to the earliest point of preparation; that is, to the point where the Paschal Cycle begins.

Thus, if Easter occurs late, the season of Epiphany has more room. But if Easter occurs early, Epiphany is shortened, and it can even be shortened so much that only two Sundays are left.

If the Paschal Cycle intrudes into the green time of the prolongation of the Christmas Cycle, the Sundays after Epiphany need to move to the end of the green time that follows the Easter season.

These conflicts, between the two cycles of the Liturgical Year, show us how the season of preparation is closely connected with the season of festivity, on which it depends in a definite way. Meanwhile, the green seasons are then counted through successive weeks one after another, throughout whatever time is left free.

And how should we interpret the green periods, with respect to the life of Christ?

After the revelations of his infancy, Jesus "grew in wisdom, age, and grace." He leads a retired life, until the time when He must initiate His mission of Divine Teacher. Therefore, He obeys the calling of God, and He goes into the desert, remaining in prayer and in fasting for 40 days to prepare Himself for public life.

His public life does not begin when He reaches the age of maturity—it depends on God, and it is has its own appointed days. All things are foreseen in prophecy and will end with the completion of man's Redemption. So the green time in the calendar does not have an end per se. Its end is signaled by the beginning of the Divine Mission.

CHAPTER 5

Easter

The Paschal Cycle occupies more than three fourths of the year. As it forms in an inseparable block around the day of Easter, which varies in its position, the entire Easter Cycle moves with it, and almost always it encroaches on the time after Epiphany.

The Paschal Season proper, which begins with Easter Sunday, commemorates Jesus from the Resurrection to the Ascension, and it also includes the descent of the Holy Spirit, or Pentecost.

Thus in total it includes: six Sundays after Easter (the First, Second, Third, Fourth, Fifth, and Sixth Sunday after Easter), Pentecost Sunday, and then the week until the following Saturday: encompassing 56 days total.

And as the Lord remained on earth 40 days after His Resurrection, the feast of the Ascension also takes its place within the Paschal season.

Note that the corresponding feast in the Christmas Cycle, the Presentation in the Temple (or the Purification) 40 days

after the Nativity, does not fall in the Christmas Season.

Nonetheless, this does not detract from the admirable correspondences of the two feasts: the God-child, who goes to the Temple of His Father 40 days after his coming in the flesh, and the Risen Messiah, who goes to heaven to sit at the right hand of His Father 40 days after the Resurrection.

There is even divine meaning and action in the two great feasts that intervene in the two liturgical seasons and mark their respective closes: namely, the kings from the Orient who were guided by the Star, and the Holy Spirit that comes from Heaven.

From these two great closing feast days come the names of the times that follow: respectively, the Time after Epiphany, and Time after Pentecost.

LENT

The time of preparation for Easter is quite long.

Lent is a period of penance that demands recollection, prayer, and fasting. It is the time that prepares one to receive the grace of Redemption, and it recalls the fast of 40 days that Christ made in the desert, to prepare Himself for his Public Life and His appearance as the Divine Teacher.

Among the earliest Christians, it was a period of preparation for the Catchumens, which included the "Penance of Admission to Baptism."

The fast was rigorous, and permitted only one meal at sunset, after the religious rituals of the day were all finished.

Moreover, this fast permitted neither meat, nor dairy, nor eggs, nor wine.

Before being admitted to Lent, the aspiring members of the Church had to humble themselves, making a public admission of their sins prostrate at the feet of the bishop.

This reminded them that they were but dust, ash, and mud, and that after death they would be returned to ash and the dust of the earth: *Memento, homo, quia pulvis es et in pulverum reverteris.* (Remember man, that thou art dust and unto dust thou shalt return.)

And they accepted ashes symbolically cast upon their heads, because "the waters had penetrated to their souls, and they had need of one who would save them." They received the sackcloth and the imposition of the Lenten penance; and they remained outside the doors of the Church. Only at the end of Holy Week could they approach the entrance, through the merits of Christ, and they received Baptism on Holy Saturday.

The Confession of the Penitents was done on Holy Thursday.

Every year all the faithful had to do the Lenten penance: which is a long Confiteor that precedes the resurrection of the soul in Christ.

With the passing of time, however, as the Fast was suspended every Sunday, the 40 days of Fast were distributed in a longer period. Normally 40 days would fit in six weeks. But when the Sundays are removed, there remain only 36 days of fasting. To make up the number of 40, there were thus added another four days from the preceding week.

This is why the Lenten Fast begins on a Wednesday, and to that day was assigned the Imposition of Ashes.

In many of the Eastern Churches, the Fast was suspended not only on Sunday but on Saturday as well. Because of this, the period of penance was greatly prolonged, and ended up including the three weeks prior to the first Sunday of Lent.

Even though the Roman Church did not adopt this practice, there remained on the liturgical calendar a period of three non-fasting Sundays preceding Lent. The Church on those days adopts the color violet, and omits the Alleluia, only taking it up again at Easter.

The period of those three Sundays is called the Season of Septuagesima, and it is a sort of adjunct to Lent.[6] The person who feels the solemnity of the Lent season will during this time perform devotions and spiritual recollections.

The three weeks in the season of Septuagesima are called: Septuagesima Sunday, Sexagesima Sunday, and Quinquagesima Sunday, and it is on Wednesday of this last week that Ash Wednesday falls.

The Season of Lent, therefore, though it has only 40 days of Fast, nevertheless encompasses a period of 70 days.

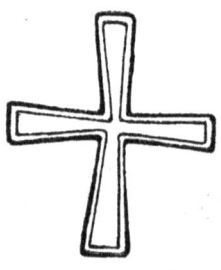

---

6   This season is not included in the current 1969 calendar.

THE VICTORY

Why does humanity invoke the Messiah?

To be redeemed and freed from servitude and from sin; to be lifted up from decay and raised from the state of death.

Now all this is not completed by the God-child who is celebrated during Christmas, but by the Messiah who completed His mission, and who brought us victory over death:

"I am the resurrection and the life" (John 11:25).

Easter, therefore, is the center of all liturgical time, the Feast of Feasts, the Solemnity of Solemnities.

For fallen humanity, Christmastime is the birth of the Liberator, but it is only on Easter that the Liberation is completed. On this day humanity celebrates the great victory over the enemy. One hears the hymn of exulting and triumph: "Alleluia! Alleluia!"; Christ is raised, and "all will be raised….in Him, with Him, and by Him."

The Resurrection happened on a Sunday, when Sunday was not yet a feast day within the week; that is, a sanctified day. For the Hebrews it was a day just like any other.

The Resurrection of Christ made the day holy for Christians: and it is in reference to that day that the times of the year are marked.

Easter therefore is the principal reckoner of time, and it is a feast of spiritual jubilation so great that one is permitted on that day to pray without kneeling, so distant is any idea of penance and humiliation.

It is "the first of the days of the year." The Liturgical Year does not really begin, as the civil one does, from the first day of the year in festivity, but from the center of the year in glory. It does not fall amidst the Winter snows, but in the heart of a luxuriant Spring, when all the Earth is reborn, around the new Man that rises again in the soul of every Christian.

Easter does not have a vigil day like Christmas, but a whole entire week, loaded with pain, during which we commemorate the price of Redemption, the Passion of Our Lord Jesus Christ.

The sorrowful services that the Church observes during Holy Week come together in the Way of the Cross; Christians, at the foot of the Cross of the Crucified God, listen to His last seven words, and at the end they remain prostrate at the sepulchre of the dead Lord.

Beginning from the evening of Holy Thursday, the altars inside the churches are despoiled of ornaments; no sound is heard any longer, neither altar bells nor church bells. Darkness surrounds a funereal silence; feeble and impassioned Lamentations, that seem more like the cry of the Marys than the voice of the prophets speaking through the mouth of Jeremiah, permeate the hearts of those who make their pilgrimages through the churches.

The very end of Lent is like the press through which the olives must pass to yield the illuminating oil. And the extreme anguish of mourning gives a measure of glorious joy that shines upon man, who has reached his Passover.

Easter is the feast of a freed mankind. Christ suffers for us, but we are the ones who benefit from it, gaining a victory for that which we have not fought. It is Christ who fights for us, graciously giving us the victory. It is His Blood that redeemed us. We do not do anything to earn it, we do not do anything but sin . . . "*Peccavi Domine!* . . ." (I have sinned, Lord!)

Therefore, the Liturgical Year concerns the life of man redeemed by Christ; and the Mass concerns Christ. In fact, the two key points of the Mass and of the Liturgical Year do not correspond, although they both recall the life of Christ.

The first part of the Mass, the instructional part, culminates with the teaching of the Divine Master, who reveals to man His doctrines, and is thus a mirror of the public life of the Messiah.

The first part of the Liturgical Year, on the other hand, has as its culmination the Incarnation of the Word and the Nativity of the Baby Jesus, who brings salvation: and humanity feels reassured: "Mine eyes have seen the Savior! Now the servant of God can go in peace."

The mystical part of the Mass has the Consecration as its culmination point: and it re-presents Christ Who dies in the extreme suffering of the Cross. It is the Messiah who is there present; so much so that the Lord truly returns among us when we commemorate His Passion. On the altar is offered a true sacrifice, with the propitiatory offering of the Divine Victim.

In the Liturgical Year, however, the mystical portion culminates in a blaze of victory, a feast of incomparable joy during which the cries of triumph resound: humanity celebrates its own Redemption.

But it is also the feast on which it is obligatory for every Christian to receive the Lord, by approaching the Sacrament of the Eucharist: "Receive Communion at least on Easter."

Man, following the life of his Savior, lives in Him; for Christ made man to enjoy the fruits of Redemption until the end of time.

THE COLOR WHITE

The liturgy reserves the color white for sacred festivities.

Thus during Easter the color white dominates, for a whole week until the completion of the octave. The very words of the liturgy speak of the color of the sacred vestments' majesty: "The Marys, going down to the sepulchre of Christ, saw a young man dressed in a white tunic."

The days of the Octave are called *"in albis,"* days in white, and Sunday of the Octave is *"Domenica in albis."*

White is the color of purification. The old man is gone, just like every crumb of unleavened bread among the Hebrews was gone, at the Passover sunrise. At the Christian Easter, everything is renewed from death, and that which is reborn is new and without blemish.

In the primitive Church the color white was also specially visible, because the catechumens, who had received Baptism on Holy Saturday, dressed in white and wore the garment of the Neophyte throughout the entire week, removing it only on the following Sunday, the Sunday "in albis."

Every act of life is also a symbol of purification or of renewal during the Easter solemnity: for example, the most ancient custom—which is still observed—of cleaning and whitening the houses, of wearing new clothes, and finally of blessing all the foods that are now lawfully eaten after the Lenten fast. We resume them not like starving men who are rediscovering food, but like new men, who have learned temperance and who do not want to cast any shadow over their hard-won purity.

Thus the foods are left out, on the Saturday before Easter, under the eyes of those fasting, without being touched. Every house is abundantly provisioned; in the city the foodstuffs are adorned with branches and with silver, but no one of those fasting for 40 days will touch them. First, the priest must come to each house and bless the foods saved for Easter, because the faithful will consume them as individuals raised in Christ.

THE PASCHAL CANDLE

On the day of Easter one sees in the churches, next to the altar, a large candle beautifully crafted, painted with bright colors and finely historiated. It is lit, and its light symbolizes the triumphant life of the Savior. It will remain lit for a long time, just as Jesus remained on earth after the Resurrection, burning for the space of 40 consecutive days.

On the day of the Ascension, in order to symbolize the glorious disappearance of the Savior, the candle is extinguished and carried away.

This is recalled by a corresponding event in the celebration of the Mass: At the coming down of Christ in the Eucharist, lighted candles are brought in that burn during the whole time that the Divine Presence lasts upon the altar; namely, until the Communion.

THE FEASTS OF EASTERTIDE

After Easter there follow six Sundays, called the "Sundays after Easter" which arrive in late Spring. They take place in May and, according to the date of Easter, in June.

The jubilation of nature thus accompanies that of man; the churches are filled with flowers.

There is, however, a day in which sadness returns. It is a vigil, and Christians recall in it the processions of penitents, chanting the Litany of the Saints: the Rogations.

However, no one dares forget that they are in a glorious season: "Make the voice of jubilation be heard, make it heard to the very ends of the earth."

It is the feast of the Ascension: the Ascension is the glory of the Lord, it is true, but men see Him disappear, and they listen with sadness to His final prayer: "Father, the hour is come; I have glorified You on earth, I have accomplished the work that You gave me to do; now I come to You, glorify your Son" (cf. John 17: 1-2, 4-5). And from the perspective of the Apostles He lifted Himself up into the air, until a cloud took Him from their sight.

The Church, on the day of the Ascension, extinguishes the Paschal candle that gave light and joy: it is the 40th day from Easter Sunday.

CHAPTER 6

Pentecost

A little before ascending to Heaven, the Lord exhorted the Apostles to action with this consoling promise: "You will receive the power of the Holy Spirit, coming upon you, and you will give testimony of me to the ends of the earth" (cf. Acts 1:8). Ten days later, in fact, and therefore 50 days after the Resurrection, on a Sunday morning, while they had been gathering in the Cenacle, surrounded by the Most Holy Virgin Mary, the Apostles, various faithful and pious women—120 persons in all—the Paraclete descended upon them under the form of tongues of fire.

The Apostles were left inspired, and they began speaking in all manner of languages, with fiery speeches that rocked the world to its foundations.

They had acquired the power to call all the peoples to the Kingdom of God, and to fight like combatants until they had conquered the works of darkness—hatred, pride, wrath—and until the triumph of the works of light—peace, truth, and love.

The new law was promulgated: the Apostles, in their

successors, would bring forth the fruits of Redemption until the end of time.

On the day of Pentecost the hand has been put to a work that is effective, militant, and infinitely fecund, working to bring about the result of a universal triumph: the Church of Christ.

EASTER OF ROSES

By the fact that the descent of the Paraclete puts into effect the work of Redemption, and signals the birth of the Church, Pentecost assumes the same solemnity as Easter. During its vigil it was the custom, in the early days of the Church, to baptize another group of catechumens—those who were ill or unprepared on the occasion of Holy Saturday.

The Mass, however, puts aside the color white, characteristic of Eastertide. On the solemnity of Pentecost, as also in all the days of the week until the Saturday following, the liturgical vestments take on a vivid red color: the color of the divine fire.

Feasts and expressive representations characterized the sacred rituals of Pentecost Sunday in the Middle Ages.

As the Holy Spirit is also represented in the form of a dove, during the Mass a dove was released that flew amidst the resounding clamor of trumpets. Tufts of flaming cotton were also let go from on high, along with roses and rose petals, that all fell in a quantity like raindrops. Because of this custom, and because the feast often coincides with the flowering of roses in May, Pentecost is called the "Easter of Roses."

The Life of Christ in the Liturgical Year

Diagram 4.

THE PASCHAL NUMBER

The distribution of Sundays around Easter is quite wonderful, as it recalls the distribution of the Apostles around Christ at the Last Supper: six Sundays precede it (the Sundays of Lent), and six Sundays follow it (the Sundays of Eastertide). Easter itself remains at the seventh place, namely in the middle of everything; just as Christ on the Paschal banquet was in the middle of the Apostles, having six on one side and six on the other.

It is also marvelous that the cycle of Sundays, if we consider the two solemnities that stand at its beginning and at its end, represent the path of man's spiritual journey.

The cycle begins with Ash Wednesday; man is himself ash. But the ash is not alive; it disperses. Proceeding always towards Christ and, walking the way of Penance (the six Sundays of Lent), man finds Resurrection and Life. Then, advancing in purity received in the grace of Christ (the Sundays after Easter), one finally encounters the Creator Spirit who enflames, edifies, and renews the face of the world.

Thus, man can build on the rock of eternal works, because "if it is not God who builds, man labors in vain" (Ps, 126: 1).

TIME AFTER PENTECOST

The remainder of the year is marked by liturgical green.

It lasts long enough to equal the time of all the feast days: it therefore lasts around half a year.

We count 24 Sundays after Pentecost[7], which are referred to by ordinal numbers: first, second, third . . . , to the 24th Sunday after Pentecost.

This last is always the end of the Liturgical Year, and it precedes the first Sunday of Advent of the successive year.

If, however, the Paschal Cycle, including the time of Septuagesima, has intruded on the Christmas Cycle, the last of the six Sundays after Epiphany, as we have seen, must give way. Then, after the long string of Sundays after Pentecost have gone by, the Sundays of Epiphany are reinserted in succession between the 23rd and the 24th Sunday after Pentecost, always making sure that the 24th Sunday is the last of the year.

The color green ought to be adopted right at the close of the Pentecost octave; but, as this Sunday is dedicated to the august mystery of the Most Holy Trinity, the Church adopts white instead.

Now the men called by Jesus Christ and sanctified by the Holy Spirit, the Apostles, must act non-stop, so also the long string of Sundays after Pentecost represents the growth of the Church and its triumph in the world.

---

[7] In the current (1969) calendar, these Sundays are called Sundays of Ordinary Time.

The Apostles' labors continue the work of Redemption. Those militant men stand against the dark enemies that tempt the soul of man and the powerful enemies of the world who can kill the body but not the soul. They fight with the arms of Christ, with souls enflamed by the Holy Spirit.

In the end, they penetrated into the very heart of the Roman Empire that wanted to destroy them; and the same Peter placed his Chair in Rome, which thus became the seat of the Vicar of Christ, center of the Catholic Church.

The furious and ferocious barbarian tribes then descended, but before the Church their hearts dissolved, and they yearned for the peace of Christ.

In this long period after Pentecost is commemorated therefore the great host of followers who fought and triumphed in the Church of Christ. In this host without number every Christian wishes to unite himself, because the purpose of virtue is sanctification. And all of us, amassed in an irresistible march, can participate in the conquests of the Kingdom of Heaven.

The Liturgical Year, which represents the life of man in Christ, is divided in two more or less equal halves: one half comprises the festivals of Jesus the Redeemer, and the other half symbolizes the life of the Christian people redeemed and made free.

This last part makes us think of the Hebrew people when they were liberated from slavery in Egypt and found themselves in the desert, where they suffered from hunger until God, pitying them because of their sufferings, let fall manna from heaven.

And what would have been our state, after the Redemption, if we were left alone in the desert of life? Jesus would not have abandoned us after having saved us.

"The merciful Lord left those who fear him a Food in memory of his miracles" (from Ps. 110: 4-5).

The life of the Christian people, thus, cannot be conceived as detached from the Eucharist.

How could men show the gratitude to reciprocate the perfection of such love?

"Give as much praise as you can, because He is greater than any praise, neither can you praise Him enough. The joy of your mind will be a continual praise: be sonorous, joyful, and happy. Therefore we, reverencing and prostrating ourselves on the floor, adore such a wonderful Sacrament."[8]

THE FEAST OF CORPUS CHRISTI

The feast of Corpus Christi is an expression of man's gratitude and love toward Jesus.

For many, many centuries there was no day of the year that was dedicated to adoration of the Sacred Host with particular solemnity. The Sacrament was reserved for the sick and for the dying; and it was kept in a secluded place and transported, when necessary, hidden at the breast, as Saint Tarcisius did.

It was a religious of Belgium, Saint Juliana of Mt. Cornillon, who had a vision of Jesus in the Holy Sacrament solemnly going forth through the streets and the squares, glorified as a King by a rejoicing people.

---

8   Paraphrase of the Sequence of Corpus Christ, *Lauda Sion*.

This vision was accepted by Pope Urban IV, who established the feast of Corpus Christi, fixing it on the Thursday after the Octave of Pentecost.

An Office and a Mass were written for it, and St. Thomas Aquinas composed the hymns that today are sung in honor of the Blessed Sacrament.

Jesus exits the Temple to go among the people, through the churches and through the squares, and to the people all are given to honor Him publicly.

The priests wear the most magnificent vestments, and they carry in hand the Monstrance, walking slowly.

On that solemn day, the windows along the streets are decorated with tapestries and carpets of velvet and gold; but the most beautiful carpet is that which was made by hundreds of hands, working all night long during the vigil of Corpus Christi, to arrange little fresh flowers in wonderful designs, that cover the streets and the squares where the Lord will pass.

In some little towns one may happen to see a myriad of little lights going around in the mountains the night before Corpus Christi. These are people who go to gather wildflowers and herbs that release a scent when they are stepped on, who will later be scattering them where the people are walking around the Holy Eucharist.

"O Lord, You have fed us with fine wheat, Alleluia! You have filled us with honey from the rock. The eyes of all hope in You; You fill with blessings all the living" (from the Mass of Corpus Christi).

CHAPTER 7

THE LITURGICAL CALENDAR

Liturgical time is subdivided after the events of the life of Jesus Christ and of the Church Militant and Triumphant; and the Sundays, which are the representative days of each week, punctuate the subdivisions.

To represent these subdivisions of time, and to remind the faithful to observe the precepts of the Church, is the purpose of the liturgical calendar.

What ought the faithful seek in it? We need to seek out the Sundays and the obligatory feasts, in order to follow the liturgical texts that the Church has established for each Mass.

We have already examined the two cycles represented in a hypothetical calendar, but now, in order to study its construction, let us consult an actual calendar, which is based on the position of Easter and Christmas in a predetermined year: 1950. (See the calendar at the back of the book).

In this calendar one can see indicated the 52 weeks of the year, and of some of the Lord's feasts that are essential in the cycle of liturgical time: namely Christmas, the Circumcision, the Epiphany, the Purification, and Ash Wednesday.

The Sundays and the other festivals are along the bottom. The seasons are differentiated by means of four liturgical colors: violet, green, white, and red; and corresponding to these are the titles by which they are distinguished in the Missal. As the month and the day are indicated on the grid, it is relatively simple to locate the liturgical feasts within the

civil year.

If, for example, you want to know on which day Ash Wednesday falls in 1950, you must find the violet period that precedes Easter: it's February 22nd.

More important, however, is knowing which Sunday corresponds to a fixed date, in order to find the correct Mass in the Missal, relative to the Liturgical Year.

For example, if it is May 7th, 1950, the calendar shows that is a Sunday, and its relative position is written to the side: the Fourth Sunday after Easter. Or, if it is March 26th, it is the 5th Sunday of Lent. The 22nd of October corresponds to the 21st Sunday after Pentecost, etc.

THE EMBER DAYS

Other little additions have been made in the calendar to make it easier to consult.

The lines at left divide the times of the year according to the four astronomical seasons: autumn, winter, spring, summer, corresponding to the 21st day of December, March, June, and September.

Thus, it is easy to compare the astronomical seasons and the liturgical seasons.

Although there is no direct correspondence between them, with the liturgical subdivisions forming an entirely original and independent way to mark the seasons of the year, the

Church did not simply ignore popular institutions without taking into consideration which aspects of them were useful and good.

The divisions of the four seasons were very intimately related to popular customs regarding climate and production of the necessities of life. Thus, they were necessarily of interest to the Church, the mother of Christians, especially since in the early centuries the passing from one season to another was solemnly celebrated.

During pagan times in Rome, the beginning of each season was celebrated with great solemnity in order to propitiate the gods at the harvest time. But similar customs the Church also inherited from Palestine, where the Hebrew people were used to consecrating the four seasons of the year by means of solemn fasting.

These customs, therefore, already existed in the time of Peter and the first Apostles. Periodic fasting at the changing of seasons also finds important justification from and is borne out by human experience, and the modern science of physiology fully confirms its salutary effects.

The Church, therefore, with maternal indulgence, from the very beginning welcomed this custom. It later consecrated it to the glory of God, by instituting, in the fourth century, times of fasting known as the *Ember Days*.

The fast consists of three days in one week: Wednesday, Friday, and Saturday, on which are celebrated special sacred offices of the Church.

The Ember Days fast, which occurs four times in one year,

corresponds to the change of sidereal seasons.

So if you look at the calendar of 1950, there are little indications in the margins, marked with the letters E.D., showing which Sundays the Ember days fall between:
> between the 3rd and 4th of Advent
> between the 1st and 2nd of Lent
> Pentecost and its octave
> between the 16th and 17th after Pentecost

The weeks of the Ember Days were fixed by Pope Gregory VII.

Consulting the calendar of 1950, we can see that the first Ember week coincides with the transition from autumn to winter. Here the fact that the Christmas feast-days are fixed, is evidence that the Christian observances correspond to the solemnities of antiquity; and we can say the same for the time after Pentecost, where there is a perfect match between the fourth Ember week and the transition from Summer to Autumn.

However, in Eastertide, which can move within the year, it appears evident that the Ember Days were tied to the cycle of the Christian year. In fact, this has caused the 2nd and 3rd Embertides to be displaced in comparison to the changes of season by two weeks. And thus for two weeks, the Easter cycle intrudes on the Christmas cycle, shifting those two weeks of Epiphany to the end of the time after Pentecost. The markings on the calendar at the back of the book, therefore, show the subdivision of the seasons.

THE LIFE OF THE CHURCH

However, we must also superimpose on the calendar the variable feasts, such as those pertaining to Our Lord, The Virgin, the Angels and the Saints, with these last in all their various categories: Apostles, evangelists, martyrs, virgins, confessors, bishops, doctors.

As the saints, to which the Church has conferred the honors of the altar, are numberless, there are not enough days in the year to remember them all separately. These commemorations thus are distributed according to the order of the civil calendar. These feasts, in fact, are not connected to the seasons, which thus gives them a stable position that they would not have if they were displaced as the variable feasts.

All this makes the religious calendar closely intertwined with the civil calendar, and could result in many people being confused.

However, the knowledge of the two calendars needs to be clear to every Christian: what separates and distinguishes them in their essential constitutions.

The figures that we give here (see Diagrams 5 and 6) represent the central theme of the liturgical season and the unfolding of these themes.

In the first figure there is no hint of months and days, no distinction of seasons: the long empty line is divided in four parts, because the Christmas cycle occupies a fourth of the year.

The symbols that subdivide the time correspond to two feasts, indicated by flaming disks to represent two suns: the upper one symbolizes Christmas, and the lower one, surmounted by a cross, symbolizes Easter.

The Life of Christ in the Liturgical Year

Diagram 5.

THE LITURGICAL CALENDAR

To the side of the drawing are written these words:

The seasons of the Liturgical Year are derived from a Sun of Truth and Justice.

surmounted with a flag that shows the liturgical colors in succession, following each subdivision of the cycles into seasons:
> Season of Preparation: violet
> Season of Festivity: white
> Season of Transition: green (after Epiphany and after Pentecost)

And this last, because its length is uncertain and undecided, is depicted as a long fringe.

The staff of the flag, of a vivid red color, symbolizes redemption and love, and is surmounted with a globe symbolizing the whole world placed beneath the cross.

In the next table is depicted the subdivision of the seasons: the two centers of spiritual suns that are the day of Christmas and the day of Easter. From each of these proceed two wavy arrows, one pointing towards the beginning of the year and the other towards the opposite side.

The upper arrows, dark and violet, represent the seasons of preparation, and the lower arrows, red like the disks, represent the progress of the seasons, with little circles along the arrows that signify the Sundays and feasts.

The four Sundays of Advent are along the arrow of Christmas that points upward, and along the other arrow are the Sundays (between two and three)—between the octaves of the Christmas feasts—and the other feasts, marked with phrases:

Christmas: *And the Word was made flesh and dwelt among us.*

Circumcision: *And they called his name Jesus.*

Presentation of the Temple (which, despite being out of place with respect to its true position in the civil calendar, belongs however to the Christmas cycle): A *light who illuminates the nations.*

Finally, the image shows a feast off the arrow line: namely, a comet at its tip, as if the arrow was gently drawn to it. This is the Epiphany, the rush of the pagan peoples from the furthest regions to the place where the Word was made incarnate: *And they adored the King of the world.*

After Epiphany there is a green background, and that space is measured on one side with equidistant numbers: I, II, III, IV. This period for the year 1950 lasts only 4 weeks. Thus the arrow ascending from Easter reaches quite high, leaving some space free. The other two Sundays, V and VI, are picked up in the second green section, all the way at the bottom.

Along the arrow above Easter are given first the three Sundays of Septuagesima, and then a dark dot that indicates the beginning of Lent (Ash Wednesday): *Remember, O man, that thou art dust.*

The six Sundays of Lent are shown along the arrow, and the last ends atop the Easter disk by the cross: *Christ, our Pasch, has been immolated.*

The larger disk represents the Resurrection: *I am the Resurrection and the Life.* At the bottom of the disk, along the red arrow, are shown the six Sundays of Easter, and between the fifth and the sixth of these, a blue dot symbolizes the feast of the Ascension: *He is ascended into heaven.*

Nothing else from the life of Our Lord is shown on the Paschal arrow. But just after the tip of the arrow is placed, as if being drawn to it, a disk with rays. This comes from afar, from Heaven, to where Jesus Christ just ascended; and the

THE LITURGICAL CALENDAR

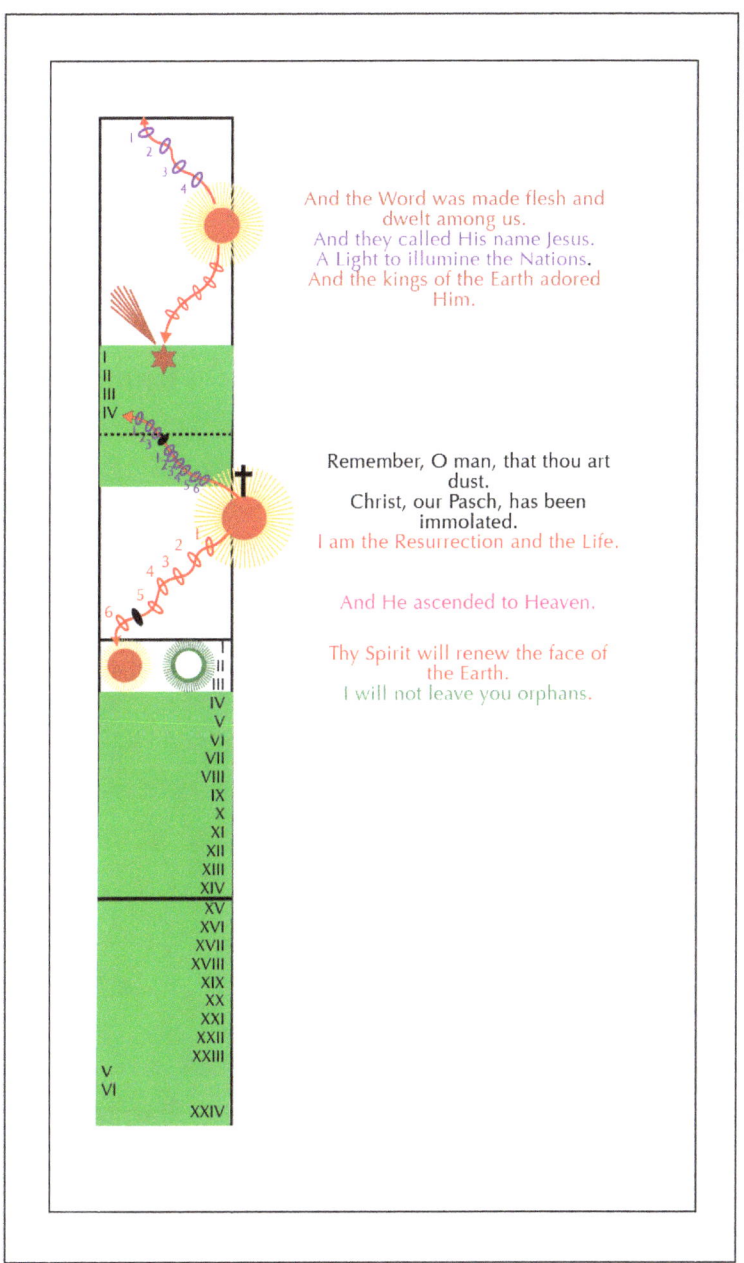

Diagram 6.

disk symbolizes the Holy Spirit: *Thy Spirit shall renew the face of the earth.*

Then, at bottom, is the green of after Pentecost, which fills the rest of the space until the end of the year: *I will not leave you orphans.*

The white disk, placed between the first and second Sundays after Pentecost, symbolizes the feast of Corpus Christi.

There follow the 24 weeks after Pentecost, including (before the last one) the Sundays displaced from the time after Epiphany.

THE LIFE OF MAN

The calendar of Jesus is also the calendar of men, because it is the earthly life of Jesus, of God made man, hidden within it.

Therefore there are two cycles that revolve around and are filled by a common source. One is the Incarnation: Jesus is the incarnate Son of God. He took flesh in the most pure womb of the Blessed Virgin Mary but, even as He is made man, He remains God, and as a God-man He carries out His mission.

The Sacred Infancy occupies the whole first cycle, in which is depicted the mysterious Person of the Child.

He takes unto Himself the burden of human flesh, and together with it the uncertainties of life and all human weakness: a marvelous period of sacrifice, accomplished in an ineffable sweetness, where the incomprehensible Greatness encloses itself in the little body of a Child, tender and helpless. In fact, as soon as He was born He was greeted by the emotions of men and Angels. He received the gifts of the shepherds and the Magi. He is the Infant plagued with the cruelty of a world that does not believe in Him and fears Him (the will and the power of Herod in the Slaughter of the Innocents). He is the Child that astounds the doctors in the Temple, displaying a wisdom that He did not learn from them.

Later, after the scintillating period of His Infancy, all

becomes obscure and He hides Himself.

The Person who is incarnated must adapt Himself to the world in which He was born: He obeys, and He works. He lives during this time a hidden life, until the age of 30.

The second cycle depicted on the calendar is that of His public life, when Jesus carries out His Mission: He therefore reveals Himself to men, to whom He made himself so similar, and He teaches them by His example to do the will of God. Only one thing is necessary for man: "to do the will of God."

THE END AND THE BEGINNING OF THE YEAR

The end of the time after Pentecost passes smoothly into the season of Advent, the green of the former meeting the violet of the latter, just as the violet that begins the Easter Cycle meets the green that follows the Christmas Cycle.

Here, however, between Pentecost and Advent, there is something extra: there is the passage from one Liturgical Year to another, at the end of the month of November.

When the civil New Year begins at the 1st of January, the Liturgical Year has already begun in the old civil year, which we do not see any trace of in the civil calendar. Meanwhile, the end of November and December in a civil year actually pertains to the following Liturgical Year.

This leads to a noteworthy fact: the weeks do not correspond to the end or the beginning of a Liturgical Year.

THE LITURGICAL CALENDAR

If, for example, we look at the two cycles of Christmas and Easter in the liturgical calendar of 1950, we find the first Sunday on the 27th of November, and the last Sunday on the 26th of November: this is explained by the fact that the two dates pertain to two different Liturgical Years.

The last Sunday of the year is always the "24th after Pentecost," even if, in reality, like in 1950, it is the 26th.

This Sunday is connected more to the first Sunday of Advent than to the prolonging of the Paschal Season, and it can be moved and distanced from the other 23 Sundays. But it can never be moved away from the Sunday that begins a new Liturgical Year.

These two Sundays therefore, are the end and the beginning Masses in contact.

It is well known that the names of the Sundays and the feasts of the year are fixed, and one can track back through the Missal the *propers* of each Mass. Let us look at these *propers* to see with what spirit the Liturgical Year begins and ends.

In the Gospel of the 24th Sunday after Pentecost, we find words of obscure, terrible meaning. These are from a prophecy of the prophet Daniel, explained and commented on by the Divine Teacher: "When you shall see the abomination of desolation, which was spoken of by Daniel the prophet, standing in the holy place; he that readeth, let him understand: then they that are in Judea, let them flee to the mountains, and he that is in the field, let him not go back to take his coat…; there shall be a great tribulation, such as has not been found from the beginning of the world until now, neither shall be.

"And immediately after the tribulation of those days, the sun shall be darkened, and the moon shall not give her light, and the stars shall fall from heaven, and the powers of

The Life of Christ in the Liturgical Year

Diagram 7.

heaven shall be moved; and then shall all the tribes of the earth mourn" (cf. Mt. 24: 15-30).

And Jesus, who explains to us the prophecy, adds: "There shall arise false prophets who shall show great signs and wonders: do not listen to them! Do not follow them! From the fig-tree learn this parable: when the branch thereof is now tender, and the leaves come forth, you know that summer is nigh. So you also, when you shall see all these things, know that Son of Man is at the gates" (cf. Mt. 24: 11, 32-33).

The Gospel of the first Sunday in Advent records a discourse of Jesus: "There shall be upon the earth the distress of nations, by reason of the roaring of the confusion of the sea and waves, men withering away for fear and expectation of what shall come upon the whole world. For the powers of heaven shall be moved" and then He repeats the parable, "See the fig-tree, and all the trees: when they now shoot forth their fruit, you know that summer is night: so you also, when you shall see these things come to pass, know that the kingdom of God is at hand" (Lk. 21:25-33).

These two Sundays, therefore, are connected by the same theme; and the year is a closed cycle, which revolves and repeats itself, like the orbit of the Earth around the Sun.

How different the Christian New Year is from the civil one!

In the latter there prevails the wishful illusion of pagan times, when nothing positive and secure directed one's way in life: "Have a good year!" it is said, "a good end and a good beginning!" One needs to quickly and thoughtlessly cross that flimsy bridge that stands between one year and the other, because there is an unconscious fear of misfortune that threatens man's happiness and life at every moment, and the danger might be averted with boisterous well-wishing.

But what good is this, and what do we need to do to obtain it?

The Liturgical Year, on the other hand, proceeds as if on a bridge of stone, along a safe road.

Men are called to meditate on visions of the dangers which threaten them, because they must have them clearly present: these are unspeakable, and they will last until the end of the world.

In the prophecy of Daniel is shown the image of the destruction of Jerusalem, which shows how fragile are the greatest world powers and the richest nations. Of magnificent temples there may be left only a wall, a ruin, that recalls the tears and lamentations of a dispersed people.

It is for the future that the end of the world and the last judgment, which will be rendered by the same Christ when He returns in power and majesty, are announced.

Reflecting on all this, and remembering that man is ashes, makes a suitable end and a good beginning for the year; because it is necessary to watch for danger in front of us, in order to avoid it, and to hold tight to a secure guide in order to proceed unharmed.

This is the vision of the Christian!

The guide who leads, not from month to month but from week to week, from day to day, will help us proceed safely to the glow of the Divine Light.

The *propers* of the two Masses, in fact, present us with comforting words to guide us. In the Mass of the 24th Sunday, St. Paul teaches the faithful with wise instructions: "*Walk worthy of God, being fruitful in every good work, giving thanks to God, who hath translated us into the kingdom of the Son of His love*" (Col. 1: 10-13).

And in the first Mass of Advent, St. Paul again exhorts the faithful with similar words:

"*Let us walk honestly as in the day; not in drunkenness and indulgence, not in contention, but clothed in our Lord Jesus*

Christ" (Rom. 13: 13-14).

The Liturgical Year is like a closed circle: the beginning and the end are conjoined in the spirit that unites them.

Along the circumference of this circle, one can imagine, are marked 52 divisions that correspond to the 52 Sundays of the year; they are like the hours marked on a watch.

The 24th Sunday after Pentecost is joined to the 1st Sunday of Advent; with a dark color over both of them.

These contrast with the red rays of the Holy Spirit at the top, and the radiant bands of Eastertide.

By and large the rays of the circle indicate the liturgical seasons, and the feasts of Christmas, Ash Wednesday, Good Friday, Easter, Ascension, Pentecost, and Corpus Christi, are marked in their proper position of weeks.

The colors indicate light and flame in the two festal periods of Christmas and Easter.

The semicircle at right, in its various colors, represents the life of Jesus; the semicircle at left, green and uniform, surmounted with the sign of the Eucharist, corresponds to the life of man.

What was the mission of Jesus?

As soon as He completed it with wonderful order, having ended His time among men and ascended to Heaven, from Heaven came a flaming ray!

This makes us think, as a distant comparison, of the phenomena that can happen in the physical world, when a mechanism uses invisible forces to accomplish marvelous effects. The very tiny and indirect actions of a wireless (radio wave communication) can actually lead to two human minds communicating over great distances.

Something parallel can be conceived in the spiritual world and in the sphere of divinity. In the mission of Jesus, there also is something apparently small: a Baby that is born. But this Baby is also the Man who, by living, loving, suffering and dying, accomplishes an ineffable miracle: He re-establishes a bond between man and the Supreme Creator.

This is the communication that took place, the ray of light: the poor Apostles, at first ignorant and fearful, then speak in all the various tongues, and they advance intrepidly toward the conquest of the world.

Christ has left us the means to ensure unfailing help for man. He has (if one were to say it in material terms) traced a wonderful and complete blueprint, with the visible signs of invisible Grace; He has given us the Sacraments. And at the center of these He has given Himself in the Eucharist.

Around all these spiritual facts turns the history of the Church.

The Church is the new construction, which in a tangible way represents the spiritual plane. She is not the divine Creator who maintains the world and who sanctifies man, but She is the "station" through which man places himself in communication with God, and finds the road toward his faraway homeland: the Kingdom of Heaven.

The Church is the earthly work instituted for us by Jesus Christ. She is not just a beautiful house in which we pray, but She is the spiritual institution on earth for the salvation of mankind.

Man has placed around this spiritual "Station" all the beauty that has been inspired by Divine Love; and he surrounded the house of god with art and wealth. She is, therefore, constructed by God Himself "with living stones," worked by His hand and firmly placed on top of the Building:

> "To Thy House, O Lord, is holiness,
> through the length of ages."
> (cf. Ps. 92: 5)

"This is the House of the Lord, solidly built and well founded upon the rock."

"Precious stones are all its walls, and the towers constructed of pearls."

"O Church, your name means Vision of peace; your doors are every hour open, and he who suffers here for the love of Christ is received there by virtue of the Savior's merits!"

Part Three

The Holy Mass

The Holy Mass

Just as we have given the child the means of orienting himself in the period of the Liturgical Year, we enable him to orient himself in the Holy Mass via:

1. a guide — "the Open Book" — aimed at having him break down and understand the different parts, and

2. a Missal, geared towards allowing him to follow the Mass without any outside help.

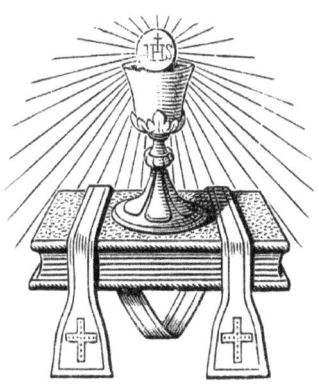

CHAPTER I

THE OPEN BOOK

BRIEF HISTORY OF THE BOOK

How did this *true book* arrive and who wrote it? It is the only book that has the honor of being put on the altar with sacred objects when the Mass is celebrated.

We know that certain sacred books were written by men, such as the four Gospels. We can imagine the Apostle Mark, Luke, Matthew, or John being attentive to writing these pages that generations will reverently read.

We can also visualize Israel's great priests recording the Chosen People's most prominent events in the Bible.

It is as if the Missal, which contains the prayers of the Liturgy, arose from the hearts of those first Christians who gathered, ardent with faith and full of holiness, in the place where they waited for the miracle of the Eucharist to be accomplished. We must remember what the Mass was in the early days: a great drama, always the same, offered anew by the entire Christian people. The faithful did not simply go *hear* a bishop preside. Everyone thought about this obligation: "Be doers of the word and not merely hearers. If you are merely hearers, you will forget the Word of God, which will escape you, like your image in the mirror" (cf. James 1: 22-23).

The first Christians did not just listen—they acted. Their action did not consist only of carrying the offering and begging for alms. Everyone was truly an actor in this drama, and the roles were divided as in a play. It is true that only one, the priest, was clothed with the power, which was given by Christ, to call upon the Divine Presence in the Sacrament and to transmit it to men who were able to receive it. But around him a rather complex action was going on, in which every Christian had to participate.

From what inspired souls did these solemn and yet simple prayers of the Liturgy emerge? These are prayers that every priest dares to express today to call out to the living God among us.

No doubt the first Christians fixed on an expression when its beauty seemed inspired by the Holy Spirit. It was written, and it was faithfully repeated for centuries by the fathers of the Church. The acts of these holy people, therefore, remained, fixed in the rite. They prove to us that these memorable priests who carried out these wonders were the victors of the world; they were, before God, like ingenuous little children who collected the crumbs and who spoke with simplicity to the Almighty.

The others shared the different tasks around the celebrant (the bishop); this one read a passage from the Gospels, and this one a letter of the first Apostles. Another chose Psalms to sing around the Sacrament, inspired by the memory of King David. Finally, the people prepared their *responses* to the bishop, because between the celebrant and the Mass of the Faithful, true dialogues were established for the glory of God. When it seemed good, they were fixed in a book so that the "Ordinary," thus established, would remain for centuries and centuries. This process very much resembled what the

Book of Genesis talks about: "God created the world and saw that it was good" (cf Gen. 1:31). So, He ordered all things that were created and good to remain forever.

In addition to the books of the sacrament, there were *responsories* for the people, *antiphonaries* for singers, *epistolaries* and *evangelaries* for the clergy. But because of the growing number of churches, many found themselves in little centers where the complex celebration that was used in the great Christian basilicas was impossible. For that reason and, no doubt as a result of other circumstances, the Mass was reduced to its most essential terms. The texts, which were, at first, scattered through various books, were united into a single one, which, for this reason, was called the *plenary*.

It is this (condensed) résumé of divine wisdom and holy inspiration that became the Missal.

THE UNIQUE BOOK

No book was as revered and loved as the Missal.

In the same way as for the sacred objects of the Mass, nothing seemed sufficient to give Christianity's sacred text its magnificence. Its cover was decorated with gold and precious stones, and its pages, carefully written, were adorned with miniatures of inestimable value. Many Missals remain among the famous jewels of the treasures of kings, as witnesses of the veneration in which this holy book was held.

The ribbons of colors that hang from some of these pages are one of its specific characteristics. When the priest, before starting Mass, goes to the left of the altar to prepare the book, we see him choose among these ribbons, and using them as bookmarks, he places them in various spots of the volume.

The Missal always has a decorative binding and is always adorned with silk ribbons of various colors. It is always luxuriously printed, although more or less lavishly.

But whether it be the Missal that is placed on the Holy Father's altar at St. Peter's in Rome or the one that is destined for the most humble chapel in the village, the sacred text is identical in everything that matters.

In any country and among people of all languages, the Missal is always written in Latin and only Latin, that is to say, without any translation. The presiders of the Latin Rite[3] in all the world's countries celebrate the Mass with the same words and with the same language in order that we really appreciate that the universal Church is one and that its center is in Rome, the Latin Empire's ancient center.

The Catholic Church is universal, one and Roman; and is led by a single pastor.

Throughout the centuries, however, imperial Rome fell, and Latin disappeared little by little in the life of nations. Many "Latin languages" appeared, and, even in Rome itself, Latin is no longer a common language.

THE CLOSED BOOK

For a long time, this book belonged to the faithful who recited the responses in dialogue with the presider.

But then, the faithful became a stranger to the rite that he loved so much and in which he had participated for centuries!

He could no longer enter with the Offering of the Species to be consecrated, and the solemn hymn of the Offertory which used to hide the noise of the comings and goings through the church had become useless. He was no longer able to go up the steps to sing the *Gradual*. His response, without which

---

3   It is important to point out to children that the Catholic Church is not restricted to the Latin world's dimensions and that there are Eastern Catholic liturgies where the languages that were spoken by the world's first Apostles and Christians – Greeks, Syrians, Chaldeans, Copts, Slavs, etc. are still used.

the bishop did not continue the dialogue to God's glory—as between a father and child—was no longer awaited as it was in the days of old. This book, which was written in a now-dead language for all Western people, became a closed book before which every Christian was illiterate.

And the voice of the holy fathers of the Church who had spoken there remained mute for the faithful. The faithful were only allowed to unite themselves in spirit with the priest and prayed without being able to understand anything about the rite which was occurring right in front of them or what the priest was saying. When printing allowed for the circulation of Mass books, only a little missal remained, which did not have any of the sacred texts. It only had exhortations and prayers that were collated by an ordinary writer who was neither holy nor inspired.

THE LITURGICAL MOVEMENT

It was His Holiness Pope Pius X who felt the need, once more, to summon and unite Christians around the altar.

"Reunite with Jesus Christ!"

But who can reunite humankind in the spirit of Jesus Christ except for Jesus Christ Himself?

"Bring the people closer to the Sacred Liturgy," the Holy Father ordered, and by "the people," he mainly designated those who had had the privilege of being distinguished by the Divine Master himself: the children.

"Unless you change and become like these little children, you will not enter the Kingdom of Heaven!" (cf Mt. 18: 3). Adults, therefore, were admitted into the sacred liturgy, accompanied by little children.

The problem was to make the text and the rite of the

Mass accessible to all the faithful. The Liturgical Movement, designed to explain the Mass and to put the text in the common language into the hands of the faithful, with sufficient explanations to make them follow the rite, developed widely in all parts of the Western Catholic world.[4]

At that time care was taken to help the children to listen to Mass, and books were made available to them which were abundantly illustrated and provided with instructive notes; but these notes and illustrations were still only verbal teachings which duplicate, one might say, the flow of the liturgy.

THE OPEN BOOK

How do we open a book?

Is it opened with speeches? Is it read so that someone will tell you what it says?

When St. Augustine felt the miraculous call in the church of St. Ambrose in Milan: "Open and read," he did not receive any teachings or revelations from this voice. He says that an invigorating exchange took place between his soul and the words which he found when opening at random the book on the altar. This exchange was helped by the silence and solitude of the deserted and obscure church. St. Augustine had already read so many books that he was one of the greatest scholars of his time. But this unique book showed him the path to holiness.

Our task must consist in linking the child's mind with the sacred text and then leaving him alone with God. We must, of course, lead him to the understanding the rite of the altar through instructions and teaching. But having arrived there,

---

[4] Eastern Christians, having never had Mass books in their hands, always participated in the liturgy using gestures, chants, and the responses of the Assembly.

the child must no longer depend on us as a necessary guide.

The Bible teaches us: When little Samuel felt called during the night, he ran towards Eli, but he was spurned by him in the name of the faith. "When you feel yourself called again, you will not come to me, but you will answer: Speak, Lord, your servant is listening!" (cf. 1 Sam 3: 4-9)

When it comes to making a book accessible to children, it is to the book that we must turn. If we want to explain it to them, we make ourselves interpreters of the book; we do not open it to them.

Thus, the Church opened the Missal to the faithful by placing the vernacular translation next to the Latin text.

For small children, we can do just one more thing. We can arrange the text in a clearer way, separating between all the successive parts, and distinguishing the sentences that have different meanings, thus highlighting details to make them more obvious and understandable. This process is similar to using movie films to illustrate movement. Instead of explaining the movement, we show it slowly so that all the successive details are clearly emphasized.

We will therefore begin by separating the parts of the Mass, isolating each one on one page, without worrying whether it is a long or short part, and writing it only in the vernacular.

So, rather than transcribing the Mass on the successive pages of a book, we will transfer each of its parts on a separate index card so that the text can then be horizontally arranged.

The texts do not stay hidden inside the volume, but are all visible. It is not necessary to turn the pages or to insert bookmarks to start the whole Mass over. This result can be obtained by arranging the movable parts next to each other and by having them all be simultaneously visible and legible.

Later, one will find differences on each of these cards. Thus, if it is a dialogue part, the words that alternate between the priest and the people (said by the child) are distinct, not only because they are indented, but also because they are written in two different colours. When, on the contrary, it comes to a text that is not spoken, like a prayer text, an antiphon, etc., the diverse parts will be separated into paragraphs so that the inscriptions are concise:

For example:

"Be courageous in the combat,
and fight against the ancient serpent,
and you will reach the Kingdom of Heaven."

Another example:

"What shall I return to the Lord
for all His bounty to me?
I will lift up the cup of salvation
and call on the name of the Lord,
I will invoke Him by singing His praises,
and I will be delivered from my enemies."

(Prayer of the Priest at Communion)

THE ORDINARY OF THE MASS

The child must already know something about the Mass. He was prepared for it by the book *The Mass Explained to Children,* which helps him grasp the fundamental subdivisons: The Mass of Instruction, available to catechumens, also called the Mass of the Catechumens, and the Mystical Mass or the Mass of the Faithful which was reserved for the baptized faithful.

The Mystical Mass is itself divided into three parts:

1. The Offertory,
2. The Consecration,
3. Communion.

Thus, the Mass is made up of separate pieces that must be

gathered together. Some of these pieces are repeated in all Masses. They make up the structure which is ordered and invariable. It is called the *Ordinary of the Mass*.

On the other hand, other parts (which were previously distributed between the clergy and the laity) vary from Mass to Mass, day by day, and are inserted into defined places in the Ordinary. These parts combined are called the *Proper of the Mass*.

So, the first subdivision in the order of the liturgical text of the Mass consists of what is common to all the Masses (the Ordinary) and what is specific to each one (the Proper).

It is actually easy to prepare a set of separate index cards when it comes to the Ordinary.

But what is to be done about the Propers that vary more than 50 times, if we only take Sundays into account? Should we consider all days, which vary around a hundred times?

We will have to limit ourselves to preparing only the Ordinary with this set. For the Propers, it will be enough to indicate the place where they are to be inserted.

The parts of the Proper are, consequently, represented by blank index cards that will only have one title: *Introit, Collect, Epistle, Gradual, Gospel, Offertory, Secret, Communion, Post-Communion*.

The work that will be done with these cards is aimed only at the full text of the Ordinary of the Mass. But in the midst of the written texts, on the blank cards, the Propers will be represented so that there is a complete picture of the structure of the whole Mass.

It is now a matter of collecting, in groups, the cards relating to the different parts into which the Mass is subdivided. In order to do this in a clear and easy way, we will use cards of different colours for each of the four parts of the Mass. For example, green cards for the Mass of the Catechumens, yellow cards for the Offertory, red for the Consecration, and blue for Communion.

Each of these cards will be gathered into an envelope with their color in order to keep them in order. The envelope will also contain the blank cards of the Propers which correspond to it.

Thus, a study guide is prepared. Although it contains the text of the Mass, it does not consist of a book to be followed, but, rather, loose stones with which to build it.

THE WAY TO USE THIS GUIDE

The child should be advised to study the cards contained in the envelope separately and successively in the order of the text. Each of the parts will be presented and carefully explained by the teacher the first time and then left for the child who must use it himself.

The child starts by putting the cards in order, one next to the other, on a table (to be sure that this order is rigorously respected, the cards will have a sequential number on the back, which serves as control of error). The text of a whole section of the Mass appears, unfolding before one's eyes. It clearly shows all the parts assembled in their successive order. In order to arrive at this result, the child must have read and reread them. He then chooses one or the other of these cards to study it in detail, either to learn it by heart or to copy it carefully in order to make up one's own small handwritten book.

Here is another example: After all the cards have been put in order, they can be mixed and put back in order by memory. It is enough to repeat the exercise two or three times to see how much the text implies of itself the order of succession of the cards. It is a logical sense that partly supports knowledge, and it is precisely this that creates the pleasure of research and redoubles the interest in repeating these exercises.

GUIDE FOR THE MASS OF THE CATECHUMENS

The first envelope contains 14 cards, including 5 Propers cards *(Diag. 8)*. They contain the following separated parts:
1. *The Sign of the Cross*
2. *Judica me* (Psalm 42) written in two colors because it is spoken between the priest and the child or the faithful
3. *The Confiteor*, repeated in two colors with small variations between the text that is recited by the priest and the one that is recited by the faithful
4. *Deus tu converses . . .* (The dialogue after the Absolution)
5. *Aufer a nobis . . .* (The prayer of the priest, who goes up to the altar and kisses the martyr's relics)
6. *The Introit* (Proper)
7. *The Kyrie* (2 colors)
8. *The Gloria*
9. *The Oration* or *Collect* (Proper)
10. *The Epistle* (Proper)
11. *The Gradual* and the *Tract* (Proper)
12. *Munda Cor* (The prayer before the Gospel)
13. *The Gospel* (Proper)
14. *The Credo*.

When the study of the text of the Ordinary is sufficiently advanced, we can consider other elements about the rite.

MASS OF THE CATECHUMENS

1. Sign of the Cross	**2.** Judica me... (Psalm 42) (2 colors)	**3.** Confiteor... (2 colors)	Mass of the Catechumens = 14 cards (9 green, 5 white). Text of the Ordinary is written in its entirety on the green cards; only the title of the Proper is written on the white cards. The child places on the card various figures and symbols. (Diag. 10)
4. Deus, Te conversus... *(Dialogue after the Absolution)* (2 colors)	**5.** Aufer a nobis... *(Prayer of the priest ascending to the altar)*	**6.** INTROIT	
7. Kyrie... (2 colors)	**8.** Gloria...	**9.** COLLECT	**10.** EPISTLE
11. GRADUAL TRACT	**12.** Munda Cor... *(Prayer of Purification before the Gospel)*	**13.** GOSPEL	**14.** Credo...

Diagram 8.

As he celebrates the Mass by reading the various parts of the sacred texts, the priest moves, sometimes to the right, sometimes to the left, making Signs of the Cross on himself or signs of blessing on sacred objects. The outward signs of the rite must be associated with the words of the text.

We already know, via the general explanation of the Mass in *The Mass Explained to Chidren,* that the priest stays at the foot of the steps at first. It is only after the *Confiteor* and the *Absolution* that he climbs these steps and kisses the sacred stone. He goes to the right to read the *Introit*, the first Proper of the Mass.

Returning to the center, he recites the *Kyrie* and *Gloria*. After this great introduction, he starts the readings—of the Epistle to the right of the altar and then, the Gospel, to the left.

Finally, the *Credo*, which is recited in the center of the altar, ends this part of the Mass—the Mass of the Catechumens.

All these movements of transfer and devotion must be shown to the child, first of all by the teacher, who presents the material to him. Next to the cards, to one side, are small colored cardboard figures which can be moved around and placed on the cards.

We start with the priest's movements.

The material includes many moveable figures representing the priest in his priestly vestments—there are yellow, green, red, and blue priests.

The yellow one represents when the priest is in the middle of the altar, the green one, when he is to the right, and the red one, when he is on the left. Finally, a blue card represents the priest as he is greeting the faithful when, turning towards them, he says: "*Dominus vobiscum.*" (The Lord be with you.) This last little blue figure displays an interesting detail.

Actually, the Mass is not only divided into four large parts that are assembled according to the cards with four colors—it also includes subdivisions. For example, when the prologue ends with the *Gloria* in the Mass of the Catechumens and the instructive readings start, the priest comes back to the people and greets them: "*Dominus vobiscum*." All the small blue preist-shaped figures, which are put in their places, display with one glance a more subtle subdivision in the liturgical text. The child can study it and then note the "*Dominus vobiscum*" himself on the text on which the little figures are placed..

HOW TO PLACE THE FIGURES

In all rubrics related to the conduct of the Mass, it is understood that the priests presides with his back to the faithful.

When a series of index cards is arranged in single file according to the order of the text, we must add a figure which represents the priest related to each of the index cards, according to the position of the celebrant when he pronounces the written words on this card *(Diag. 9)*.

If the priest has not yet climbed the steps of the altar, the figure is placed at the bottom of the card. If he has already climbed the steps, it is placed above the card, with his feet touching its top edge. In this last case, the placement is either in the center, to the left, or the right of the card as indicated by the color of the priest-figure.

The double indication of color and location to demonstrate the same feature might seem superfluous. But a movement of the figures—which are movable and cannot be fixed—would risk causing error. It is the color that guarantees that we were not mistaken in choosing the material. We have an idea about the priest's movements merely by assembling the figures.

The cards for the Mass of Catechumens with the figures in place.

Diagram 9.

In observing the arrangement of the cards and figures in their entirety, we see that the figure of the *"Dominus vobiscum"* is at the end of the *Gloria*. The priest's greeting divides the Mass of the Catechumens in two: the preparatory part—or great introduction—and the instructional part. The latter starts with a series of Propers (*Collect*, *Epistle*, *Gradua*l), which are read to the right of the altar and which reach their high point in the reading of the Gospel, which is done on the left. This part of the Mass ends with the *Credo*, which is recited in the center.

As soon as the child has arrived at this point of the instruction, he can *attend* Mass, which will complete this instruction better than a teacher's guidance. He will know how to follow a text and observe the priest's movement and positions by trying to recall what he has already studied.

This is why it is very desirable that a Mass be celebrated in a place especially designed for children. This Mass would have the particular feature of displaying a maximum of perfection, a scrupulous care of each detail, and a slower rhythm than usual.

The children who are still studying the Mass of the Catechumens must be placed behind the priest to follow his specific movements. Those who have already gone through the study of the Mystical Mass must preferably be placed to the right of the altar in order to see the movements that we will later describe more clearly.

By following the Mass, little children will realize what they have already learned and what remains for them to study. The Mass will lead them to the material, just as the material will lead them to the Mass.

THE PRIEST'S GESTURES

The next step is the study of the various gestures that the priest carries out in celebrating the Mass, such as blessings, Signs of the Cross, genuflections, etc. The little symbols of the material to be placed on the texts corresponding to these gestures make up something like a mystical punctuation mark in the sacred text.

In fact, we see red dots, here and there, on the cards. They indicate the precise place in which this gesture occurs. They can be found placed between two parts of the same word, dividing it. They do not therefore indicate the kind of gesture that occurs—the child must recall it. On the other hand, it is the material, composed of various small crosses and various signs, which represents all these gestures in detail.

Among the principle gestures made by the priest during the celebration is the cross that blesses, and this gesture is repeated throughout the celebration of the rite. This predominant gesture is shown in the material by a small red cross (see *Diag. 11A*).

Here is an example: We find five red dots that are inserted between the words on one of the cards that has to do with the central part of the Mystical Mass, which starts with "This is why, in memory of . . ." and ends with: ". . . the chalice of Eternal Salvation." We read the following direction on the back of this card: "five crosses of blessing." It is obvious that these five dots must correspond to five small red crosses, as we see in the sample cards in Diagram 11A, B.

Most of the other gestures are also represented by symbols *(Diag. 10)*. It is the frequent attendance at Mass that makes this knowledge more precise. Nonetheless, the number of small symbols to be placed on any particular card is indicated on the back of that card, which provides control of error.

The Holy Mass

STRUCTURE	COMBINATIONS
cross of blessing on himself or the faithful	 *cross on the host*
cross of blessing on the objects	 *cross on the chalice*
cross of blessing on the bread and wine	*cross with the host*
genuflection	 *cross with the paten*
 *figures of the priest*  *Dominus vobiscum*	 *cross with the host on the chalice*
 *kiss on the altar and book*	
strike on the chest	
 *chalice* *paten* *host*	

Diagram 10.

THE OFFERTORY

We will study the following parts in the same manner as the Mass of the Catechumens.

The cards for the preparatory part of the Mystical Mass will be found in the yellow envelope *(Diag. 12)*.

There are eleven cards, including two white ones. They include or represent the following parts:

    1. *The Offertory* (Proper)
    2. *The Offering of the bread*
    3. *Mixing of the wine and the water*
    4. *The Offering of the wine*
    5. *The Lavabo* (prayer that the priest says in purifying his hands)
    6. *The Oblation to the Holy Trinity*
    7. *The Orate fratres* (invitation to the people and their response)
    8. *The Secret* (Proper)
    9. *Dialogue prayers (2 colors)*
    10. *Preface*
    11. *Sanctus.*

We can, without even having received any particular teaching, logically understand the reason why several figures representing the priest are thus arranged in this part of the Mass. When the priest pours the water and wine in the chalice and purifies his hands by washing them, it is certain that he must be on the right of the altar. The Secret and Offertory, which are prayers of the Proper, must also be read at the right of the altar, in front of the Missal. All the other prayers, invocations, and offerings are naturally done in the center.

The ninth index card starts with a "*Dominus vobiscum*" that takes place right after the Secret. So, the Offertory can

This is why, Lord, in memory
of the Blessed Passion of Christ,
Your Son, Our Lord,
of His Resurrection from the dead,
and also
of His Ascension into the glory of Heaven,
we, Your servants,
and with us, Your Holy People,
present to Your glorious Majesty—
a chosen offering
among the goods that You have given us —
the Perfect ✢ Victim
the Holy ✢ Victim
the Spotless ✢ Victim
the Sacred ✢ Bread of Eternal Life,
and the Chalice of ✢ Eternal Salvation.

Diagram 11A.

8

Unde et memores...

1 Yellow Priest
      5 Crosses of Benediction

Diagram 11B.

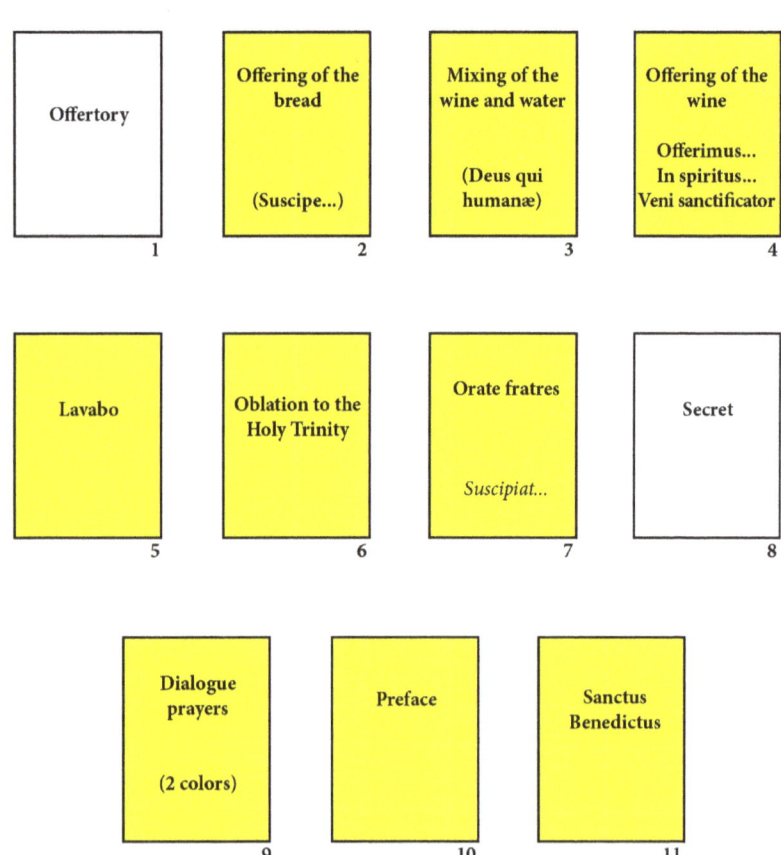

Offertory = 11 cards (9 yellow, 2 white). On the yellow cards is written the whole text; on the white cards is written only the title of the proper. The child places on the cards various figurines and symbols (Diag. 10).

Diagram 12.

be divided into parts: the second part—the *Preface* and *Sanctus*—represents the introduction to the Sacrifice.

The succession of the text itself is clear and can, by intuition, give the order of the cards. Before offering the chalice, water and wine must be poured, since it is the species to be consecrated that is offered, and not the empty chalice. The solemn Oblation, which is done in memory of Jesus, is like a finale of each part of the offerings. The invitation and meditation on the Secret clearly indicate that this spiritual section closes the whole series of offerings through the offering of our hearts.

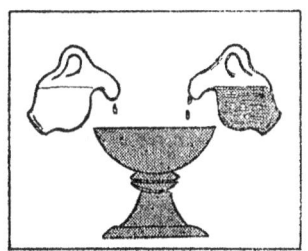

Diagram 13.

The position of the separated cards of the "*Dominus vobiscum*" is also very clear. The invitation of the priest—*Sursum Corda (Lift up your hearts)*—is evidently addressed to the people who are still immersed in the Secret. The dialogue that follows, which is written in two colors, prepares for the great speech of the Preface, which ends with the Hosanna: "*Sanctus, sanctus, sanctus.*"

It would be enough for the child's reflection, therefore, for him to arrange the index cards and, when in doubt, the number written on the back ensures the placement of each of the cards.

An interesting and possible problem to be solved, therefore, arises for the location of the cards. It is precisely because this problem does not surpass the limits of the effort that it is of great interest to the children. This must encourage the teacher not to intervene unnecessarily.

By observing the cards in their respective positions, we clearly see the Offertory's divisions.

The "*Dominus Vobiscum*" separates the last three cards

from the other part which is, more properly, the Offertory. The latter is presented as a part of the Ordinary, bounded on each end by a Proper: the Offertory and the Secret. The Offertory verse is that song which masked the noises of the comings and goings between the Mass of the Catechumens and the Mystical Mass in the early Church. The Secret makes up the silent and meditative offering of one's heart to God.

The spoken prayers, which start before the Secret, resume right after this interval of silence.

The cards are not headed by a title as shown in Diagram 12, but only by the text, which does not necessarily indicate the action. Thus, the prayer of the cards which corresponds to the action of pouring the water and wine in the chalice, starts in this way:

> *God, who, in an admirable way,*
> *created human nature in its nobility,*
> *and has restored it*
> *in a way that is even more admirable,*
> *Allow us, according to the mystery*
> *of this water and wine,*
> *to take part in the divinity*
> *of the One Who deigned to share in our humanity,*
> *Jesus Christ, your Son, Our Lord.*

And while he purifies his hands, the priest recites some verses from a Psalm:

> *"I wash my hands among the innocence…*
> *Deliver me, Lord, and have mercy on me."*

In order to offer an outer aid for the recognition of this text and, at the same time, to make the exercise more varied, we have prepared small cards, separate from the big ones. Certain figures from the sacred objects that are used by the priest at the altar are placed on them, for example, the cruets with the water and wine *(Diag. 13)*, the paten containing the host, etc.

THE SACRIFICE

The following part is related to the Sacrifice, and it is represented on red index cards. When we open the envelope containing them, we immediately notice that no white card having to do with the Propers is found there. So, we have arrived at this point in the Mass where only the priest acts and where the faithful, in silence, remain concentrated in expectation and in adoration.

The priest continues to remain in the middle of the altar, which he does not do in the other parts of the Mass.

There is no indication of *"Dominus vobiscum"* to separate this part from the preceding ones. The people understand that it is forgotten at such a solemn time. The Hosanna to the Lord will resound now, and one cannot detach it from the heart that wants to follow Him closely during His Passion.

But the text resumes with "So . . . " as if to continue an interrupted speech: "So you, O Lord . . ." *"Te igitur . . ."* The T of this *"Te,"* which is printed in a capital letter, is thought to be the Cross that is placed at the head of the central action of the Mass.

Here begins the Canon, that is to say, the Rule, because the prayers that make it up have been determined since the beginning. These venerable prayers are inscribed on our cards in a concise form, to distinguish and highlight each one of their phrases.

The parts of the liturgical text follow one another in this way *(Diag. 14)*:

    1. The first prayer before the Consecration (*Te Igitur*)
    2. The first Diptych (*Memento*: Commemoration of the Living)
    3. Invocation of the Saints (*Communicantes*)
    4. The second prayer before the Consecration (*Hanc Igitur*)
    5. The third prayer before the Consecration (*Quam Oblationem*)
    6. The Consecration of the Host
    7. The Consecration of the Wine
    8. The first prayer after the Consecration (*Unde et memores*)
    9. The second prayer after the Consecration (*Supre quae*)
    10. The third prayer after the Consecration (*Supplices*)
    11. The second Diptych (Memento: Commemoration of the Dead)
    12. Invocation of the Saints (*Nobis quoque*)
    13. The offering of the consecrated Bread and Wine (Minor Elevation).

By observing the cards that are arranged in the diagram according to the canonical order, we perceive that there is a part that is entirely reserved for the Consecration: the three prayers that precede it, the three that follow it, and the Minor Elevation of the Species which depends on it. Other parts, like the Commemoration of the Living, the Commemoration of the Dead, and the Prayer to the Saints, are uninvolved with the Consecration.

The canon is interrupted by these prayers, says the Missal, and the Mass is as if suspended. Diagram 14 shows the precise points during which the Mass is suspended. The

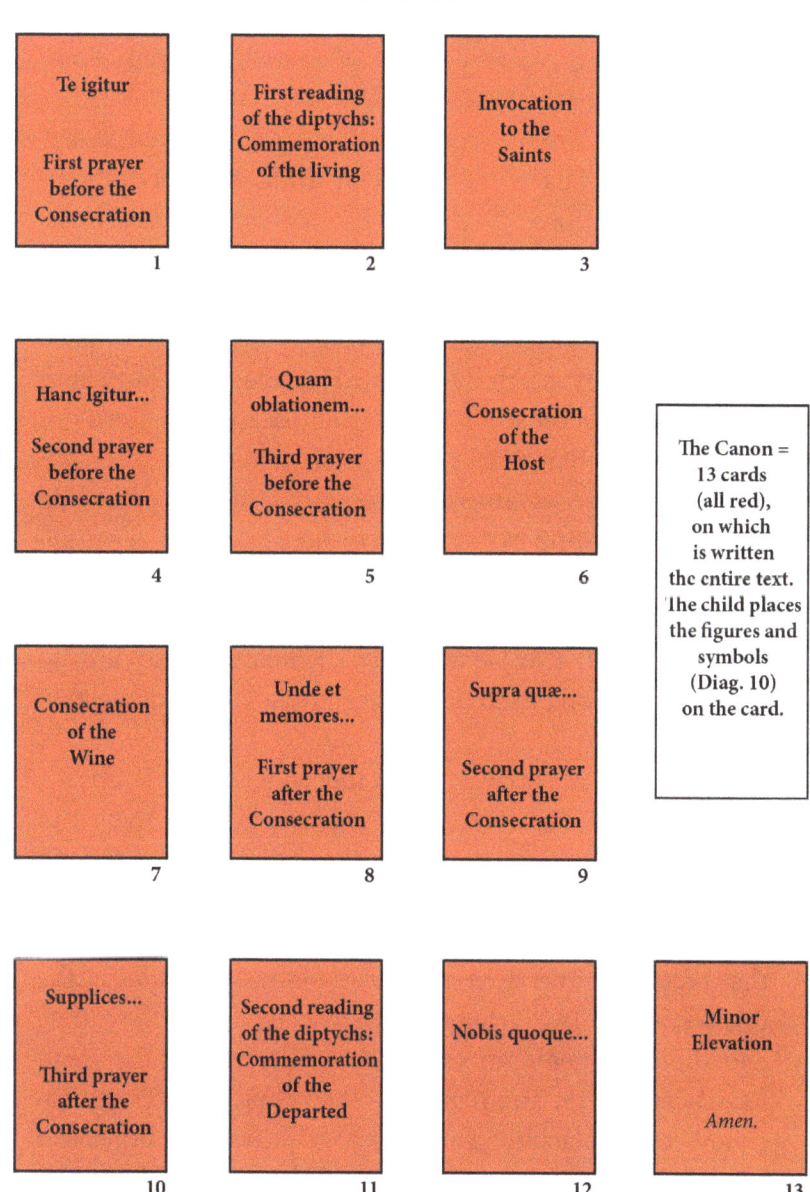

Diagram 14.

interruptions are after the first card and before the last one.

As far as the interruptions are concerned, we see that in both parts, each one is made up of a Commemoration and an Invocation to the Saints.

As the cards are movable and all the parts of the text stay right in front of us, we can easily set aside the interruptions. Then the three prayers before the Consecration become close, as are those that follow. The cards of the Commemorations and the Invocations can be replaced in a different framework, leaving their respective locations relative to the center intact. We can logically attach the last card immediately above both consecrations because it accurately represents the Offering—it is the Minor Elevation.

We therefore arrange all the cards in the preceding diagram according to the order of the text, in the position that results from the moves we have just discussed (*see Diag. 15.*). Moreover, to make the little crosses that are inserted in the text more visible, we will place them outside the cards to which they belong to so that their number and arrangement remain clearer.

Diagram 15 makes it clear that there is a perfect symmetry, not only in the distribution of the parts, but also in that of the signs. One can see that the cards that are related to both Consecrations and their Offering (the Minor Elevation) that is on top of them are in the center. There are three prayers that precede it and three that follow it on both sides of the Consecration. Two groups of the Invocation of the Saints and the Commemorations of the Living and of the Dead have been put on another level. The result is the canonical arrangement, placing the memory of the living and the dead toward the center and the memory of the saints and apostles toward the outside of the diagram.

There is one sign of blessing above each of the Consecration cards. There are five crosses of the adjacent prayers on both sides (the last one before and the first one after the Consecrations). The second prayer has no cross on either side. The first of the three that precede the Consecration and the last of the three prayers that follow it have three crosses each (the last of these crosses is related to a sign of the priest on himself). Thus, each group of the three prayers includes eight crosses. Let us now observe the card of the Offering of the Consecration—we see eight crosses, an equal number.

Other things can be observed about the numbers: there are thirteen cards, one of which, the essential and principal one, represents the Offering. This causes us to make a connection between the Lord and His Twelve Apostles.

Four of these cards are distinct and placed on another level. They recall men and sanctification in the Commemorations and in the memory of the Saints.

If the fathers of the Church had wanted to develop this symmetry, they would certainly not have fixed the liturgical texts with this interruption of the diptychs that veils such a perfect structure.

It is often said that everything from God has balance and is symmetrical. We can admit that this symmetry was attached because the Mass is divine and alive and established with the Holy Spirit's directions. The central part, around which the whole Mass is arranged, is the offering of the consecrated Victim, that is to say, the Chalice and Host that are elevated together (the Minor Elevation). This gesture recalls and represents Jesus Christ crucified. He is the one who said: "And I, when I am lifted up from the earth, will draw all people to myself" (cf. John 12: 32).

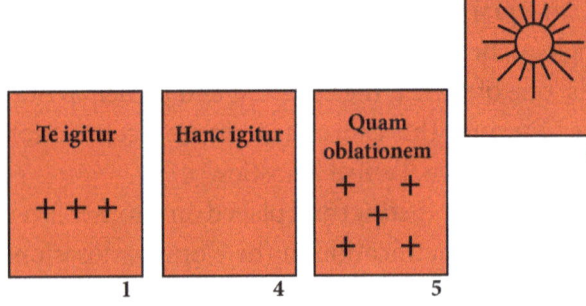

Te igitur + + + 1	Hanc igitur 4	Quam oblationem + + + + + 5

Commem-
oration
of the
Living

2

Invocation

Saints

3

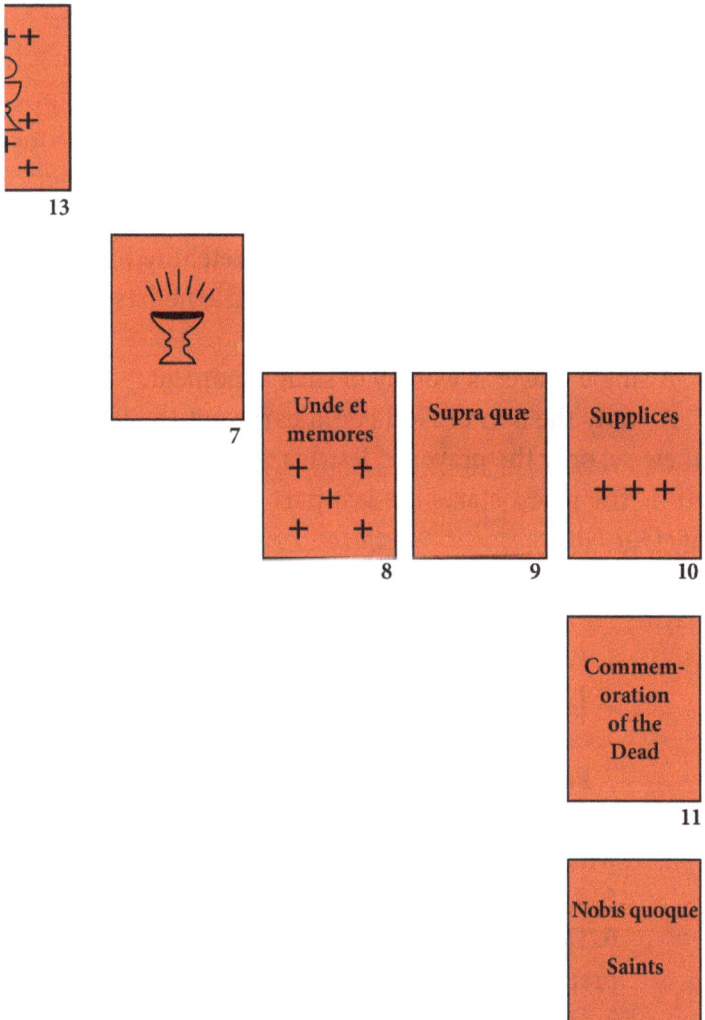

Diagram 15.

COMMUNION

Finally, we move on to the study of the last part of the Mass for which we use the group of blue index cards. The first task is to arrange them in a row and then to arrange the priest's figures in order to have an idea about the priest's movements and the "*Dominus vobiscum*" that subdivides this group.

After the solemnity of the Sacrifice, greeting the crowd is not what preoccupies the priest. Stretching out his arms in a gesture of adoration, he prays while he has the Divine Presence before him.

A single prayer is worthy of such a moment.

As only the Son of God could carry out the Redemption, likewise, only the prayer of Jesus is worthy to be returned to Him. The priest starts the last part of the Mass by reciting the *Our Father*.

The sequence of this part of the Mass is established in this way:

1. *Pater Noster* (Our Father)
2. *Libera Nos* (At the end of which the Host is broken over the chalice)
3. Pax Domini (A prayer invoking the peace of Christ)
4. *Haec Commixtio* (Preparation of the Chalice in which a fragment of the Host is immersed)
5. *Agnus Dei* (Lamb of God)
6. *Domine Jesu Christe* (The first prayer of the preparation of the soul for Communion)
7. *Dominie Jesu Christe* (The second prayer)
8. *Perceptio Corporis tui* (The third prayer)
9. *Panem coelestem* (The Communion of the priest in the Body of Jesus Christ)
10. *Sanguis Domini* (The Communion of the priest in the Blood of Jesus Christ)

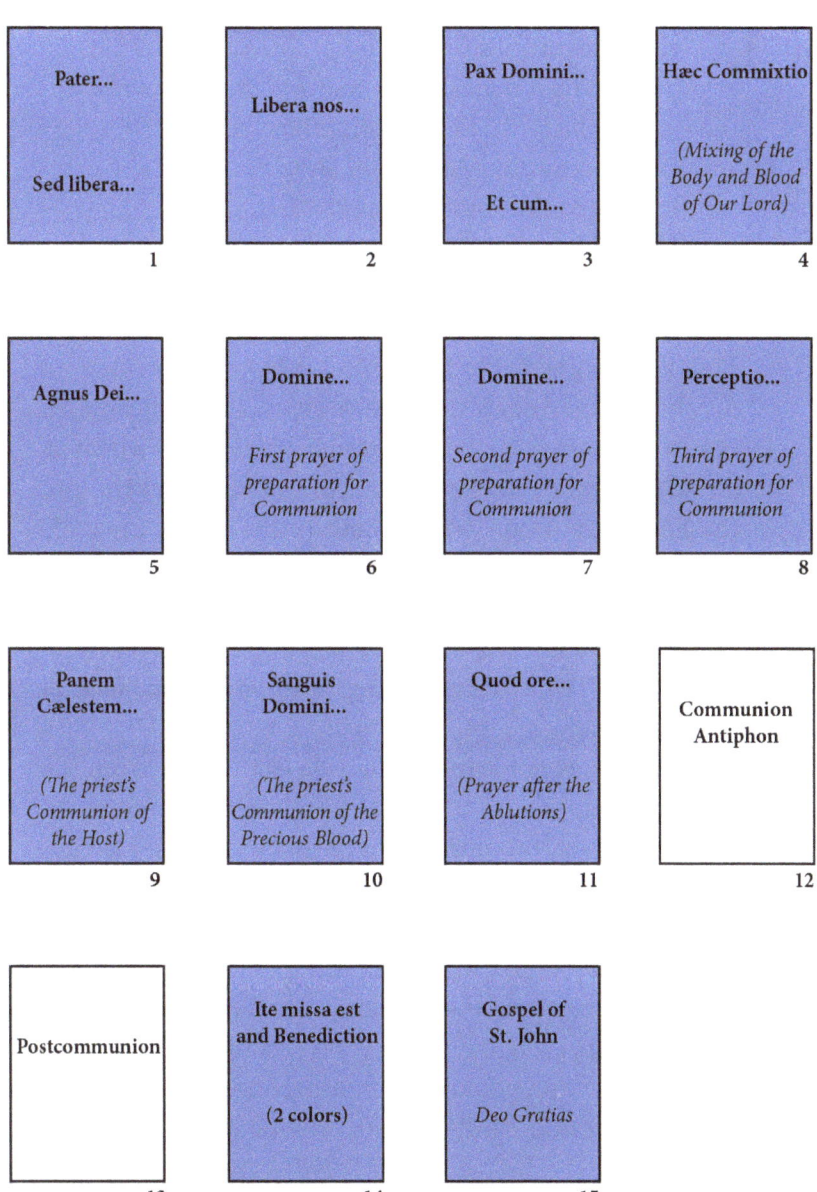

Diagram 16.

11. *Quod ore sumpsimus* (The prayer of the priest while he purifies his hands)
He will then replace the burse and the veil on the chalice as it was at the beginning of Mass.
12. Communion Antiphon (Proper)
13. Postcommunion (Proper)
14. *Ite Missa Est* (The priest greets, dismisses, and blesses the faithful)
15. The Gospel of Saint John followed by *Deo gratias* (Thanks be to God).

Arranging the index cards in a row as is indicated in Diagram 16, leads to the *"Dominus vobiscum,"* which is found at the end of the last Proper of the Mass—at the end of the Postcommunion prayer. Both of the following cards are not part of the text related to Communion. They only make up the end of the whole Mass: the dismissal (*"Ite Missa est"*—Go, the Mass is ended), the last prayer of greeting to the Most Holy Trinity (the blessing), and, finally, the Gospel of St. John.

The priest does not leave the middle of the altar from the Consecration up to the time that he gives Communion to the faithful. Then, the number of moves increases. He goes several times to the side of the Epistle (right side) and, finally, returns to the side of the Gospel (left side), precisely as at the end of the Mass of the Catechumens.

When the priest prepares the Body and Blood of Our Lord for Communion, each of his gestures is accompanied by some words. So we have prepared some figures concerning the detail of these gestures on cardboard strips. One exercise consists of recognizing the link between the gesture and text and, consequently, putting the diagrams on the blank spaces that were arranged for this purpose on the corresponding cards.

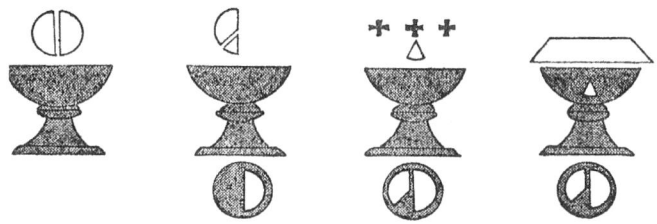

Diagram 17.

Diagram 17 relates particularly to the breaking of the Host and the mixing of a fragment of the Host with the Blood of Our Lord.

THE ENTIRE MASS

After the study of the four separate parts, all the index cards can now be placed together—the different parts in successive rows, one above the other.

The overall picture shows the complete structure in the order of the liturgical text. The green cards, which have the text of the Mass of the Catechumens, are at the top. Then, one sees the yellow, red, and blue cards, which relate to the three subdivisions of the Mystical Mass: the Offertory, the Sacrifice, and Communion *(Diag. 18)*.

The Mass of the Catechumens, which is a separate and distinct part, is arranged in an arch, in the manner of a vault.

The whole Mystical Mass, surmounted by a small image representing the Last Supper, takes place underneath.

There is, first of all, the Offertory's yellow index cards, followed by the Sacrifice whose cards are arranged according to the symmetry of its elements. In the middle, there is an

The Holy Mass

The Open Book

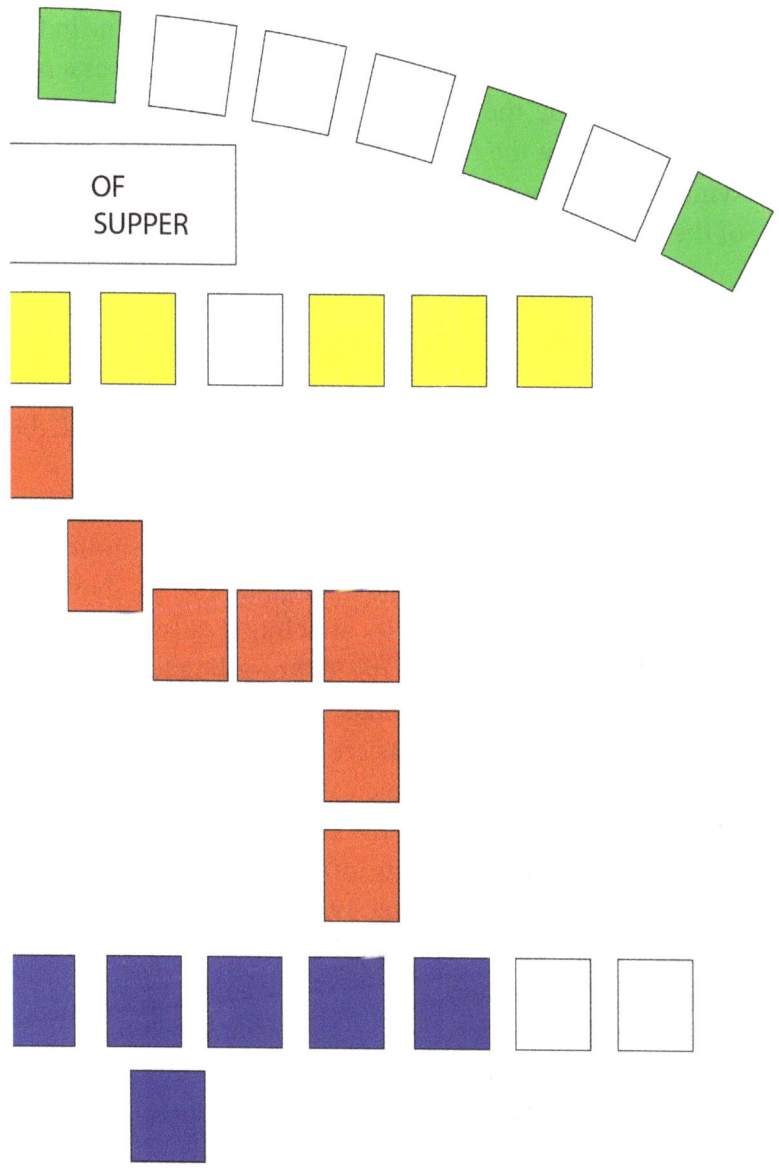

Diagram 18.

image of Christ on the Cross, which remains at the center of the whole structure. It rises above the card which represents the Minor Elevation. The long blue column of the line in the last part—the Communion—consequently, appears as a row of support while the cards of the conclusion are arranged underneath, like the base of the structure. How much this symbolic building made up of words, and which is a reflection of the Church of Christ, is favorable to meditation!

SUMMARY OF THE MATERIAL

When the study of the text and rite by means of the written cards, representative signs, and tables is sufficiently fixed, the Mass has become a mental habit.

Then, only a few signs are needed to remember what has been studied, and the representative material is no longer needed. This is the goal of the final guide that is shown in Diagrams 19 and 20. The series of points recalls the series of cards. They are vertically arranged. According to the priest's position, the point is at the center, to the left, or to the right.

As all the successive points are assembled in a line, from the first one to the others, one can almost follow the priest in his movements in front of the altar during the celebration of the Mass. The four parts of the Mass are separately represented in four lines *(Diag. 19)*.

Line A - The Mass of the Catechumens.

Line B - The Offertory.

Line C - The Sacrifice (the parts are arranged according to the text).

Line D - Communion.

The part of the Mass indicated by each line is labeled under the line. (The first moment of the particular part of the Mass is the point at the top of the page, and then the movement progresses down the page.)

Then, there is a final chart in which the four partial charts are assembled in a single drawing *(Diag. 20)*. No indication of the parts of the Mass is shown in that one. The only informative sign is a strip on which a lit altar candle is shown on the side. This candle starts at the point which represents the Consecration of the Host and ends at the point that represents receiving Communion. It symbolizes the time during which the Divine Presence remains on the altar.

These charts could be used to mentally resume the study of the Mass and to return to the order of its development. Countless applications can be made with it—as much for details as for the overall structure. We can adapt the position of the child who serves at Mass and the position of the faithful who attend it, and we can, likewise, observe the process of the Mass as a whole.

The stability of the priest's position in the middle of the altar, from the Hosanna up to Communion, could not be more evident than in front of this straight column which rises without the slightest deviation.

Likewise, the central place of the Consecration in comparison to the preceding straight path and the one that follows it, is also very clear if we consider the Mass started after the introduction.

The arrangement on the centerline of all the parts that relate to the Ordinary of the Mass is also to be noticed. Only the Propers move from the center. The few exceptions of the parts of the Ordinary that are subject to movement to the right relate exclusively to prayers that are accompanied by gestures that must be physically performed to the right of the altar: the mixture of the water and wine in the chalice and the purification of the hands.

The various episodes of the Savior's life can inspire a series

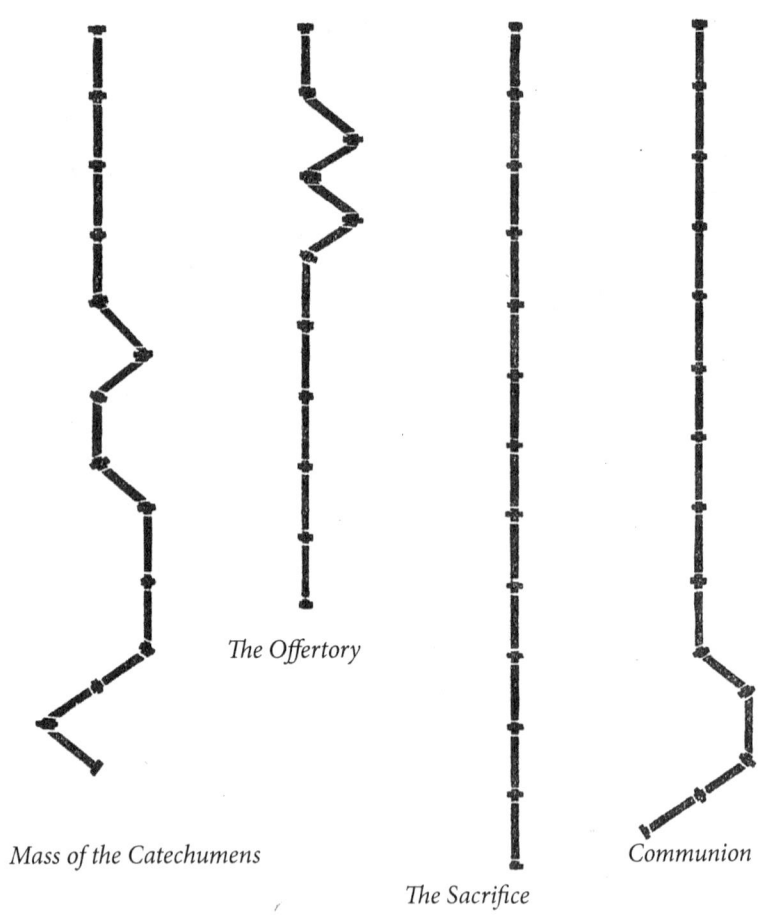

SUMMARY OF THE MATERIAL

Diagram 19.

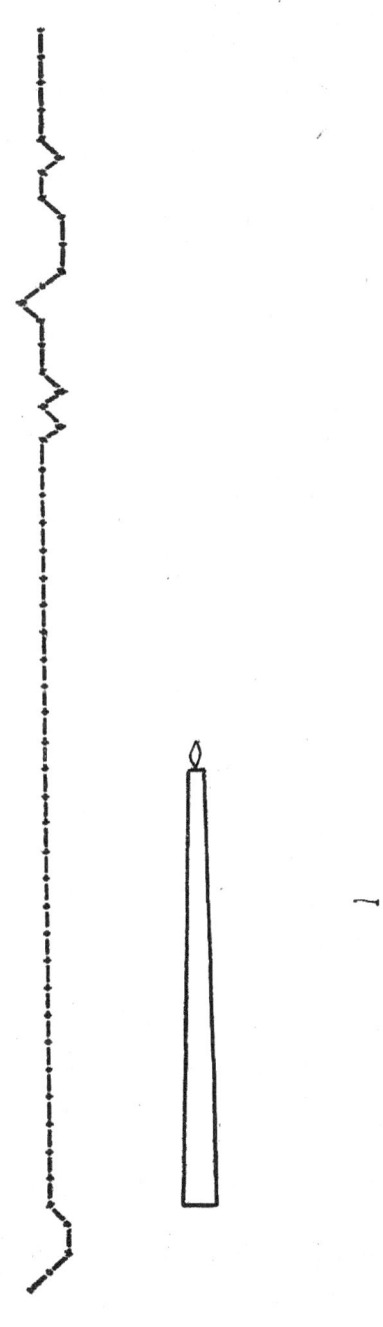

SUMMARY OF THE MATERIAL

Diagram 20.

of meditations or evocations that follow the development of His life as well as that of the Mass. Jesus' Eucharistic Presence on the altar starts with the Crucifixion and ends with the tomb. When we meditate on the five wounds, the Agony, and the Lord's Death, we can feel Him present and receive Him in our hearts.

Another kind of meditation, which can link the rite to the episodes of Christ's life, has to do with the boundaries of attendance that make a valid participation in the Mass. When we arrive late or we are really in a hurry to leave, can we be sure that we have validly listened to a Mass? We know we need to be present for at least a moment before the book is deposited from the right to the left of the altar for the reading of the Gospel and not leave before the "*Ite Missa Est.*" So, in effect, we must stay from the passage during which Christ publicly reveals Himself with His divine teachings up to the one where He leaves the earth in His Ascension. That is to say, it is essential not to miss the time when the Lord reveals Himself to the world as the Divine Master of men.

The parts of the Mass when the faithful may be seated can also be observed in our drawing. After the *Gloria* (birth of Jesus), the priest's "*Dominus vobiscum*" gives those who were bowing down while waiting for the Messiah's birth the freedom to sit down. The faithful remain seated from the birth until the Gospel. The Mass meanwhile represents the hidden life of the Messiah when John the Baptist preaches and baptizes people in the Jordan River (the Epistle and other prayers).

After the Gospel and the Credo, people can sit during the Offertory. Right after that, the Messiah reappears in His glorious coming to Jerusalem in the people's Hosanna. The faithful fall on their knees without getting up again because, being prostrated, they accompany Him to Golgotha and assist Him up to the time when He is put in the tomb.

The one who leaves right after the *"Ite Misa Est,"* that is to say, before the blessing and, consequently, before the last Gospel, is like someone who breaks away from the group of Apostles while they wait for the coming of the Paraclete with the Most Blessed Virgin Mary in the Cenacle. He turns his back at the end of the drama that continues in humankind when the Holy Spirit's fire inflames men and makes them act according to the Divine Master's commandment: "Go therefore and make disciples of all nations . . ."

Representative Object for Mass of the Catechumens:
The Missal

Representative object for Mass of the Faithful:
The Chalice and Host

Diagram 21.

CHAPTER 2

The Missal

The books of the Mass which are written according to the liturgical text and are intended for use by the faithful are the prayer book and the missal.

The prayer book contains, along with the Ordinary of the Mass, the Propers of all the Sundays and Holy Days of Obligation—those Masses that the faithful must attend. In addition, they include prayers and devotions. Written almost entirely in the vernacular, they do not always offer the Latin text alongside the vernacular translation.

The missals, however, are most often written in two languages, their pages shared between two columns with the Latin text opposite the vernacular. They include, in addition to the Ordinary, the Propers of every day of the year. In the first part, one finds the complete Propers of the season—those of the Masses that relate to Our Lord, and not only on Sundays. The second part includes the Propers of the Commemorations of the Saints arranged in the civil calendar's order. Finally, one sees the Propers of the votive Masses.

These liturgical books are bound, and their outer form makes their religious character apparent. Therefore, these books are carried by the faithful only to follow the Mass. Always at our disposal, but put away right afterwards, the wisdom of their content is a guide for life and a comfort for the soul that each one of us needs at some time. It is the heritage of our fathers and Saints, and those who have sustained the Christian community. Since our Baptism, we have sworn to be faithful to it.

The Mass, which we celebrate at the altar, includes the content of the Ordinary and the Proper of the day. Its solemnity penetrates the soul and inspires a devotion. Saint Augustine says that "the music of the hymns and canticles penetrated my ears and, from there, descended to my heart, spreading the truth" (cf. *The Confessions*).

Pope Sixtus V says that "the Divine Offices lead souls to meditate on the most sublime things and inflame the heart with devotion."

When the Church offers the celebration of the Divine Mysteries to the faithful, we find her an unmatched master in the art of arousing interest. Then each person must continue the work that is started because the eyes, once opened to the truth, yearn to see it continually. When faith is enkindled, it wants to keep burning. The Mass book that is between our hands is precisely the one that is needed for the soul, which works and meditates in solitude after having been enlightened at the foot of the altar. Having received the Word in the splendor of the Temple, we can reread it in the haven of our room or in the silence of the woods or in the accomplishment of our ordinary tasks when we suffer from those moments of dryness that make us thirst for God's Word. A Sunday Mass gives us enough to nourish our meditations during the whole week that separates us from the following Sunday.

So, here is a practical problem: Preparing a Mass book—for the faithful and especially for children—that is not only an "Open Book," that is to say, intelligible, but also a book that is structured in such a form and in such dimensions that allows one to always have it close at hand.

THE ORDINARY

The book that we have exclusively prepared for children includes the text of the Mass without any addition or prayers or preparation. These missals offered to the faithful by the Church have only what the officiating priest says during the celebration from the initial sign of the cross to the Gospel of Saint John, translated into the local language. That represents the minimum that is necessary to follow the Divine Office and only takes up a little volume. However, we divide this volume into two separate books. The thinner one includes the parts that are related to the Mass of the Catechumens, and the other one pertains to the Mystical Mass. These two small volumes, continually recall the first basic subdivision of the Mass and the separation of their content. The first part includes the instructions and great readings of the Epistle and Gospel while the Mystical Mass is almost exclusively made up of prayers that were once reserved for the faithful who were already initiated.

Both small books, whose content so profoundly differs, must be visibly distinct from each other. We have bound the Book of the Catechumens and decorated it with the reproduction of a splendid open missal. We have given the other one a solemn purple binding on which the symbolic signs of the Sacrifice of the altar are etched (Diag. 21).

Both are the same dimension and are so small that they can be hidden together in a small folder. We have prepared this folder of very ordinary appearance, without any external sign, covered with soft leather or silk with two pockets inside, one on each side, where the two small books are inserted. The folder closes like it's made of paper. Nevertheless, out of respect for its religious content, it is decorated, on the inside, with signs that relate to both different parts. For example, there are fish where one puts the Book of the Catechumens, and there is a chalice with the host, in place of the Book of the Faithful. For the children, you can transform the folder into a small satchel.

The text of both books is presented a little like the cards that are used to work on the Mass except when the text is too long (as for the double Confiteor, the Credo, etc.) where it is written on two pages. In fact, the Mass book is no longer intended, like the cards, to make a distinction between the various elements which make up the Mass, but to set out in a clear and comprehensible manner all the sentences of each element. It is arranged in a concise style when the text refers to people or prayers. In the parts that are related to the Consecration, the pages themselves represent a stone on which are written the words of incomparable dignity.

The simple sheets are only written on one side so that the back remains blank. In addition, as with the card material, a sheet remains blank here, which corresponds to each Propers. On the page particular to each Proper, one finds an illustration with the title: *Introit, Collect, Epistle*, etc.

These illustrations, which correspond to the variable elements of the Mass, are the only ones in the book.

In fact, the missal is not the book that must *illustrate*, but only *relate* the Divine Word and completely concentrate all thought on it. The book bears the Word of God, and Divine Theater unfolds its actions before the eyes of the faithful; the faithful person is the actor. What would be the use of illustrations?

On the pages that are related to the various Propers, the simple drawings are not intended to illustrate a text, but to indicate an empty place. The drawings represent historical recollections.

For example, one finds an image showing a crowd (an ancient procession) entering the wide open door of a church on the Introit page.

A crowd of faithful people, who are united around a bishop who is going to carry the common prayer to the altar, is shown on the Collect's page.

We see one of the Apostles who is reading an ancient writing on a scroll on the Epistle's page.

On the Gradual's page, there are faithful people who are fervently praying and kneeling on the steps of the altar.

On the page for the Gospel, the large open book is shown, with the censer that surrounds these pages with a cloud of incense on one side and lit altar candles on the other.

During the Offertory, the image shows people who are collecting money and surrounded by the crowd who is singing. Others are bringing various offerings such as a vase with wine, ciboriums with hosts, garlands of flowers . . .

The faces of faithful people immersed in meditation are linked to the Secret.

In the Postcommunion, we see people with raised arms and faces that reflect an attitude of devotion.

The texts of the Propers are not permanent parts of the book, but they are included in the book, each one in its place, when it is prepared (as described below) for a particular day. They serve to show that there is an unchanging part in the Mass and another part that is variable.

The Propers are distributed on sheets that have the same dimensions as the book's pages. They are decorated with a ribbon whose color is different for each part of the Proper. For example, Introit—green; Collect—white; Epistle—blue; Gradual—yellow; Gospel—red; Offertory—brown; Secret—purple; Communion—light blue; Postcommunion—gray.

THE HOLY MASS

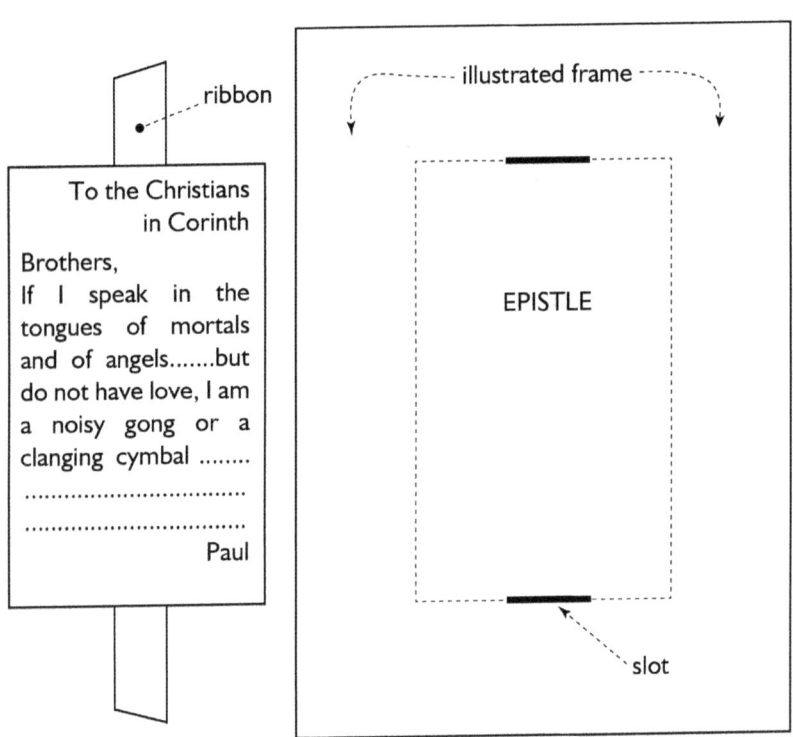

Diagram 22.

Two small notches are found on each illustrated page of the book *(Diag. 22)* in which the Proper's ribbons are inserted. By pulling the ribbons, the page of text lays exactly over the illustrated page that disappears below.

When all the Propers are put in place, the illustrations of both small Mass books remain hidden. The rest is complete (including the Propers of the day) and decorated with ribbons, just like the book of the altar. So that the ribbons are not superimposed, they are attached to the sheets in a staggered arrangement that corresponds to notches similarly staggered on the illustrated page. The small book of the Mass of the Catechumens, prepared with the Propers, thus appears adorned with five juxtaposed coloured ribbons that stand out at the top and bottom of the pages.

The Proper parts of the Mystical Mass are arranged in the same way. The small book that contains the Ordinary and the Proper of the Mass of the Faithful appears decorated with four ribbons.

We must, in the latter, notice other details that have to do with the central part of the Mystical Mass in the Commemoration of the Living and the Commemoration of the Dead.

In order to show children that the Mass is celebrated not only to fill all those who are present with grace, but also for those who are absent or have left the earth, we have prepared movable pages to be attached for each of these occasions.

There is a border at the top of the page, which is prepared for the Commemoration of the Living, that recalls the style of the ancient diptychs that are shown in early churches. Underneath, two blank spaces are arranged on which the child can write the names of living persons for whom he wants to pray during the Holy Mass.

On the corresponding page of the Ordinary under the words: "Remember, Lord, your servants . . ." there is a space as big as the diptych. On the sides, two notches allow for the insertion of this diptych and its exact adaptation to the page so as to cover the whole blank space. The printed text resumes on the lower part of the page: "and of all here present . . ." under the names written by the child.

The same holds true for the Commemoration of the Dead. Here, the page is decorated with borders of detailed figures that recall the souls of the deceased: the palm, etc. For the page in the book related to the Commemoration of the Dead, a blank space reoccurs. It has two sideways notches in which the page of the Commemoration is inserted. There, the child can write the names of the deceased that he hopes to recall during the Mass. The book's corresponding page has the words of the text printed in front: "Remember also, Lord, your servants . . ." The sheet that has the names that are written by the child also appears immediately above the resumption of the printed text on the page . . . "who have gone before us marked with the sign of faith and who rest in the sleep of peace."

Both sheets of Commemorations, which are removed from the book after the Mass, are stored separately. In this way, the child recalls his prayers and those whom he remembered before God during the whole Liturgical Year.

When the two small books have been prepared in this way with the Propers of the day and the commemorative diptychs, they are stored in the two pockets of the folder, the ribbons carefully folded on the cover.

Such a Mass book must, consequently, be reconstructed from time to time. It requires the activity of the small child more than the use of his senses. Up until now, we have thought it necessary to use the senses of the small child to maintain his attention and open his intelligence. The books which were meant for him were full of pictures. Our book, on the contrary, attracts the child to activity by bringing its various parts together. But, undoubtedly, in order for this activity to take place, there had to be preparation. It was this preparation that led the child to become interested in constructive work.

The book itself (and, in this case, it is only an educational guide) continues to teach and stabilize his initial knowledge. In fact, being made up of two parts, it does not cease to recall that the Mass has two parts—the Mass of the Catechumens and the Mass of the Faithful. The fact that, from time to time, one must insert pages that are taken from outside the book is a reminder that, in the Mass, there is an Ordinary and invariable part and another moveable part which is the Proper of each Mass. The series of ribbons indicates that the Propers are mostly in the Mass of the Catechumens. Since it is the instructive part, its teachings change each time while continuing the instruction throughout the year. In the Mass of the Faithful, there are few variable parts, while the text of the Ordinary is much more voluminous.

The book's repeated structure makes up a true teaching. If we asked one of the children who uses this missal: "How many variable parts are there in the Mass of the Catechumens and how many are there in the Mass of the Faithful," he would unhesitatingly answer: "Five in the first and four in the second." And it would not be the fruit of the arduous lessons that the teacher gave him. It would be because he has manipulated the movable ribbons and sheets and has so often seen the five ribbons of the first small volume and the four ribbons of the second one. He has, without any effort, assimilated this knowledge.

This education rises to a moral plane. The Mass must not

simply be listened to and attentively followed. It calls for a preparation.

In fact, we cannot lightly access the celebration of our religion's most sacred act. The priest who will celebrate it prepares himself by prayer as he puts on priestly vestments. What could be better adapted to the child than the layout of his Mass book, the identification of the Propers, and the recollection of his loved ones for whom he wants to offer the Sacrifice, and whose names he has traced?

THE PROPERS

The Propers of the Mass—its variable parts—are made up of Psalm verses, prayers, and passages from the Old or New Testament. The Mass includes many excerpts from the four Gospels throughout the Liturgical Year. It also includes Epistles of the Apostles, as well as many accounts of their glorious actions drawn from "Acts," Psalm verses, historic stories taken from the Book of Kings, and passages from the Prophets and the poetic Book of Wisdom. There are, finally, such a great variety of magnificent Christian prayers that the Mass as a whole can be regarded as a collection of prayers.

All the parts were chosen or composed by the Church as best adapted to the spirit which forms the Mass—different according to the liturgical times or the particular purposes it proposes. The adaptation around the immutable structure of the Holy Mass throughout the diverse times of the year—waiting, penance, suffering, and rejoicing—is due to the diversity of the Propers that vary according to the circumstances, determining the "Mass of the moment." It is through the Propers that this unchanging structure adapts to the variations of each day, both to the commemoration of the Saints as well as to the supplications of men to God, determining whether Masses are celebrated in honor of the Lord, the Virgin Mary, Angels, or Saints.

Although the goal that the Church sets in the arrangement of the Propers of the Mass is only to honor God and to appeal to Christians to live in Him, it nevertheless fulfills a true instruction of the Holy Scriptures that is intended for all people.

While being the indissoluble spouse of Jesus Christ, the Church becomes a teacher for us and a Holy Mother who offers us her sublime teachings. In fact, by choosing from this rich source of wisdom—the Old and New Testament—the pieces best adapted to express the particular spirit of the day, she sets herself the goal of leaving a deep, unmistakable trace of it in the souls of her children.

Christians receive this real and vast instruction while having the impression of being in a constant feast in a place of spiritual grace. It is particularly because of the Propers that we need a book near us to *study* the Mass, one might say, in school-language. But when it is the Church that teaches, its teachings must be *meditated on* because that is the form of study that suits the soul eager for the Word of God. The Propers are linked to a day, and they pass, except that they return each year as if they are fresh, new prayers. To our amazement, these passages often seem to answer a question we are pondering. They so frequently bring the comfort that we secretly look for! These verses cast a ray of light into our spirit or reflect a feeling that we did not know how to express. They leave us feeling overwhelmed by their elevation. For a moment they draw us in, and then they disappear. It's like a crown of precious stones placed to adorn the time of a feast but immediately returned to its case.

We have limited the first study of the Mass to the

preparation of the Sunday and feast Propers, times that have a fixed date, as we have indicated in the liturgical calendar. This collection reduces the content of the Propers to what is more or less in the prayer books. However, our study includes a little less, since the prayer books also include the Holy Days of Obligation in honor of Our Lord, and our book's only aim is to set down clear bases for the instruction of the Mass and times of the Liturgical Year.

Keeping within the limits that we made to the Mass book for children, that is, not taking into account *all* the Propers (which follow one after the other in the common missals without any relation between them), a united and logical continuation has emerged like a series of lessons that flow naturally from one to the other. This stabilizes a base of knowledge from which the child can then start orienting himself in the more complete domain of Propers that pertain to each day of the year.

The Propers of the Mass of the Catechumens are:

1. *The Introit* – Psalm verses that in the modern rite take the place of whole Psalms that were sung by the crowd of the faithful in the early Church.

2. *The Collect* – the prayer that precedes the Epistle that the priest offers to God for the present group of people and for the Church.

3. *The Epistle* – is a letter of an Apostle or, sometimes, an excerpt from the Old Testament.

4. *The Gradual* – is made up of Psalm verses or passages from the Bible that remind us of those that the faithful or clergy sang, while kneeling on the altar's steps.

5. *The Gospel* – is always a passage from one of the four Gospels.

The Propers of the Mystical Mass are:

6. *The Offertory* – Psalm verses or passages from the Bible

that are similar to those that the faithful sang during the noisy exit of the catechumens and the presentation of the offerings.

7. *The Secret* – the prayer that the priest and the faithful offer to God in a silent meditation and that includes the intention that was formulated during the Collect.

8. *Communion* – varies and can consist of a Psalm verse, a quote from a Gospel passage, or a prayer.

9. *The Postcommunion* – is always the prayer of the faithful who have received Communion and who implore grace. It recalls the intention of the day.

DOXOLOGY

Whatever the Psalm offered by the Church may be, it is sung for the glory of the Most Holy Trinity. It always ends with the recitation of these words: "Glory be to the Father, to the Son, and to the Holy Spirit, as it was in the beginning, is now and in the ages of ages. Amen."[5]

This prayer, incidentally, is said after the Psalms that the religious repeat in the daily Divine Office, outside of Mass. We must constantly recite it in homage to the Most Holy Trinity. It is not printed in books, but only indicated at the end of the verse by the words: "*Gloria Patri* . . ." We must, nonetheless, repeat the whole phrase. Knowing it by heart is, therefore, required. We have to repeat it in our own language. The priest repeats it in Latin: "*Gloria Patri et Filio et Spiritui Sancto, sicut erat in principio et nunc et semper et in saecula saeculorum. Amen.*"

But at the end of the *prayers*, on the other hand, the *Gloria Patri* is not recited. We ask something of God through Jesus

---

[5] The official translation used in the US is "is now and ever shall be, world without end, Amen

Christ's merits because the communication that man can have with God is done through the grace of the Redemption. Jesus Christ has reconciled us with the Eternal Father. By humbly speaking our request to the omnipotent God, we hope to have Jesus Christ answer us—He who is our Lord, the Son of God who, with the Holy Spirit, is part of the Trinity. We must remember all of that each time that we pray: "Through Jesus Christ, our Lord . . ."

This formula is not required for each prayer that is spoken to God by the Christian, but it is like the finale of all the Propers that are prayers in the Mass. The Mass is like the court of a great king, where a ceremony is mandatory and where we have to observe formulas of respect. But the Church, being lenient towards us, observes the formula in lieu of the faithful who are incapable of responding to it. It is the altar server who responds. However, the faithful who have studied the rules and know them may have the honor to participate directly in the formulas of the ceremony according to the customs accepted in their diocese.

We do not repeat the entire formula of this phrase in books, but we indicate it by the words "*per Dominum*" or by the initials *Per D. N. J. C.*

Since these formulas must be known by heart and are invariable, they cannot be described as variable parts even though they are always in conjunction with the Propers, which are variable. At the end of a Proper that is a Psalm, we find the words: "*Gloria Patri . . .*" and at the end of that which is a prayer, we find "*Per Dominum . . .*"

To make the variety of the Propers clearer, we have decorated the pages of the chants and prayers differently. A musical instrument—a lyre, organ, etc.—is drawn above the Psalms that, for the most part, are sung. A candelabra or lit lamp is drawn above the prayers, which connect us to God, the source of light. As the child inserts the ribbons on the illustrated page that bears the title of a particular Proper, he sees the relationship between the illustration and the page of text that he is inserting. Very quickly he will know if this Proper is made up of a Psalm or a prayer, and he will not forget it.

Once put together, the separate sheets allow for an overall study. By placing the Psalm sheet and the prayer sheet next to each other and arranging them in the order of their succession in the Mass, we note at first glance how many Psalms and how many prayers there are.

We see that there are four Psalms and three prayers: three in the Mass of the Catechumens and four others in the Mystical Mass. The Psalms dominate the Mass of the Catechumens, and in the Mystical Mass, it is the prayers.

EPISTLE AND GOSPEL

Particular care was taken in the preparation of the Epistle and the Gospel. The sheet on which the word "Epistle" is written presents the text as a handwritten letter with the address, heading, and signature arranged in the usual way, for example:

To the Corinthians,

My brothers,

If I speak ...
... but do not have love, I am a noisy gong or a clanging cymbal ...

Paul.

The form of the letter makes the meaning of the Epistle of

the Mass clear to the child. It reaches the faithful and is read aloud to them. It is one of those letters written in the Apostles' own hand and sent directly to spread the Lord's doctrine and "to feed His lambs." Those who wrote them spoke to Jesus Himself and heard His inexpressible and divine voice, except for Saint Paul, who was vehemently called by God Himself and received a miraculous mission from Heaven.

Those were the first men that the Holy Spirit enkindled. These glorious heroes, though they were ill, persecuted, imprisoned, and martyred, did not stop working through a thousand dangers, living by the toil of their hands. Through their letters, they revived the faith of their distant brothers who formed the scattered circles of the early Church. This is one of those letters that is reaching us!

We also form the groups of the faithful who are on the lookout for a voice that revives our faith. Gathered around the altar where the Holy Mass is still celebrated, we are, like them, after twenty centuries, anxious to receive the inspiring encouragement of a man who is closer to God than we are, stronger than we are. We gather around the letters of Peter, Paul, James, or John, who write us and call us their brothers and dear friends. This distant letter, which was written in a dead language on a scroll or a papyrus in Hebrew, Greek, or Latin, lives again today in our native language. Interspersed in our little book, we can take it with us, and read and reread it often, as we do a very cherished letter that we have received. In this way, the exceptional content of the Epistle, mysteriously surprises us. We do not yet know what it is going to tell us, but when we go to Mass, we repeat to ourselves in rejoicing: "There is a letter there for me."

Facing the Gospel, the passages related to the Proper of the Masses are printed with great decorations. The priest says a prayer asking God to purify his tongue, just like the prophet Isaiah whose tongue was purified by God with a burning ember. We cannot confuse that prayer with the Gospel. The Word of the Gospel, which represents the voice of the Messiah, is read in the Church only after the book has changed places on the altar because Christ's Word cannot be heard where others are sounding. During its reading, a cloud of incense arises in solemn Masses, and altar candles are lit.

The distinction made by the Church for the Gospel cannot be overlooked in a book whose mission is to bring to the child the knowledge and distinction of the different parts of the Mass. The sheets that relate to the Gospel must, therefore, be different from all the others. Each word must be meticulously embellished with the same love as that of the Benedictines and religious of Saint Bernard who decorated them, letter by letter, and managed to make them a work of art.

What must also emerge from this reading is that it does not include a complete text, but a passage taken from a book. This is why this excerpt is always preceded by the instruction: "From the Gospel according to . . ."

One could imagine replacing the book of the Gospel, on successive pages, by a large scroll of parchment unrolling little by little. Thus, the volume appears to be rolled over and under the text to be read. We want to show the Gospel as an ancient writing which harmonizes with the roll on which it is written since this detail always appears: "*In illo tempore . . .*" ("In that time . . .")

Therefore, three ideas—the homage, the fact that the account is only an excerpt, and that it talks about ancient events—must appear in the Mass itself, thanks to the representative pages of the Proper.

THE CHART OF THE PROPERS

The Propers of each Mass include nine pages that are decorated with ribbons. Sometimes, one page is not enough for the Epistles and Gospels. One has to use a double page that is folded in two. We often also add hymns that are characteristic of the Mass of the day or instructions for variations in the Ordinary of the Mass—e.g. a special Preface.

All that is related to a Mass is collected in a closed envelope. In this envelope, we can also add little notes that provide some observations that help us understand the spirit of the Mass in its entirety. Thus, the envelope of the Propers is full of surprises.

For a first study, the Propers of sixty Masses are prepared in separate envelopes; later on, the number can be increased by adding some Masses of the main commemorations.

These sixty envelopes correspond to the feasts of our Lord indicated on the liturgical calendar, that is to say:

- the four Sundays of Advent,
- Christmas,
- the Sunday in the Christmas Octave,
- the Circumcision (Octave Day of Christmas),
- the Sunday that follows the feast of the Circumcision,
- Epiphany,
- the six Sundays after Epiphany,
- the Purification (Presentation of Jesus),
- the three Sundays of Septuagesima,
- Ash Wednesday,
- the six Sundays of Lent,
- Easter Sunday,
- the six Sundays after Easter,
- the Ascension,

- Pentecost,
- Corpus Christi,
- the twenty-four Sundays after Pentecost.

The sixty envelopes are joined together five-by-five in a double row of six overlapping bags. Into each envelope is inserted a strip of strong cardboard, surmounted by a disk in a liturgical color. The particular Sunday is indicated on this disk. To retrieve an envelope, simply pull the disk from above. In order for the signs identifying the Mass to be clearly displayed, the cardboard strip of the five envelopes intended for the same satchel is arranged in a different place according to their order of succession. The first one is at the end; the third one is in the middle; the last one is at the end on the right. The second one, and the fourth one are inserted on one side and the other from the middle.

By uniting the five overlapping envelopes in this way, the disks continue to be distinctly visible even if the envelopes are replaced out of order.

A chart of disks results from the ensemble of bags that are loaded with envelopes, and, at first glance, clearly indicates the succession of the times of the Liturgical Year. Moreover, the indications noted on the disks make it possible to recognize the titles of the successive Sundays of the year. Next to this chart, is the liturgical calendar established in groups of 5 days (see *Diag. 23*), and this makes a pretty ornamental band the exact length of the chart. In this way, we can read what Mass corresponds to the date. For example, May 8, 1955 corresponds to the 4th Sunday after Easter. The envelope will be found among the white discs of the Easter feasts with the instruction: "4th Sunday after Easter." The disk is pulled from above, and the envelope that hides the magnificent gifts of the Propers of this Sunday comes out.

Every year we must change the calendar, but the chart always remains the same since the Sundays never change places, time, or names in their mutual relationships.

We have attained something immovable in the Liturgical Year since the times are centered on God, who is the Center of the Liturgy, whereas the calendar based on nature's outer phenomena is constantly changing.

All that is very clear to the mind of the child who is going to find the Propers on the chart, according to the date indicated on the calendar.

CONCLUSION

The results obtained with our education system have led some to believe that our optimism had been exaggerated, and that according to us, there is only good in man. Yet we are in the habit of declaring that the child does "badly" when he does something that bothers us or that changes the routine of the habits in which we rest and find our well-being. But have we ever asked ourselves what the good and bad actions of a child are? Have we never been mistaken in judging the child compared to us rather than judging him compared to the Divine Plan? Do we not forget many sacred principles when we are face to face with this tiny being that Jesus Christ said was our guide to the Kingdom of Heaven? The Bible tells us that man was made in the image of God and that Original Sin disturbed the Divine Plan. However, with education, we must help the child to be ready to receive the grace that restores man in the image of God in the original plan.

That does not mean that we must make the child *in our image* or offer ourselves as an example of perfection. Between us and the baptized child, there is the distance created by our sin; therefore the child is better than we are. "Truly I tell you, unless you change and become like children, you will never enter the kingdom of heaven" (Mt 18: 3).

It is evident that we must help the child *to go to Jesus*, which does not mean that he must *come to us*.

As a model to imitate, too often we have shown him the sinner in ourselves. Let us have more charity and show him more justice. Let us give him what he needs for the development of his whole being, and let us give him the freedom to follow those laws which are inscribed in the deepest part of his soul: to perfect oneself, to work, to love.

TABLE OF DIAGRAMS

Diagram 1	Symbolic Representation of the Cross	166
Diagram 2	a) Orbit of the Earth Around the Sun	169
	b) Path of the Moon Around the Earth	169
Diagram 3	Liturgical Colors	171
Diagram 4	The Paschal Number	200
Diagram 5	The Central Points of the Seasons of the Liturgical Year	212
Diagram 6	The Unfolding of These Seasons	215
Diagram 7	The Circle of the 52 Sundays	220
Diagram 8	Index Cards for the Mass of the Catechumens	242
Diagram 9	How the Priest Figures are Placed on These Index Cards	245
Diagram 10	Symbolic Signs of the Gestures	248
Diagram 11	Model of Double-Sided Index Cards	250-251
Diagram 12	Index Cards for the Offertory	252
Diagram 13	Cruets	253
Diagram 14	Index Cards for the Canon	257
Diagram 15	Index Cards for the Canon, in a Symmetrical Order	260-261
Diagram 16	Index Cards for Communion	263
Diagram 17	Breaking of the Host	264
Diagram 18	The Entire Mass	266-267
Diagram 19	Summary in Four Separate Parts	270
Diagram 20	Summary in a Single Drawing	271
Diagram 21	Representative Objects	273
Diagram 22	A Page of the Proper With Its Ribbon, and a Page Prepared to Receive It	280
Diagram 23	Liturgical Calendar: Life in Jesus Christ	302-303

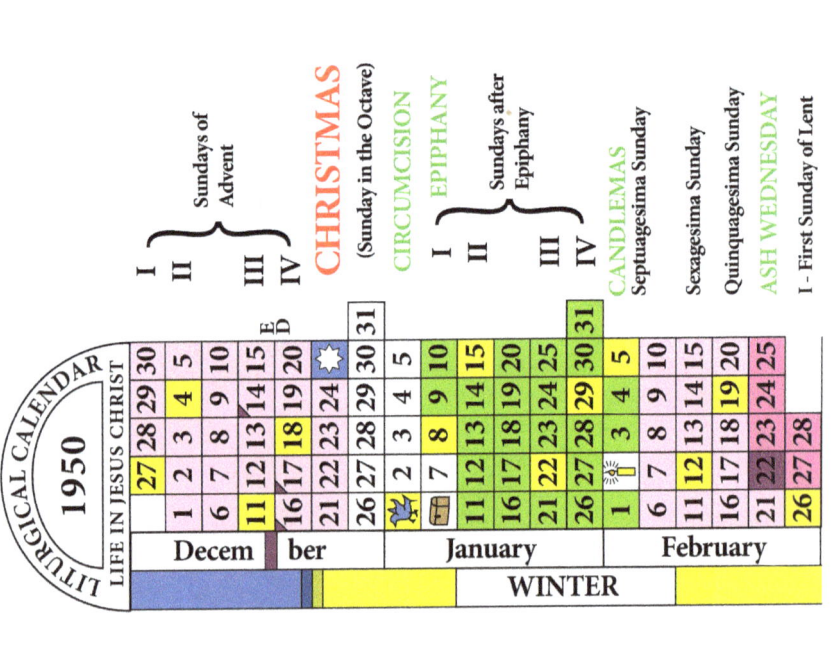

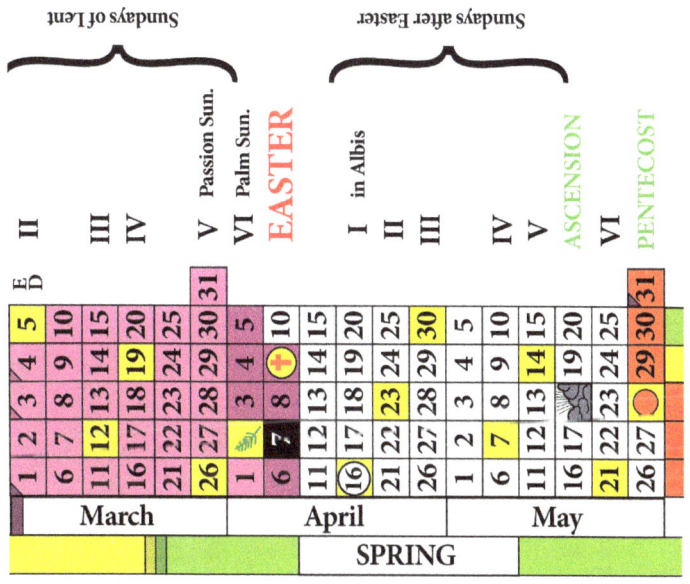

Diagram 23.

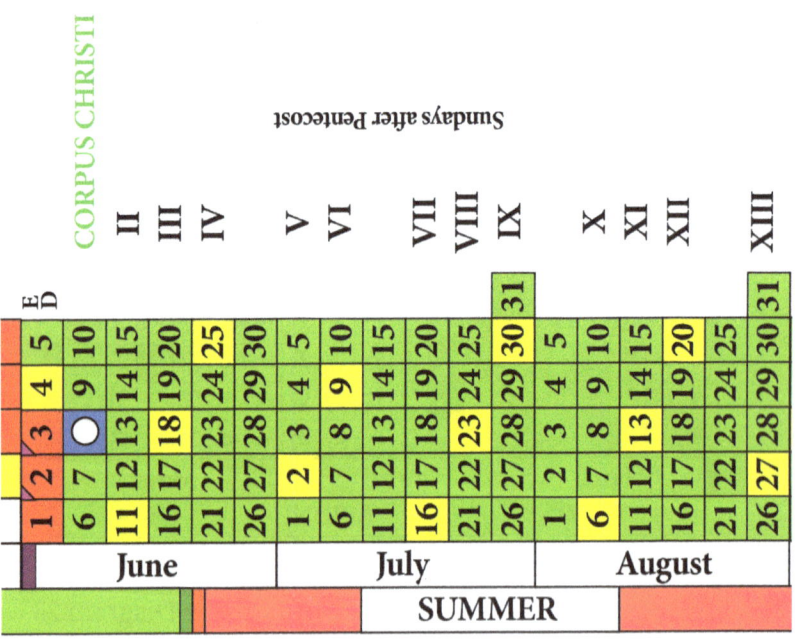

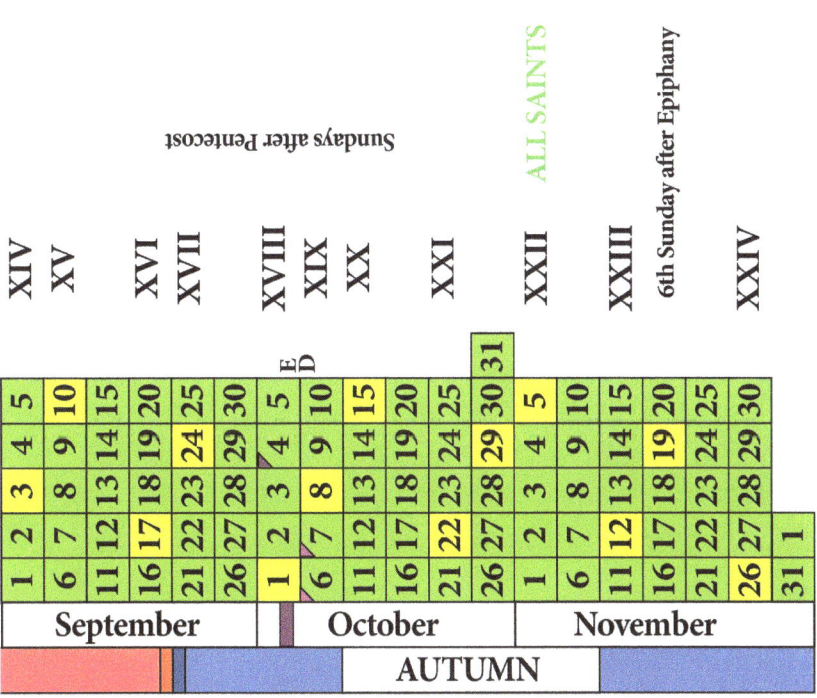

www.ingramcontent.com/pod-product-compliance
Lightning Source LLC
Chambersburg PA
CBHW071658170426
43195CB00039B/2231